Open University Press
English, Language, and Education series
General Editor: Anthony Adams
Lecturer in Education, University of Cambridge

This series is concerned with all aspects of language in education
from the primary school to the tertiary sector. Its authors are
experienced educators who examine both principles and
practice of English subject teaching and language across the curriculum in
the context of current educational and societal developments.

TITLES IN THE SERIES

Narrative and Argument
Richard Andrews

Time for Drama
Roma Burgess and Pamela Gaudry

Computers and Literacy
Daniel Chandler and Stephen Marcus (eds.)

Readers, Texts, Teachers
Bill Corcoran and Emrys Evans (eds.)

Developing Response to Poetry
Patrick Dias and Michael Hayhoe

The Primary Language Book
Peter Dougill and Richard Knott

Children Talk About Books: Seeing Themselves as Readers
Donald Fry

Literary Theory and English Teaching
Peter Griffith

Assessing English
Brian Johnston

Lipservice: The Story of Talk in Schools
Pat Jones

The English Department in a Changing World
Richard Knott

Oracy Matters
Margaret MacLure, Terry Phillips and Andrew Wilkinson (eds.)

Teaching Literature for Examinations
Robert Protherough

Developing Response to Fiction
Robert Protherough

Microcomputers and the Language Arts
Brent Robinson

English Teaching from A–Z
Wayne Sawyer, Anthony Adams and Ken Watson

Reconstructing 'A' Level English
Patrick Scott

Collaboration and Writing
Morag Styles (ed.)

English Teaching in Perspective
Ken Watson

The Quality of Writing
Andrew Wilkinson

The Writing of Writing
Andrew Wilkinson (ed.)

DEVELOPING RESPONSE TO FICTION

Robert Protherough

Open University Press
Milton Keynes · Philadelphia

Open University Press
12 Cofferidge Close
Stony Stratford
Milton Keynes MK11 1BY, England
and
1900 Frost Road, Suite 101
Bristol, PA 19007, USA

First published 1983
Reprinted 1986, 1989

British Library Cataloguing in Publication Data
Protherough, Robert
  Developing response to fiction.
  1. Reading
  I. Title
  428.4   LB1050

ISBN   0 335 10405 3

Text design by W.A.P.

Typeset by S & S Press, Abingdon, Oxon.
Printed in Great Britain by
M. & A. Thomson Litho Limited,
East Kilbride, Scotland.

To the memory of my mother

who introduced me to stories

Contents

Part Three: Programme

Acknowledgements

The ideas which form the basis for this book have been growing for years. My thinking about what happens when we read novels and stories has been given shape by work with children in a number of schools, by experiences with students and in-service groups, by conversations with colleagues and – of course – by reading. Those to whose ideas I am most conscious of being indebted, in very different ways, include John Dixon, Geoff Fox, David Jackson, Nancy Martin, Margaret Spencer, Leslie Stratta, Frank Whitehead and Andrew Wilkinson, but like other teachers I have learned from many more individuals than can be acknowledged here.

What are described in Part One as the Hull enquiries sprang out of what local teachers said they most urgently wished to know about fiction in school. The ensuing investigations were chiefly carried out in five comprehensive schools, and I am grateful to teachers like John Bryson of Kelvin Hall High School, Mike Smith of Howden School and their colleagues for their help. My particular thanks are due to John Fawcett of Cottingham High School, and Judith Atkinson of Wolfreton School, and formerly of Sydney Smith High School. They and members of their departments carried out the major sections of these enquiries, made children's work available to me, and have allowed me to work with classes and to interview individuals on a number of occasions.

I am also grateful to the five experienced teachers who contributed the case studies which form the central part of this volume, and ensured that it is firmly grounded in actual practice. I have been encouraged by their willingness to share their experience and to return later to reflect upon it.

Versions of two sections of this book, appearing in chapters two and three, have appeared elsewhere, and I am grateful for permission to reproduce this material. 'How children describe their reading of stories' was printed in a volume of *Aspects of Education, The Development of Readers*, published by the Institute of Education at Hull University, and 'How children judge stories' appeared in *Children's Literature in Education*.

The production of the final text owes much to my wife Margaret who has uncomplainingly typed successive drafts and tried to point out where my writing was more than usually opaque or clumsy. John Skelton of the Open University Press has been most helpful and supportive, and I am grateful to him and his readers for helpful criticisms and suggestions. The errors that remain, like the opinions expressed, are my own responsibility.

Introduction

When we talk about the reading of fiction there is a deep ambiguity in that innocent phrase 'developing response'. Does *developing* simply describe what *happens*, a universal experience, or what somebody *does for* others, a teaching objective? How far is the development of response to stories to be seen as an essentially natural process, like increasing in height and weight, and how far as an ability which has to be acquired by being taught, like learning to use a computer? Those studies which describe children's changing taste in books as they grow older tend to stress the first sense of development; volumes about what to do with novels in school emphasize the second. This book attempts to bring the two closer together: to relate classroom practice directly to a clearer awareness of what children are actually doing as they engage with stories at different ages. It argues that understanding of response, of what stories do to children, should be central to any teaching of fiction.

The key question for teachers could be framed like this: when a novel is being 'taught', what is being 'learned'? The debates of literary theorists about the relationship between the reader and the text raise insistent pedagogic questions, but rarely answer them. Stanley Fish and others have argued cogently that meaning, significance and value are not to be described as qualities of a text itself, but as events, experiences of readers. Critical activity should be concerned with 'an analysis of the developing responses of the reader'. It is surprising, then, that Fish and others fail to take the step of moving beyond the abstraction of 'the reader' to consider those 'developing responses' in a range of actual individuals, and particularly in those young people who are actively engaged in learning how to come to terms with a novel. A theory centred on the reader and reading should surely be prepared to demonstrate what knowledge and abilities real readers actually deploy in responding as they do and to show how these abilities develop in practice.

Teachers in school may be forgiven, then, for thinking that semiotics, discourse theory, structuralism and deconstruction, with their specialized terminologies, are irrelevant to classroom practice, and yet all these are essentially concerned – as teachers are – with how texts should be *used*. By what principles do we select those novels that we put into the hands of children? How do the activities we practise help them to read with more enjoyment and understanding? What qualities are assessed by examinations in literature, and how effectively do they achieve this task? Our reluctance to discuss such basic questions as these is often concealed beneath a show of gritty pragmatism; we claim to be constrained by the lack of resources, by the pressures of the examination system, by the lack of interest of our classes, by the failure of those who taught them in earlier years . . . Certainly these pressures exist, but it is the unthinking use of familiar methods acquired by tradition and the uncertainty about what fiction is *for* in schools that most militate against success.

This volume, therefore, brings together observations of children reading and teachers teaching with the ideas of specialists concerned with reading and learning, to show how these relate to each other, and to suggest what the implications are for work in schools.

The first part is intended to provide the rationale for what follows. It draws on a number of linked small-scale classroom investigations, carried out in comprehensive schools in and around Hull over a number of years, involving local teachers and research students at Hull University. It also considers recent work on reading theory by psychologists, literary specialists and educationalists, to show how this can simultaneously illuminate and be illuminated by what is going on in classrooms. Each of the three chapters focuses on one particular view of a total process: the development of response in young fiction readers. The first concentrates on the nature of response, and its importance for ideas of curriculum. The second is concerned with the definition of fiction and of the fiction-reading process. The third is about reader development, and provides a tentative model for discussing how children between 11 and 16 learn new ways of responding to a wider range of fiction. These three chapters are interdependent.

The second part shifts the focus from children's reading and perceptions of reading to the way in which teachers see the process. Five case studies, written by experienced and able English teachers, describe programmes of fiction study with pupils of different ages, giving specific examples of children's responses in talk and writing, and analysing in retrospect the successes and failures of different classroom strategies.

The third part is the application of the previous two, and grows directly out of them. It begins by considering how novel reading is affected by the school context, by being 'taught' and examined. Within this framework, it proposes a programme for the teaching of fiction in schools: the principles that should underlie it, ways in which it might be structured, the implications of choosing texts and methods that might be practised. Although it draws on the work of a wide variety of individual teachers and departments, this part is not chiefly concerned to present inert 'good ideas' as though they can be imported into any classroom ready-made. The intention is rather to exemplify the sort of principles and strategies by which teachers can work out their own coherent programmes for the particular

groups with whom they are working, to counter that damning judgement
in the Secondary Survey: 'Most schools are not promoting reading as fully
and effectively as is needed for any part of their ability range.' (5.8)

Part One

Principles

1 Focus on Response

We judge a work of art by its effect on our sincere and vital emotion, and nothing else. All the critical twiddle-twaddle about style and form, all this pseudo-scientific classifying and analysing of books in an imitation-botanical fashion, is mere impertinence and mostly dull jargon.

D. H. Lawrence. *Phoenix*

WHAT DO STORIES DO?

Some 11-year-olds in their first term at a comprehensive school just outside Hull have been listening to a story about a country boy who is watching, reluctant but fascinated, while a pig is being slaughtered.[1] They jot down their immediate reactions to the story, and then talk about it in groups. Their comments include these, and many others like them:

'It made me feel sick imagining it and specially the knife when it cut the pig's flesh.'
'My legs went like jelly.'
'I was moved, thought it cruel.'
'I could feel the pig getting cut, and the blood running down.'
'I will never eat bacon again.'
'I thought about if I was the pig, it would be horrible.'
'It made me furious at the slaughter.'
'It reminded me of school dinners.'
'I kept thinking about the blood in the bucket and how horrible it must have been.'
'I hated Mr Powell because of his job slaughtering animals.'
'When he blew up the pig's bladder and threw it at them it hit the boy in the face, it made me want to wash my face over and over again.'

In the same school, boys and girls in a third-year mixed-ability group have been hearing Doris Lessing's story *Through the Tunnel*, about a boy's dangerous underwater adventure.[2] Their initial remarks, before they begin to examine the story in more detail, include such typical responses as these:

'I imagined it was me whose eyes were bursting and filling up with blood, a horrible feeling.'
'I felt my stomach tightening.'
'I felt frightened, I couldn't do anything about it.'
'It brought back memories of being scared, overpowered by water.'
'It made me wonder whether he would ever find the end of the tunnel, and were there any dangerous animals.'
'I felt a bit dizzy.'
'It was awful when his head was swelling, his eyes bursting.'
'I put myself in that situation, I could not hold my breath for over a minute.'
'I felt the skin on my back being ripped and stinging with the salt water.'
'I could imagine being in that position, wanting to breathe and air so far away.'
'I felt a sensation of the sea against my face.'

Looking at these children's words should remind us vividly of the simple, basic truth: stories do things to people. Alternatively expressed, we know that things happen to people when they read, and that any theory about the place of fiction in schools has to begin with this fact.

> Most people have no clear idea of art's consequences, whether for good or for bad. They suppose that a spectator who is not inwardly gripped by it, because it is not good enough, is not affected at all. Quite apart from the fact that one can be gripped by bad art as easily as by good, even if one *isn't* gripped something happens to one.[3]

Yes, 'something happens to one'. Some of the children in the two classes mentioned have been conscious of physical changes: feeling sick or dizzy, legs turning to jelly, stomach tightening. Others felt an emotional reaction: fury, hate, horror or fear. Some were prompted to remember moments in their own experiences and to associate with them (memories of being scared or of school dinners), others to reason and speculate ('It made me wonder . . .') and others to shift their attitudes ('I will never eat bacon again'). Many underwent empathetically the experiences and feelings of characters in the stories (the pig being cut, the boy struck by the bladder, gasping underwater, sharp rocks ripping the skin). Sometimes things like this that happen in reading are significant and observable; sometimes they are virtually imperceptible.

When as adults we are challenged to explain why certain books are important to us, our instinctive response is to describe the experiences of reading them. We present the tears we shed, the excitement we felt, the changes in our way of thinking or the new insights as a kind of litmus paper changing colour, to prove that something happened. The emotional importance of the experience can sometimes outweigh all later critical judgements. Hull teachers have recorded, for example, a lasting affection for Biggles while simultaneously being forced to acknowledge 'the class orientation of the stories, their automatic superiority and dated ideas', or

for a circus tale even while remarking, 'I now realize that it is trite, sentimental rubbish.' Young readers operate in just the same way. When Hull
children bear testimony to the power of favourite stories, the same phrases
keep recurring. There is an impact which may be purely emotional ('it
upset me', 'it horrified me', 'I cried my eyes out') or may go on to affect
attitudes ('made me look differently', 'changed the way I see', 'made me
realize more clearly', 'changed my attitude'). Pupils in the Exeter area
seem to describe their reading experiences in very similar terms: *Bevis* 'al-
tered my whole approach to life', *F67* 'made me want to cry', after *The
Belstone Fox*, 'I gave up hunting'.[4] Similarly, 15-year-olds in the APU (Assessment of Performance Unit) sample seem to define the importance of
fiction in terms of what it does to them: reading 'helps me', 'calms me',
offers 'escape' or 'release', allows the reader to 'live a different life', or
'become involved in different times and situations.'[5]

Nevertheless, although we may be prepared to acknowledge the crucial
importance of personal response, teachers are frequently uneasy when it
comes to discussing just what it is that novels do to their pupils. For one
thing, they are conscious of struggling against the main stream of the secondary curriculum, with its emphasis on suppressing the personal in
favour of 'facts', emphasizing thoughts rather than feelings, and even dis-
couraging the use of the first person in writing. For another, they are sus-
picious of a gulf between the actual responses of children and what as
teachers they feel *should* be made of the stories read. Most of all, they are
uncertain of what their own role should be in 'teaching' a novel. They are
uncomfortably aware that there are no clear links between teaching and
pupil response, no secure models of how that response develops and not
even any consensus about the kind of language in which to explore these
processes. Almost any group of teachers talking about children's reading
will cover a spectrum from pious but woolly rhetoric to a brutal
utilitarianism. One study group at a NATE (National Association for the
Teaching of English) conference spent some days asserting 'for all pupils
the value of reading fiction' and the importance of 'personal involvement
in the world of the book'. The group's report, with admirable honesty,
admitted however that much of their time was 'circling', because:

> It is difficult to be confident about what takes place when a child reads a
> book. In discussing this process our language sometimes becomes a trifle
> misty:
> '. . . it doesn't really operate on an intellectual level but somewhere else . . .'
> '. . . after a child makes contact with a book things may never be quite the
> same'
> '. . . you're getting at what it is to be alive . . .'
> '. . . some books do some things for some people . . .'

It is clearly essential to begin trying to clear away some of that mist, and to see more clearly what happens when children read books, how they develop that ability, and what differences a classroom setting makes.

SOME PROBLEMS OF DISCUSSING RESPONSE

The difficulties of such an undertaking are enormous. Some of them are inherent in any consideration of the reading process and others spring directly from the teaching situation. For example:

1　There is no neat, assessable product. Literary response is not like the ability to write or to talk into a recorder: it's a private engagement between reader and text that goes on in the head, and can only be translated selectively and imprecisely to someone else through a retrospective analysis and a struggle with words. Lawrence said: 'Nothing is more difficult than to determine what a child takes in, and does not take in' – and he said it about the fact that the hymns from his childhood somehow meant more to him than the great poems he encountered later.[6]

2　Response is unique. 'Each of us reads in his own characteristic way,' says Norman Holland who has demonstrated in detail how differently students can seem to understand and to react to the same text.[7] Back in the 1920s, June Downey pointed out a number of ways in which readers' responses (to poetry, in this case) appeared to be conditioned by their personalities.[8] They read in different modes, and preferred different kinds of works: those which appealed particularly to their own predispositions in each case. When the members of a class listen to the same story, what they are hearing is *not* the same: each is bringing together what the mind selects from the text with that individual's existing experience – of life, of language, and of literary conventions.

3　It is hard to disentangle the pupils' responses from the teacher's. We all know the importance of our own enthusiasm – we use it professionally. You hear teachers say: 'My children all loved *The Hobbit* or *Elidor* or *The Machine Gunners*', and perhaps they did, but were they responding to the story or to the teacher? Over 60 years ago, research showed that in almost all classes studied children preferred those books that their teachers were enthusiastic about.[9] The variations in the popularity of certain books between different schools or forms or libraries certainly seem to suggest that, especially with young children, teacher attitude is significant. Indeed, even the way in which pupils respond to a text in different countries has been shown by an international survey to be partly conditioned by the ways they are taught.[10]

4　Response cannot be accurately predicted. A teacher may make sound professional judgements that a book will be successful with a given class and still be startled by the intensity of some children's reactions. Our habits of assessing group reaction can blind us – except in dramatic moments of tears or outrage – to how wide the range of reactions may be. Because all children have their unique blend of experiences, attitudes, backgrounds and interests which they bring to the text, we can never be quite sure how they will react to such charged moments in modern juvenile novels as the racial tensions in *My Mate Shofiq*, the acceptance of mother's suicide in *Grover*, the encounter with drugs in *That was Then, This is Now*, or the feelings of rejection and aggression in *The Pinballs*. Some readers may be upset or horrified, some may be strengthened, some may enjoy the story superficially, some may detach themselves from it, some may be changed – for good or ill – and we can never be really sure in advance.

5   Individual response can be modified by being one of a group. When one class of young children heard how Charlie Bucket found the gold ticket that would change his life, some of them broke into cheers which the others took up. A number of children prefer to read humorous books with other people, because the shared laughter increases their enjoyment. One said, 'If I think it's not funny, and other people laugh, then I think it's funny'. In some cases, the effect of the group may be to inhibit feelings: the child who chokes back tears because they will seem 'soft' to classmates, or the easily-influenced pupil who stops enjoying a story because majority opinion in the class is that it is 'boring'. In others, children's initially unfavourable reactions to a story can be modified by the enthusiasm of their classmates.

In view of these difficulties, it is perhaps not surprising that the conclusion of one major book on literary response was: 'We know nothing about the process of reading and the interaction of man and book.' For the teacher, though, that *interaction* is of primary importance. At one end of the process there are the literary specialists, indefatigably examining texts in great detail to assess what readings are and are not admissible, and the new reading specialists, with their slide-rules to work out measures of readability and density of text. At the other end are the psychologists, with their stimulus-response models, busy wiring-up readers to measure the sweat on their palms, heart rates, eye movements, hormone balance. The teacher is the third man, in the middle, a kind of literary pander, forever introducing kids and books to each other in the hope that they'll fall in love. Where does the teacher fit into the process? The following sections consider what teachers see as the purposes of teaching literature, the relationship of their views to the existing curriculum and the extent to which they not only anticipate but also teach 'for' particular effects. All of these are most easily defined in terms of response.

WHY TEACH FICTION?

Despite their awareness of difficulties in assessing response, teachers still instinctively validate their choice of texts and of methods in terms of their pupils' reactions. Frequently the judgements are generalized and global: a story is 'good' because it 'went down splendidly with the third year', or because it 'produced some marvellous written work', or because 'they all want another story by the same author'. This is not to undervalue such judgements: they are an essential part of teaching. However, they frequently overlook the differences in the consciously or unconsciously formulated criteria by which the judgement is made.

To consider our aims, the purposes which we think the reading of fiction may serve is – in another sense – to predict and eventually to assess potential response. A teacher who decides to use *The Turbulent Term of Tyke Tyler* primarily to combat sexual stereotypes, or to enlarge children's sympathies for those of different abilities or backgrounds, or as the springboard for a programme of work on the topic of school, or simply as a sure-fire read for last period in the afternoons, is implicitly deciding the criteria by which children's response will ultimately be measured. The choice of fiction to read with children, or to offer them for their own reading, is inevitably bound up with the teacher's or parent's views of what reading is *for*.

Discussions with teachers, and available surveys of their opinions, suggest that their perceptions of the major purposes of reading literature can be structured in three main groups. Different teachers will, of course, attribute different comparative degrees of importance to each of these. To provide an oversimplified map, the functions can be distinguished as follows:

(a) *Personal*
  (i) At the simplest level, stories offer enjoyment, pleasure, relaxation; they develop positive attitudes towards reading.
  (ii) They develop, in some undefined sense, the imagination.
  (iii) Socially books can
      (a) aid personal development and self-understanding by presenting situations and characters with which our own can be compared, and by giving the chance to test out motives and decisions.
      (b) extend experience and knowledge of life ('broaden the mind' and 'widen the horizon') by introducing us to other kinds of people, places, periods, situations.

(b) *Curricular*
  (i) Books have linguistic functions: they develop the pupil's own use of language. There is some evidence of correlation between individuals' stan-

dard of writing and amount of reading, and of the idea that vocabulary is learned best in literary contexts.
 (ii) Stories are a basis for other English activities, especially talk and creative written work.
(iii) They carry over into other subjects (often through thematic or topic work) linking with painting, music, drama, or helping to 'bring alive' the past or other countries, or presenting material for the discussion of moral and ethical values.

(c) *Literary*
  (i) At the simplest level, books enjoyed strengthen interest in literature; they progressively make more demanding works available to the reader.
 (ii) They deepen literary appreciation by increasing awareness of concepts, forms and structures used in fiction.
(iii) They enable the reader to discriminate, evaluate on a wider base.
 (iv) They help to establish an understanding of the nature of literature and of the course of literary history.

To put this even more briefly: to lay particular stress on

personal functions assumes that stories give pleasure and develop understanding.
curricular functions assumes that they aid learning of things external to the book itself
literary functions assumes that acquiring literary and critical values is good in itself.

Such a simple model as this can be used to define what is perhaps the greatest single problem in the teaching of literature in schools. Briefly, there is an apparent gulf between the responses teacher say they value and wish to encourage and those which much of their work and most of the examining process actually elicit.

What do English teachers want the reading of literature to achieve for their pupils? In an interesting enquiry Malcolm Yorke asked a sample of teachers to rate nearly 100 objectives for teaching literature on a scale ranking from 'extremely important' to 'totally unimportant'.[12] He found a striking similarity between the attitudes of teachers of different sexes, ages, and types of school. With little variation, they agreed in placing first a series of affective aims from the *personal* section of the model suggested above. It was most important that pupils should derive emotional pleasure and release from their books, develop positive attitudes towards reading, develop personally and socially through empathy, become tolerant and gain insights into relationships. It was also of some importance that books should trigger the pupil's own creativity, foster communication skills, increase vocabulary and so on (aims from the *curricular* section). What were rated very low were those objectives that might be termed *literary*:

developing the ability to discriminate, learning to appreciate literary conventions, forms and techniques, gaining knowledge about books and authors.

THE BROKEN-BACKED CURRICULUM

An examination of response helps us to understand the lack of cohesion between the different stages of teaching fiction in school and between the ways in which teachers and pupils perceive the learning process.

At the primary stage or early in the secondary school pupils may respond to novels in such terms as these: 'It was the best book I've ever read, and I'm going to read it right through again', or '*Watership Down* made me cry because at the end they went back home and found their place covered by a big city', or 'Kizzy made me look differently at new children in school'. Further up the school, they are more likely to write: 'Although the narrative structure may owe something to the Gothic novel, the psychological realism is wholly individual', or 'This is in nature a prophetic satirical novel, much more bitter than the sugar-coated pill of *Animal Farm.*' These are different modes of response, legitimate in a different context. The model of what is thought appropriate in examination work shifts abruptly from what is felt to what is thought, from personal reaction to cool analysis, and from instinctive evaluation to a carefully learned technique of judgement.

The absence of a more personal reaction at this level is understandable, though not inevitable, because of the nature of the examination system. Certainly the JMB write of their A-level English examination that among the five areas which it 'attempts to assess', one is 'the candidate's response to literature, jointly affective and evaluative (i.e. his personal response and his understanding of the causes of his response)'. Experienced examiners, though, must surely feel that only very rarely does authentic response come through in a situation where the student has 45 minutes, without the text, to deal with topics like:

> What does the River Thames contribute to the interest of *Our Mutual Friend?*
> In what sense can you regard Peacock's work as a corrective to the excesses of Romanticism?
> What are some of the ways in which Virginia Woolf in *To the Lighthouse* departs from the conventional methods of the English novel?

Even more at O-level, questions on novels frequently put a premium on parroting and insincerity, often limiting responses to the predetermined measures by which they will be assessed. They seem to have little to do with those aims of emotional enjoyment and personality development which teachers see as so important.

Worse still, when Her Majesty's Inspectors found that reading had been 'impoverished' in secondary schools by a concentration on examination requirements, that emphasis was not found only in examination forms, like the unfortunate group that had written from dictation, a 23,000 word plot summary of *Far From the Madding Crowd*.[13] Despite all the demonstrations of the failings of traditional comprehension tests as a way of learning or of testing understanding, few course books for young children avoid using passages of fiction to be accompanied by lists of boring questions and associated exercises supposedly designed to increase vocabulary and to develop understanding. Pupils are not infrequently asked to write a 'review' of the book (a highly sophisticated exercise) or to answer sets of questions from worksheets or commercially produced 'literature cards'.

> What do you think has made this the most famous horse book ever written? (*Black Beauty*)
> Find out from this book when it was first published . . . Does it seem to you at all old-fashioned? (*Ballet Shoes*)
> 'The ending is tragic but true to life. Any other ending would have been false.' Do you agree? (*Red Pony*)
> Compare *The Canyon* with Steinbeck's story *The Pearl*. What similarities are there between the stories? In what ways are they different?
> What part do the sharks play in the book? What do you think they are meant to symbolize? (*The Old Man and the Sea*)

Experiments described by Gunnar Hansson have shown that older students themselves see major differences between the ways in which they respond to literature and those in which their teachers and other literary 'experts' react (and ultimately expect them to react). When the students were asked to rank a number of criteria for making judgements about text, and then to rank those which they thought were most important for teachers and scholars, the two lists were not only very different, but different in a significant way.

> When the students rank for themselves, the most important criteria are the emotional impact of the work, the author's imagination, the moral significance of the work, and the author's sincerity. All these criteria, which pay attention to human qualities in literature . . . are placed low down in the supposed ranking by experts and teachers. Instead, a number of purely *formal* criteria, such as form and style, aesthetic order, and symbols and metaphors, are considered to be very important. . .
> Results of this kind may make us wonder about the way literature is taught at school, and what gives the students their opinions of what is more or less important to their teachers.[14]

In some schools the whole programme is broken-backed: an abrupt change comes about the ages of 13 to 14. Before and after that break, different aims operate, books are read in different ways and different responses (expressed in different language styles) are demanded from pupils. To exaggerate for clarity: after the break children study the book, the whole book and nothing but the book in obsessive detail which extends to the notes at the bottom of the page. The purposes of the work are essentially literary. At earlier stages, the book is frequently seen as a springboard into something more interesting, a means rather than an end in itself, because the purposes are what we termed curricular or personal.

This shifting of emphasis away from the book itself can be illustrated from an American work for teachers, *Response Guides for Teaching Children's Books* (1979).[15] Here are some of the teaching ideas:

> Suggestions for work on *Charlotte's Web* by E. B. White:
> Design and construct a web out of string, yarn, or other material. Place it conspicuously in a corner of the classroom. During the class involvement with the book, the web can be used as a setting for vocabulary words to be learned.
> In pairs, practise looking terrific, then radiant, and finally humble.
> With several other students, plan and perform a pantomime of Wilbur trying to spin a web. . .
> If possible, spend an hour or so carefully observing a spider in its web. Take notes on its habits, appearance, and prey and report to the class.
>
> *The Lion, the Witch and the Wardrobe*
> Using coat-hanger wire, thread, and other materials, make a mobile that represents one of the contrasts in the book, such as good against evil, or winter against spring.
>
> *Call it Courage*
> Try building a fire by rubbing two sticks together. Write a report on your efforts and results. Did you succeed? Why or why not? Was it as hard as it was for Mafatu?

Such work seems *curricular* springboarding – the other activities take over from the book rather than developing a response to the text. *Personal*, affective springboarding by contrast can be defined as an obsession with what is happening inside children as a result of their reading, what the book is going to do to their personalities or their morals. A sensible awareness that books *do* things to people can lead to more questionable conclusions like these:

(i) The stronger the meat we offer the better, because it will produce *more* emotional reaction. So we choose books centring on brain-damaged children (*I Own the Racecourse*) or spastics (*Let the Balloon Go*) or baby-battering (*Squib*), illegal immigrants (*The Runaway Summer*) and drug-taking (*That was Then, This is Now*), or endlessly on sex.

(ii) The movement between literature and life should all be in the one direction in the classroom: the book is a key to unlock personal experience. I've seen rather too many lessons recently in which the story has been used as a simple device to trigger personal anecdotes:

How many of *you* have stolen things from shops?

How did it feel when *you* were bullied?

What really makes *you* mad with your parents?

Did *your* boy-friend ever behave like this? How do you stop him?

Oh . . . well, *why* don't you stop him?

(iii) The teacher's role is therapeutic: books are to be prescribed to change social attitudes. This, the view of the earliest writers of children's books, will be considered in the next section.

This brief examination of some aspects of discontinuity in our teaching of fiction at secondary level suggests that there are three chief reasons for concern:

1   There is often a wide discrepancy between the avowed purposes both of our formal curriculum statements and of what we say informally, and the methods and materials we actually use. Student-teachers often specify in their lesson-notes that 'pupils' enjoyment' should be the first aim, and yet the actual approaches used inhibit any kind of pleasure. The claim that literature will 'extend experience and knowledge of life' can easily be made unreal by the inappropriate choice of books, or by close attention to trivia and exercises.

2   There is often a gulf between the kinds of responses encouraged in the middle years and those seen as appropriate in examination forms. Not infrequently even in the fourth year pupils begin the detailed study of texts in which they will be examined at the end of the fifth. The responses which teachers *say* they wish most to develop are precisely those which are most difficult or impossible to assess by examination, and this makes for discontinuity in the programme.

3   Crucially to separate out subjective emotional responses and apparently objective critical thinking is surely to diminish and to weaken both. The responses of pleasure and the sense of personal development should be inseparable from knowing more about how stories work and from increasing the ability to compare and discriminate. The kind of polarizing that enquiries, such as those cited here, suggest to be common, is potentially damaging.

TEACHING FOR EFFECT

The effects of books on readers can be – have been – presented in very different styles and terminologies, varying from autobiographical anecdotes to statistical analyses. Frequently they reveal most about the tellers or writers and their situations rather than about the books themselves. The effect of reading can be described in terms which range from seeing it as a wholly unpredictable magic or as offering subconscious gratifications to personality building or bibliotherapy or a means towards social adaptation, or even as a direct moral influence causing shifts of belief, attitude and behaviour. The teacher's role in giving children books varies correspondingly from being a sort of magician to acting as psychologist, doctor, artist, preacher or social worker. In offering books to children, what is the teacher expecting to happen? Compare, for example, these assertions:

> . . . imaginative literature is therapeutic and does have a magical effect on people's minds and on their ultimate behaviour.[16]
>
> It is to make good some of the deficiencies of experience that people read fiction . . . to satisfy those needs, relieve our anxieties and assuage our guilt.[17]
>
> . . . we need now the courage to accept literature . . . (as) a source of rich and special pleasure, good in themselves, needing and perhaps having no further justification.[18]

It is true that some investigations have suggested that books can 'improve' children's attitudes to blacks or other ethnic groups and that the fears of dogs and darkness which young children have could be significantly reduced by hearing and discussing stories.[19] According to one large-scale survey of the relevant research, though, studies of the supposedly beneficial effects of reading on pupils' personality and conduct are 'meagre, limited in scope, and often indeterminate in result'.[20]

The more direct the influence of books on life is suggested to be, the more care teachers need to exercise in claiming it, as they move from books as a simple source of pleasure, through vicarious experience, to a means for changed attitudes and moral development, and eventually to modified behaviour. Reading *of itself* does not make better people, regardless of what is read, how it is read and understood, and the circumstances in which it is read. It didn't take George Steiner, with his hypothetical Nazis in concentration camps reading great poetry while torturing and killing, to make this clear. These personality-stretching effects may take place ('thanks to Betsy Byars my moral stature has increased by several inches') but it would be an unwise teacher who structured lessons deliberately to achieve them. They are more often incidental benefits that don't come by planning.

It may be salutary to read the caustic comments of an author like Patricia Beer, who argues that her own 'addiction' to print in the 1930s filled her with ' a deadly mixture of notions which were false, distorted, irrelevant to my own situation, or all three'.[21] Kathleen Raine has similarly described the dangers of imaginative reading on a girl's suburban upbringing, the confusion of things learned from books with actual lived experience. Her reading meant being animated by:

> . . . energies, desires, impulses, which because they can have no outlets, no expression in the real, generate only fantasies and discontent.[22]

There is no easy way of assessing whether intense emotional responses are ultimately beneficial. In an autobiographical passage, Fred Inglis has effectively caught the uncontrollable feelings with which as a boy he used to read key passages from Kipling's *Rewards and Fairies*:

> I used to read those lines time and time again, and each time the queer, crisp ripple of excitement tingled along my spine; the brimming tears which never quite fell, the chokey lump in the throat, were the result of having too much response to the passage and that response not knowing what to do with itself.[23]

About the best that we can safely say is that *some* books are good for *some* children in *some* ways on *some* occasions.

This brings us back to the role and the responsibility of the teacher. How far can one legitimately 'teach for' a particular kind of response? Is there a difference between vague hopes or aspirations and firm objectives? If pleasure is the highest aim, then can the teacher enhance it? Does it imply choosing books that are immediately attractive rather than those that are more demanding? How does the teacher assess whether or not a book is producing the personal responses hoped for? If fiction can have good effects on the personality, then does it not follow that it can also have bad effects? Some of these issues will be considered practically in part three. Here the concern must be with *intention*.

The failure of most simplistic statements of aims is that they assume that meaning, significance or even morality are directly conveyed through a book, that they can be imprinted on a passive reader's mind or soul. Teachers who see their task as to 'instruct' children in the 'meaning' of a book, or to make them by reading less sexist or racist, are ignoring the individuality of those children and the variety of their reactions. Fiction is not an exercise in explanation or persuasion but a potential experience, the nature of which is in part dependent on the reader. Any author who writes with too determined an intention produces not literature but propaganda. In the same way, a teacher who deliberately uses a story in order to create a particular effect on children runs the risk of debasing or even destroying the story. We have seen how powerful the effects of fiction can be. Indeed, it could be argued that a story does not take on its full meaning and significance *unless* something happens to the reader. D. W. Harding has suggested that 'Responding to a great work means becoming something different from your previous self.'[24] It is just that teachers cannot stipulate in advance what the work will do, or even assess very accurately in retrospect whether or not it has produced the personal responses hoped for.

It is these special qualities of response which mark off the study of fiction (indeed, of literature generally) from all other areas of the curriculum. When he examined over 20 documents describing literature

programmes in secondary schools, Alan Purves found that they never fell
neatly into cognitive or affective domains, because response was simultaneously cognitive, affective, perceptual and psychomotor. Criticism
involves not only analytic, intellectual activities but also ones concerned
with feelings and attitudes.[25] The experience of a story has no fixed boundaries in the way that most items on a syllabus have; to a degree it is unpredictable and uncontrollable. Norman Holland has pointed out that
responding to a story is in many ways similar to responding to any fresh
experience in real life:

> When someone responds to a new experience (poetic or any other kind), he
> does so by means of the personality and previous experience he brings to
> it.[26]

It will be argued in the next chapter that in thinking about our lives, in
striving to make the world intelligible, we shape our own stories out of our
accumulated responses to real events and to those we read and hear about.
The actual and the fictional are inseparably interlocked within us.

CONCLUSION

It has been suggested that when teachers are engaged in choosing books
for pupils, or establishing the aims of reading programmes, or deciding
how to use a novel with a class, or attributing values to the reading of
fiction, they do so inevitably in the light of their existing knowledge of children's responses, and their predictions based on this. In most cases that
knowledge is implicit and frequently unformulated: 'it goes with the ter-
ritory'. Student-teachers find it hard to acquire such expertise because it
is internalised, it does not exist for them in any coherent, assimilable form.
In an important article more than 10 years ago, Geoffrey Yarlott distinguished between the many 'assumptions' made about literature teaching
and the little that was known 'objectively'. He repeatedly described
teachers' operations as intuitive:

> We have little but intuition to guide us therefore in choosing literature
> appropriate to the pupil's level of emotional development.
> Until we know more about the factors involved in children's comprehen-
> sion of literature . . . we must rely mainly on intuition to support our critical
> sense. . .[27]

More recently, Chris Woodhead summed up an article on the teaching of
literature:

> We are not yet clear about what counts as an appropriate educational objec-
> tive in this area of the curriculum, and there is at present considerable

uncertainty amongst English teachers as to the books and methods which are most likely to succeed with pupils of different ages and abilities.[28]

Any improvement on intuition and any clearer curricular framework will have to depend on increased understanding of children's responses to their reading. The next sections, therefore, concentrate on the processes of reading fiction and on the ways in which responses seem to develop.

2 Focus on Fiction-reading

'Oh, Sara,' Ermengarde whispered joyfully, 'it is like a story!'
'It is a story,' said Sara. 'Everything's a story — I am a story.
Miss Minchin is a story.'

Frances Hodgson Burnett, *The Little Princess*

WHAT IS FICTION

The problems of defining fiction can be neatly illustrated by looking at the words of two fiction writers. From one side, Penelope Mortimer is a novelist who argues that, 'I really don't believe that there is such a thing as fiction',[1] while from the other Alan Sillitoe claims that 'everything written is fiction, even non-fiction'.[2] Nothing or everything? Fiction is one of those terms which we use with a tacit assumption of shared understanding, but also with an uneasy awareness that it is a category which cannot be defined by particular qualities, nor marked off by secure frontiers from other written modes. The wider argument that literature itself is not linguistically autonomous, distinguished from other forms of discourse[3], has been accompanied by increasing unease about other convenient, conventional boundaries between fiction and non-fiction, between prose fiction and fiction in the form of television, film and radio, between quality fiction and non-quality, between adult fiction and children's fiction, and between the fiction children read and the fiction they write.

We recognize a novel as such according to the ways in which our expectations have been conditioned. Experimental works (*Tristram Shandy*, *Moby Dick*, *Slaughterhouse 5*) have been denied the title 'novel' by some critics of their own time because they seemed not to fit existing categories. The coming of faction, of dramatized history on television, simply made more obvious the already existing breakdown of tidy definitions which discriminated between reality and fiction, true and false. As readers we have been repeatedly challenged by such occasions as when Truman Capote calls *In Cold Blood* a 'non-fiction novel', or when Norman Mailer introduces himself as a third-person character in his own narrative, or when B. S. Johnson drops the mask of the protagonist in *Albert Angelo* to reveal himself at work. One of Andrew Sinclair's novels which breaks down barriers between biography and fiction has a character who proclaims, 'All writing is untrue . . . writing can only be a better or a worse fiction. . . .'[4]

In the light of the first chapter, it seems more helpful to shift attention from theorizing about what fiction *is* to what fiction *does*: to look at the process of readers reading novels and responding to them. When Hull children are asked about the meaning of fiction, they tend to make functional distinctions, to describe what happens when they are engaged with a story.

'In a story I get involved . . . I just read other books for information.' (boy 11)

'When I read stories I see pictures, whereas when I read other books I collect facts in my head.' (girl 11)

'In stories I feel the excitement and different feelings but in factual books I read with no feelings but with interest as the facts flow into my head.' (girl 13)

'Information books don't come alive for me as novels do.' (boy 13)

'I usually just flick through a factual book when I need some information, find the piece I want and read it quickly. With a story of my own choice I get into it, and if it's a good book I try to make the last page last forever.' (girl 13)

Children realize in a common-sense way that our knowledge of things is tied to the ways in which we encounter and use them. We are rarely, if ever, in the position of reading a book to see whether or not it is a novel; almost always we approach a book with a particular set of expectations because we know it is a novel (from its position on the shelves, or from what people have told us, or because of the name of the author, or the fact it says 'a novel' on the title page, or the general lay-out of the book). Fiction is what we call books that we read in a particular way, or from a particular stance. This chapter considers what is involved in that process of reading fiction, and why it should be thought of as important.

WHY IS FICTION IMPORTANT?

In his late 1950s study of the psychology of reading, Simon Lesser suggested that the almost universal activity of reading about imaginary people and events had received surprisingly little attention and was rarely seen as either important or praiseworthy. He suggested a variety of possible reasons for this: it seemed too easy and effortless, fiction was thought to be less 'important' than non-fiction, readers were afraid of yielding to fantasy or ashamed of the kind of satisfaction they derived.[5] Such dispar-agement is less common today, particularly as fiction is placed in the con-text of other narrative modes, like film and television and of our own story-making, in our heads and talking to others.

The importance of fiction for human beings can be asserted by argu-ments of different force and subtlety, most of which can be termed func-tional or developmental. The first group of these, that is, claims that such reading has beneficial effects on children's behaviour and on their general ability to read effectively and to work in other subjects. Appropriate fiction can significantly affect what is learned in other areas of the curriculum and outside the school. Children's views of the past, their ideas of other countries, their apprehension of scientific discovery can be radically affected by the stories they read and hear. The second group of arguments pushes back further to suggest that 'storying' is an essential element in consciousness – indeed is part of what it means to be human – and ulti-mately that the quality of living is related to the narrative models which have become available to an individual.

Functional arguments tend to rest on the overwhelming evidence that it is chiefly fiction which impels children to read, to learn and to continue reading in later life. The Bullock report said firmly, 'It was clear that the narrative mode provided for all children by far the strongest motivation towards the reading of books', and suggested that adult illiterates were characterized by the fact that they had never developed any sense of plea-sure to be gained from reading stories. The large-scale survey carried out for the Schools Council by Frank Whitehead and others reported in *Chil-dren and their Books*,[7] makes it clear that narrative – primarily fiction, but also including biography – 'accounts for the overwhelming majority of children's book reading' in the age range 10 to 14. Non-narrative only accounts for about a seventh of the freely-chosen reading of boys and girls surveyed. Put another way, of the 246 most widely read books – those mentioned by 10 or more children as having been read in the past month – almost all were novels, and only one was non-narrative: *The Guinness Book of Records*. Put yet another way, all the writers named by a significant number of children as their favourite authors, at age 10, 12 and 14, were novelists. Reading abilities and habits are formed primarily through encounters with fiction.

Developmental arguments are grounded in the apparently universal appetite for stories which asserts itself long before children can read or write. The act of reading or hearing a story mirrors our experience of life itself: we read as we live along a time-scale, continually seeing things in a new perspective as we look back at what has gone before to make sense of the experience, or look forward to an unknown future. In our speculations about how life or story may turn out, in our hopes and fears, we realise that the possible range of choices narrows as we go on, and that there is an inevitable end, near or far, satisfactory or unsatisfactory. The notion that narrative is an essential element in our understanding of reality, that 'We cannot think, act or desire except in narrative',[8] indeed that 'we may live more by fiction than by fact',[9], has now become a commonplace.[10] Barbara Hardy has written particularly effectively about narrative as 'a primary act of mind' through which human consciousness operates. 'In order really to live, we make up stories about ourselves and others, about the personal as well as the social past and future.' She describes how we give meaning to our experiences by shaping them, arranging them in sequence, looking for causes and effects, providing beginnings and endings, establishing similarities and distinctions – in other words, by turning our lives into stories.[11]

Our own narratives are constrained by the culture in which we live, by our intelligence and personality and the language at our disposal, by our past history and by our hopes and dreams for the future. They are potentially enlarged by the anecdotes we hear, the narratives of television and newspapers and the enormous resources of printed fiction. Frank Kermode and Umberto Eco, among others, have argued that we can only make sense of existence by using the structural devices we have learned from fiction, that to examine and analyse life we must 'think of it as a traditional novel'. Additionally, though, Kermode sees a major function of literature as challenging and unsettling the fictions by which we conventionally live, exposing the poverty of the roles we assume and enlarging our sense of what is conceivable and possible. Great fiction thus subtly changes the people that we are.

If we share these views of story, and if we believe that there is a developmental continuity between the stories we hear and tell ourselves as children and those we read and tell ourselves as adults, this is of major importance for the teacher. The presentation of fiction in school is not just an academic exercise if the quality of narrative is intimately related to the quality of life. The ultimate importance of the fiction we read to children or put in their hands lies not in any 'moral' it may convey, but in the fact that through it young people are helping to develop a sense of themselves and of their shifting place in the world as they grow up.

CHILDREN'S DESCRIPTION OF THE READING PROCESS

When we look at the ways which children themselves talk or write about reading, the ways in which they experience a story or novel once they are capable of reading independently for pleasure, we see that it is almost always in terms of a direct relationship between their own lives and the imagined life of the book. They repeatedly use spatial images, talking of the way they *move through* the events, *enter* or stand *beside* a character, observe incidents *there* before them. People and incidents are realized in terms of familiar individuals and places; motives are tested by 'how would I feel?' or 'what would I do?'

In distinguishing between the accounts of different children, the key factor is the amount of distance between the reader and the people and events of the story. At one extreme is the sense of total immersion, of being 'lost', 'wrapped up in', 'carried away by' the story. At the other extreme is the relative detachment, promoted in examination forms, which we call loosely 'critical reading'. An examination of children's responses in some of the Hull enquiries suggests that there are five major ways in which they see the process of reading fiction. These five can be arranged on such a scale of 'increasing distance', without suggesting that the fifth mode is necessarily 'better' than the first. Although younger children (aged 11 to 12) are much more likely to be classed in modes 1 or 2, and although modes 4 to 5 draw mostly on pupils of 14 or over, there is no neat correlation between age and stage. Particularly at 13 or 14, a group that covers the ability range is likely to contain individuals whose preferred responses belong in each of the five categories. Partly to make this clear, most of the replies quoted here are drawn from that age group.

What does seem to be associated with maturity in reading is the ability to operate in an increasing number of modes, according to the work being read and the mood or needs of the moment, rather than assuming that there is only one way of reading. Most of us can remember the times when we were enjoying simultaneously Dickens, *The Magnet*, Arthur Ransome, Kipling, *Rover* and *Hotspur* with no sense of incongruity, but also reading them for different purposes with quite different kinds of attention. In this respect, 'progress' in reading might be defined as the increasing ability to match modes of reading to the material being read.

There were, of course, children who either did not understand questions about how they read, or who were not willing to respond to them. A number retorted simply, 'I just read it, that's all' or 'If it's interesting I keep reading it and if it's boring I stop!' The assumption there is of an automatic decoding process: fiction makes little impact, or none that the reader is prepared to acknowledge. Some of these replies indicate that pupils have been put off reading by being forced to read books they found too dull, difficult or babyish. Virtually all the other responses, however, can be classified as belonging to one of the following modes.

Mode One: Projection into a character

The simplest and commonest way of experiencing what one 16-year-old boy described as being 'immersed ... *in* the book ... identifying with some of the characters' is imaginatively to become one of them, to lose yourself in that character's personality and situation. The same idea is repeated over and over again:

'I put myself in the person's place I am reading about.' (girl 13)

'I often imagine I am one of the characters, the hero or heroine.' (boy 13)

'I often think I am a character in the book and feel the feelings that she does.' (girl 14)

'I think I sort of move into the characters and can experience what they feel.' (boy 14)

Sometimes they mention books which they like to read in this way: frequently Enid Blyton's stories for younger girls and James Bond books or other thrillers for boys. An interesting view of the extent of the identification is given by a girl of 14: 'I imagine myself as the character and if I stop reading the book without finishing I find it hard to pick the story up again because I have forgotten my past.' The notion of 'becoming' conveyed in '*my* past' is vivid. This is not an experience limited to younger children. D. H. Russell cites studies which quote older, able students who identified with the protagonists of novels. Reading *The Catcher in the Rye*, one reported that 'after a few pages I found I was not merely reading the book, I was also living it.' Another said of *Portrait of the Artist as a Young Man* that 'In reading Joyce's novel I *was* the 'young man'.'[13]

Mode Two: Projection into the situation

Many readers describe the experience as being 'there' in the book with the characters, but not as identifying with any one of them. They see themselves as spectators on the outskirts or margin of events, emotionally involved but unable to affect the action. They often perceive themselves as 'close' to the characters, their 'friend'.

'I usually imagine I am actually there and I know the characters very well.' (girl 13)

'I feel as though I am there, witnessing the events ... I am the characters' friend.' (boy 13)

I usually begin to feel I know the characters, that I'm there in their conversations, looking on.' (girl 13)

I think that I am there with the characters, listening and seeing everything they do and say. Sometimes I feel that I am one of them.' (girl 14)

Not infrequently readers conceive themselves as being present but invisible to the characters:

> 'As I read a book I imagine that I am very close to where the events are happening, but I always remain unseen.' (girl 14)

> 'I see myself as an invisible spectator who sees everything that happens.' (boy 13)

One or two perceive themselves as a kind of 'extra' character, alongside the ones in the book: 'I quite often find myself as a character in that adventure, though the character is never mentioned in the book.'

Mode Three: Associating between book and reader

Whereas in the first two stages readers are to differing degrees trying to enter the book and to lose themselves in it, here they are more concerned to establish links between themselves as readers with their own actual experiences and the people and situations of the book. The movement is in both directions: they visualize the book in terms of their own world, and they imagine how they would feel and act if they were people in the story. The first movement is expressed in such terms as these:

> 'Often part of the scene I read about I imagine to be going on at a place I know and am very familiar with e.g. my best friend's house.' (girl 14)

> 'When I read, the things which pass through my mind are similar experiences of my own.' (girl 13)

> 'When I read about other people's feelings, I try to think to a time when I have had the same feelings and I sort of get involved.' (girl 13)

> 'When I read about people's emotions, I think to myself, "Is it like me?".' (boy 13)

The second movement is described like this:

> 'I put myself in their position and see if I would think or do the same as them.' (boy 13)
> 'I think what would I do or say in that situation.' (girl 13)
> 'I wonder how I would react in the same situation.' (girl 14)
> 'I always put myself in their place and think about what I'd do in their position.' (girl 15)

In other words, readers may realize the secondary world of the book by importing into it elements from their first-hand experience, or they may use the book as a testing-ground for their own feelings and ideas, or indeed both.

Mode Four: The distanced viewer

A number of readers described their experiences as being somehow 'above' the characters, watching them play out their roles as if on a kind of chessboard. 'I just see it all by looking down,' said a 15-year-old girl. Other critics have quoted children who described this mode of reading as being like watching a play on television, or a film, or a football match from the stand. The reader is firmly outside the action, but emotionally involved in what happens and wishing to be able to influence the outcome. One 13-year-old said, 'I sometimes get so close that I start to think of ways of stopping or starting what is happening.' Within this view of reading they may express feelings of empathy or a more distanced awareness of what 'ought' to be happening.

'I feel differently for the characters: if they are unhappy I pity them, if they are mean I hate them, etc.' (girl 14)

'I feel I want to know what their feelings are, if they are in trouble help them.' (girl 14)

'When I read a book, I hope that the baby doesn't get injured and that the villain gets killed and so on.' (boy 13)

'They seem to come real and you feel to know them . . . I keep thinking to tell them to do the right thing.'(boy 13)

'I think how the characters should have done something different.' (girl 14)

Mode Five: Detached evaluation

This mode of reading is rarely mentioned except by older pupils. A 14-year-old girl is perhaps operating in this way when she says, 'I understand, rather than feel, the emotions of the characters.' She seems neither to be identifying nor to be empathising with the figures in the story, but to be analysing them more coolly. Another says, 'I like to see how the author tells the story, creates the mood . . .' A boy who reads science fiction 'to see how convincing the inventions are' is, in a different way, also reading from a stance that is likely to inhibit emotional involvement with the story. Critical reading seems to be a form of behaviour learned in school. Gill Frith quotes a girl of 17:

What enters my mind when I read a book

When I read a book, the things that go through my mind are whether I can understand the characters, the way in which they act and why they act in a certain way. Whether the plot is moving fast enough or whether there is not enough action but too many descriptive passages. I often guess as to what will be the outcome of a certain scene and whether the scene will greatly influence other scenes . . . If I find the book interesting I will tend not to take in what I am reading at the moment but think about what will be happening on the next page or in the next chapter.[14]

The concepts here seem to be those that have grown out of literary studies. One boy was aware of the difference between the ways in which he responded while actually reading a novel and at the end of the process, looking back. He saw the more detached mode as essentially retrospective. While reading, the characters 'are part of you and you of them in the action, and as you are reading you want to help them and live for real the life the character has. Afterwards one thinks more carefully and considers what that character considered. . . .' (boy 15)

More perceptive readers were aware, as adults are, not only that different people react differently to the same text, but also that individuals respond in varied ways to different works, or even to the same work at different moments. One 14-year-old girl began a lengthy analysis of her own reading habits:

'I feel with the characters, sometimes I am an onlooker watching the adventure, sometimes I am one of the characters. I feel great sympathy with the characters if they die or become blind, crippled etc. I enjoy trying to work out riddles and mysteries if they are written like that. . . .'

She swiftly moves through phrases that could be categorized as belonging to different stages, fully aware of herself bringing the text alive in a variety of ways.

Even such a straightforward consideration of how children perceive the reading of stories raises a number of more difficult questions. What is it that keeps some children stuck at mode one wish-fulfilment reading? Do we place too obsessive an emphasis on mode five, critical reading, in the sixth form, rather than being concerned for extending the range of responses? Should we try to relate the choice of novels more directly to the preferred modes of groups and individuals? Are there certain modes which make subsequent discussion of response less appropriate than others?

MODELS OF THE FICTION-READING PROCESS

The ways we work with fiction in school will inevitably be conditioned by how we see the relationship between readers and the text. That is one reason why understanding how children themselves perceive this, described in the previous section, is so important. For teachers, there are two traditional but unsatisfactory models of the process – unsatisfactory both because they are inadequate as descriptions *and* because they lead automatically to unsuitable work in the classroom.

The first of these is the extreme objective model, which suggests that the text has a 'meaning', to be simply conveyed to passive recipients. It is assumed that they will or can all receive the same meaning and that they can be tested to see whether this has taken place. The teacher is the arbiter between 'right' and 'wrong' readings (a convenient view for someone who has to 'take' the same book with a whole class). It has been strengthened by some of the more naïve communications models with their simple diagrams of transmitters, messages and receivers. Here the reader is seen as a blank tablet waiting to be imprinted almost automatically with the text. The story (or poem) is seen as 'representing' some kind of ideal absolute reading (sometimes identified with the author's 'intention') to which all individual readings will more or less approximate.

The second is the extreme subjective model. Here the work is seen as lifeless or even non-existent until its 'meaning' is supplied by the reader. Since all readers construct their own private meanings, which are the only ones valid for them, there are no such things as right or wrong interpretations or judgements. The immediate reactions of pupils do not need to be discussed or developed; they are of equal validity because, 'it's all a matter of opinion'.

Teachers in school, and particularly in sixth forms, have been in a good position to see the damaging effects of such critical polarizing between extreme subjective and objective positions. Their students, after all, swing in a relatively unsophisticated way between the subjective notion that literary preference is not unlike supporting a football team ('I know what I like', 'it's all a matter of taste') and the objective assumption that there is a 'correct' interpretation or judgement which must be accepted, however insincerely, and afterwards parroted. Ultimately, to argue that the text is the *same* for all readers or *different* for all readers is equally unproductive. Both arguments make teaching (in the sense of shared learning and development) and discussion pointless.

There is, however, another model available between these two extremes. Although their views differ in a number of respects, scholars like Louise M. Rosenblatt, Barbara Hardy, Wolfgang Iser, Frank Smith and Norman Holland agree in the kinds of terminology which they use to describe the dynamic relationship between reader and text. It is an activity variously termed a transaction, a re-creation, a performance, an interplay, a participation, an interaction, a construction or an encounter. The literary work does not have to be seen as either entirely internal, equated with the mental and emotional experience of a reader regardless of its relevance to the text, or entirely external, an entity which exists independently of being read. Iser says that the 'convergence' of text and reader can never be precisely pinpointed, 'as it is not to be identified either with the reality of the text or with the individual disposition of the reader'.[15] Reading itself is to be seen as a creative activity, as the increasing number of studies of readers reading demonstrates.

In the process of reading a story, the narrative is 'constructed' or 'performed' through a series of interactions at any given moment. The potential information in the text is realized in terms of the individual reader's actual and second-order experience of the world. Any particular moment in the narrative is construed in terms of the accumulated, self-correcting impressions which have snowballed up to that point. The reader's shifting viewpoint makes the different attitudes, viewpoints and perspectives of the story act upon and modify each other. This process is carried out in part through the reader's awareness of the literary conventions and techniques employed. We comprehend and weigh up the values and concepts implicit in the text in terms of our own social and ideological views.

In practical terms, we can see how this happens when we talk with children who have read only a small part of a novel or who are keeping journals of their reactions as they work through the book, or when we show them a story in short sections and ask them to describe what they understand from each section in turn. We see them establishing a network of connections between their life experiences and the pages of the text, formulating notions of what will happen and remaking them, judging and commenting in a personal way. Children of 11 and 12 in Hull repeatedly use the same phrases in describing their changing perspectives of stories: I guess, I still haven't worked out, I'm sure that, it gave me a clue, perhaps it could mean, *now* I think, I suppose, it's definitely, I expect, I don't agree, it didn't seem true, I hope. There is a perpetual two-way movement between the reader and the narrative.[16]

Such practical studies show clearly that neither the mechanistic image of blank minds being imprinted by the text nor the building-blocks image of readers making at random some self-gratifying meaning out of a text that simply provides raw materials is adequate. In Horst Ruthrof's phrase, 'The reader is changed by a work which he has partly constructed himself'.[17] Because of this process of mutual modification, our second reading of a novel is never the same as the first. We have changed, and so have our expectations of the story.

This view of readers as 'producers' of the text rather than as 'consumers'[18] (similar to Brecht's view of ideal audiences as actively 'transforming' a play rather than being carried along passively by it[19]), points to the unique quality which books possess, as opposed to other everyday objects. Seen as an 'aesthetic object'[20], the book exists as a potential experience, to be 'realized' or 'performed' by readers. It diminishes – or even eliminates – the sense of division between the thinking mind and the objects of thought, between 'in here' and 'out there'. Forty years ago, F. R. Leavis said that the text was only 'there' in terms of the reader's response: we can have it 'only by an inner kind of possession'.[21] In the late 1960s, George Poulet termed books 'interior' or 'subjectified' objects: 'You are inside it; it is inside you, there is no longer outside or inside.' To a degree, the work lives its own life within us, we think the thoughts of another, we and the book 'start having a common consciousness'.

> Thus I often have the impression, while reading, of simply witnessing an action which at the same time concerns and yet does not concern me. This provokes a certain feeling of surprise within me. I am a consciousness astonished by an existence which is not mine, but which I experience as though it were mine.[22]

Similarly Norman Holland sees the reading experience going on in 'a space which reader and work create together'[23], and Wolfgang Iser says that instead of seeing novels from the outside, our viewpoint 'travels along *inside* that which it has to apprehend. This mode of grasping an object is unique to literature'.[24]

Although Poulet, Holland and Iser realize the concept in significantly different spatial images (the text is 'in' us, 'thinking' us in Poulet; we travel 'through' it in Iser; we meet in a mutually created third ground, a 'potential space' in Holland) they agree on the essential interactional qualities of the model of reading that is being presented.

The significance of such a model of books and reading for teachers is profound, for it relocates the centre of attention. The sterile antithesis between 'subject-centred' and 'child-centred' education is related to the two outmoded models of the reading process. Years ago, John Dixon wrote in *Growth Through English* that what was vital was the 'interplay' between the world of the child and the world of the writer:

> ... a teacher must acknowledge both sides of the experience and know both of them intimately if he is to help to bring the two into a fruitful relationship.[25]

This marks the significant difference between simply decoding the words of a text and actually hearing or reading a story. A child's enjoyment only begins when she or he is 'productive' or 'creative', when the text brings into play the reader's or listener's own faculties. 'It's boring' and 'It's silly' are the cries of children who are not willing or not able to participate, for whom the text is making too many demands or not enough. In these terms, one of the marks of the best fiction for children is that it leaves the readers sufficient room to remake the book as they read it, bringing to it their own experiences of life and of other books, giving characters and incidents a concrete form, filling in what is implied rather than stated, speculating and questioning, judging and sympathising. Trivial, undemanding books spell out everything; they leave nothing for the reader to do; stock formula stories eliminate all sense of the unexpected. One of the reasons that we rarely find filmed versions of novels satisfactory is that they eliminate the imaginative opportunity for us to 'construct' and visualize characters and incidents for ourselves.

In down-to-earth terms, the responses of a class of children to a story could be graphically represented by a series of overlapping circles. No two will be identical: a story will have as many versions as it has readers. On the other hand, no two will be totally dissimilar: everybody is transforming the same structures with particular potential for being realized. Readers are not only aware of the imagined characters and events evoked by the words on the page, but of the feelings, ideas, attitudes and associations which those words and events simultaneously arouse in them. As these are built into the 'meaning', it may become apparent that some of these personal responses, memories and associations will be less relevant than others, and some may have to be rejected. Louise Rosenblatt sums up the complex activity by saying that the reader's creation of a story or a poem out of a text has to be an 'active, self-ordering and self-corrective process'.[26]

THE RANGE OF INTERPRETATION

There are clear implications for our teaching practice if we hold that meaning is something which develops in the reader's interaction with the text rather than something which is in the text and has to be pulled out of it, like plums from a pie. Unfortunately the tradition, both in teaching and in criticism, has often been to emphasize the retrieving of some pre-existing meaning which the author has verbalized. Such a tradition grows understandably from the roles which teachers and critics see themselves called on to fulfil, essentially providing an interpretation of a work, which others can adopt ready-made.

> Many, perhaps most critics write, not as though they themselves were actively discovering forms and synthesizing ideas in what they read, but as if they were just passively reporting what is 'objectively' there.[27]

The significant issue for the teacher in considering the interaction between reader and text is: how much variation in interpretation is permissible? I. A. Richards once wrote crisply:

> In interpreting anything, we are letting parallels from our past guide our choice or construction of a meaning. In good interpretation the right parallels are at work; in bad interpretations wrong ones are.[28]

Quite right, of course, as far as it goes. The difficulty is that individual readers and critics fail to agree which readings come under those neatly polarized headings good/bad, right/wrong. In the mid-1960s, enquiring into students' reading of novels, James Wilson found it impossible to separate out valid interpretations from invalid ones. Although some responses were unsophisticated, partial or evasive, he wrote, 'it would have been difficult to demonstrate that these interpretations were mis-interpretations'.[29] We are forced to ask whether a highly personal, idiosyncratic reading of a story is necessarily a *bad* one. And if so, bad for whom? If we say that one of our students has misread a story, then how do we justify that opinion? When D. W. Harding grappled with these issues, he based his answers on the notion of consistency (relating the interpreta-tion of a passage to the whole text and to other language contexts of the period). He admitted, though:

> No objective demonstration of a mis-reading is possible, except perhaps where a critic has misunderstood the plain sense of a word or mis-read the author's sentence structure. Otherwise only discussion of the probabilities and mutual attempts at persuasion are open to us. But these are vital. There really are probable and less probable senses and implications of the poet's words or the playwright's sequence of scene and action.[30]

It may be helpful, then, to sketch out simply the different levels of response or interpretation in terms of their apparently objective 'right-ness' at one end of the spectrum and their essentially subjective associa-tions at the other.

1 Matters of fact which are demonstrable from the text and about which any argument can be resolved. These include such elements as dates and places, relationships of characters, the actual actions and words spoken.
2 Clear implications, construed from the attitudes and values of the work as a whole. These include such judgements of character, awareness of irony, evaluation of choices of action and so on that would be generally agreed by mature readers.
3 Manifest literary effects (which may be defined by some readers as those 'intended' by the author). These cover the use of repeated images or sym-bolic patterns, the sense of structure, deliberate openness or ambiguity, shifts of viewpoint, and so on.
4 Shared associations. These assume readers who have first-hand or second-hand awareness of events or subjects, necessary for a full under-standing of a reference. The size of the sharing group who know eighteenth century hymns or Japanese prints, who recall the world of Bloomsbury or the sound of a V.1 is inevitably hard to define and changes with time.
5 Significance based on a particular stance. The reader may share the author's viewpoint – Christian, Marxist, structuralist, feminist – or differ from it, in which case any pattern of interpretation may create a different sense of the 'real' meaning.

6   Private associations. Most readers are conscious that texts evoke personal memories, images and ideas which are unlikely to be shared with others. Although these are not objectively 'there' in the text, they need not necessarily be 'wrong' because private. Some texts – love lyrics for example – seem designed to trigger off personal identifications.

Put another way, texts are organized so that readers can be certain that they are answering 'correctly' some of the implied questions about meaning, but less certain about others. When Dickens begins *Little Dorrit*:

> Thirty years ago, Marseilles lay burning in the sun one day. A blazing sun upon a fierce August day was no greater rarity in Southern France than at any other time, before or since

only one answer is possible to questions like:

> In what month and how long ago is this opening description said to be?
> In what country and city is it set?
> Was this unusual weather for that place and time of year?

The same answers would be given to the implied questions on the tenth reading as on the first. When, one page later, we read

> In Marseilles that day there was a villainous prison . . . Like a well, like a vault, like a tomb, the prison had no knowledge of the brightness outside . . .

there is more than one answer to questions like:

> Why is the prison described as 'villainous'?
> What is the effect on the reader of the sequence of images used to describe the prison?

A reader encountering these words for the first time is likely to answer in different terms from one who has just finished the whole book, or from one who has also studied what critics say about the theme of imprisonment in *Little Dorrit*.

We all know from experience how much our views change as the result of re-reading and of discussion with others. We can all remember reading *Emma* or *Mansfield Park* in quite different ways in school, at university and at different times in our teaching career. The fact that I now view *Mansfield Park* or *Little Dorrit* differently from the way I did, implies that I may well see them differently again in a few years' time. Of course, the 'I' that did, or will do the reading is not the same as the 'I' that is writing these words. At the moment, however, I am convinced that my current reading of the novel is the 'correct' one. This does not mean that I cannot entertain interpretations and judgements that differ from my own, but that they will either seem to some degree mistaken or foolish, or they will cause my own values to shift and accommodate them. In the latter case, this will not be because they are objectively 'right' but because *now* I have made them part of 'my' reading.

Our aim must surely be a classroom in which students are encouraged to look with interest at their own perceptions of the text, and to consider why it is that some of their responses are unique and others are shared with the rest of the group. We want them to become more conscious of the links between instinctive responses and apparently considered ones. Instead of seeing their snap judgements, false starts, changes of opinion and even mistakes as evidence of immature work, we should accept them as part of a developing response to the work, as signs of learning in progress.

3 Focus on Development

In our dealings with literature, I believe that we instinctively do, in
fact, all work on the assumption that there exists in our students a
developmental sequence . . . Along what dimensions might it be possible to describe this sequence? . . . Certainly we should expect our
pupils, as they grow older, to respond more sensitively to the literature they read [and we should] look at the kinds of experience which
young readers can take, with benefit to themselves, from their reading of literature at different stages.

Frank Whitehead, *The Dartmouth Seminar Papers*

THE NEED FOR A THEORY OF DEVELOPMENT

How is it that children develop the ability to come to grips with and to
enjoy increasingly difficult fiction? Of all the problems associated with
reading this is perhaps the one about which we know least and the one
about which teachers most want guidance. It is over 50 years since one
early study in the USA sought to distinguish readers of grades 8–10 from
those of grades 11–12 in terms of the way they understood ideas in books,
empathised with the characters and entered vicariously into fictional
events.[1] That work has hardly been followed up at all, despite the repeated
use of terms like *development, sequence, stages* and *changes* in the Dartmouth
papers. The study group there reported that 'There is a need for more
exact knowledge . . . about changes in the literary responses of boys and
girls as they grow up,'[2] and this has been echoed by such authorities as
Margaret Spencer (the 'developmental dimension in reading . . . is all too
little explored'[3]) and D. W. Harding:

The full grasp of fiction is a sophisticated achievement. Children come to
it gradually, and . . . little seems to be known about the steps by which they
reach it.[4]

When members of the Inspectorate claim, with reason, that in the critical study of imaginative literature, 'it is necessary to match the material
studied to the stage of development of the children'[5], they fail to go on and
say what model of development or what particular stages they have in

mind. The terms in which scholars write of the process of developing
response are essentially metaphorical: maturation, deeper insight, refined
imaginative grasp, greater capacity for critical assessment, developing
inward order, increasing sense of form, refined responses, developing
mastery of conventions, extending sympathies, deepening insights.[6]
These overlapping terms like *developing, maturing, growing, deepening,
refining, elaborating,* propose a focus for our attention, but do little more.
The generalizations are rarely fleshed out with examples of what a *better*
reading of a story involves. What are our criteria for saying that one child's
response is more 'developed' than it was a year ago, or that it is more
'mature' than this other child's? What are the marks of a 'refined grasp' of
a text?

Students in training repeatedly say that one of their greatest difficulties
is to know what they can reasonably expect of average 11 or 13 or 15-year-
olds in terms of their ability to enjoy, understand and evaluate stories.
They complain that no structure, even a tentative one, is available to them
as it is in other curricular areas. They may be aware of Piaget, Bereiter,
Kohlberg, Moffett and Wilkinson, for example, suggesting different
means of considering children's cognitive, moral and linguistic development. Kerschensteiner, Kellogg and others have attempted to show an
evolutionary process in children's drawing and painting. Significantly,
however, in the vast mass of work that has been done on reading during
recent years, patterns of change in response to fiction have been essentially ignored. Indeed, research into response has tended to concentrate
more on what can be measured than on what teachers need to know. Most
significant work has dealt with one of three questions:

1   What sorts of errors do students make when they read?
2   What kinds of test may measure literary appreciation?
3   In what modes do students express their response to reading?

It may be helpful to summarize what answers have been offered to these
questions by a great deal of enquiry.
1   Much of the most influential work on interpretational response has
concentrated on readers' errors, and the apparent reasons for them,
rather than comparing these with more perceptive readings of the text, or
looking at those particularly interesting interpretations which cannot simply be termed 'right' or 'wrong'. This is true, of course, of the seminal
work by I. A. Richards, in which he listed the classes of error made by
Cambridge undergraduates in responding freely to poems, and of his later
book in which he observed that passages of everyday prose were 'wildly
and inexplicably misread' by students and adults.[7] It applies equally to E.
L. Black's *The Difficulties of Training College Students in Understanding what
they Read*, which suggested seven reasons why future teachers showed

such 'disappointingly low levels of attainment' in comprehending prose.[8] Other studies with a differing apparent emphasis, have also tended to stress misreadings, limitations and 'sources of difficulty' in understanding.[9]

This vein would seem to have been sufficiently worked now. It is significant that from Richards to Ring the stance has been one of almost shocked surprise at how badly apparently intelligent people read. Because the studies have not examined the range of responses, to establish what marks off 'better' readings, and have tended to assume the rightness of their own interpretations, their practical value for teachers has been limited. The influence of Richards was particularly felt in the movement towards close study of short texts or passages, seen at its best perhaps in *The Use of English* and its associated teacher groups. This rested on an assumption that such work would significantly improve the reading of those engaged on it. Because of the failure to see the process in developmental terms, it is hard to assess whether improvement did in fact take place (and what kinds of improvement: in interpretation? avoidance of error? enjoyment? discrimination?).

2   Attempts to find a more objective base for any consideration of children's ability and development have tended to concentrate on batteries of diagnostic measures. Before the last war there was an influential article entitled *Tests of Literary Appreciation*, which was based on the application of five tests to over 200 children of different ages. All the tests were comparative: ranking compositions by children or literary figures in order of merit, or picking the better out of two or three passages. In these cases, the 'right' answers were obtained from 'literary experts'. It is perhaps not surprising that the authors concluded that 'The capacity for literary appreciation correlates highly with intelligence'.[10] Such discriminatory tests were not new: they had been in use early in the 1920s, and in 1933 students were asked to distinguish 'the good from the less good, and the less good from the very bad'.[11] More recently, Robert Zais suggested grading students by their ability to discriminate between story synopses, supposed to represent the least, moderately and most sophisticated tastes. These judgements had been 'validated' by a panel of 20 English teachers.[12]

In these and other similar studies, words like 'measure' and 'scale' constantly recur, but it is dubious how far they are effective in terms of reliability and validity. Much of the difference between individuals tested seems to be accounted for by characteristics of the texts studied and by the form of the questions or other testing instruments used, rather than by the literary 'ability' displayed by respondents.[13] The vague term 'literary appreciation' is rarely defined, the tasks set are unlike the actual reading experiences of children individually or in a class, and they usually imply a restricted view of what responding to literature involves.

3   It is clearly easier to employ straightforward descriptive rather than evaluative measures when examining readers' responses. Much of the most helpful work of recent years has sought to categorize students' free spoken or written responses to texts, distinguishing simple retelling of a story from interpreting it, judging it, relating it to the reader's own experience, and so on. Working with adolescent students, grades 9–10, and interviewing them while they were actually reading four short stories, James Squire analysed their responses in six categories. He found that the dominant mode was interpretational (accounting for more than 42% of all responses), followed by narrational re-telling and self-involvement, relating the reader to the characters in the story.[14] When the same categories were used to analyse the responses of older students to novels, James Wilson found that interpretational responses were even more dominant (65·6%) and that literary judgements (12·2%) were more common at this age than narrational and self-involvement (both just under 9%).[15] Among similar category systems, the most influential has been the simple but elaborately worked-out scheme of Purves and Rippere. This established in considerable detail, four main categories: engagement, perception, interpretation and evaluation (plus 'miscellaneous').[16] The model was subsequently used by many others, including Cooper (1969) and Michalak (1976), and some of its applications will be considered in the final section of this chapter, *The Teacher and Developing Response*.

The chief shortcoming is the absence of any qualitative judgement. That older students increase the proportion of interpretational reponses ultimately only becomes significant if we know what the merits of those responses are. Any evaluative investigations of the ways in which taste, judgement or critical response 'improve' with age are dependent on the criteria for evaluating 'better' and 'worse' readings or judgements. The most effective studies, like those of Britton (1959) and Harpin (1966)[17], compare student reactions with educated adult judgements, and suggest that, in general, with age students conform more closely to adult norms.

THE HULL ENQUIRIES

Teachers who were introduced to the kind of work outlined in the last section during in-service reading workshops at Hull University identified a need for what they saw as alternative strategies. In brief, they wanted the emphasis to be less on externally devised, scientifically controlled investigations and more on ordinary classroom work in normal teaching conditions. They were concerned with the ways in which children responded to stories as part of their continuing school programmes rather than on special occasions. They wished the outcome to be some kind of model, however tentative, of the ways in which children seem to develop the ability to respond to fiction at different ages. The hope was that by straightforwardly asking children about how they saw the reading process, what they made of stories recently encountered, and why they liked or disliked certain books, without pre-determined categories or hypotheses in mind, certain 'patterns' of response might emerge.

Those who engaged in the work were well aware of some of the problems involved. Writing or talking about response is not necessarily an accurate reflection of what is experienced. Less fluent children may seem to react inadequately, not because of limited response to a story but because of inability to express it. Some of the many difficulties in assessing response have been outlined early in chapter one. Sequences of development are rarely smooth and regular, and there are wide individual differences within any generalized scheme of 'stages'. Nevertheless, experience shows that teachers work on the assumption that there is some broadly defined succession of themes that can be responded to, motives that can be discerned, effects that can be experienced. Two particular Hull enquiries are reported here: one concerned with how children judge stories at different ages and the other with how they construct meaning and significance in stories.

HOW CHILDREN JUDGE STORIES

The beginning of the section '*The broken-backed curriculum*', in chapter one, quoted some of the responses to novels which pupils make at different ages. They demonstrated something of the shift from the personal and instinctive to the artificial and detached, and began to raise questions about how far it is our teaching that moves them in this direction. We hear surprisingly little about how children evaluate the books they read, what criteria they apply or how the ability to judge develops. There has been a great deal of work on *what* children enjoy, their favourite authors and titles and topics, but little on *why* they have these preferences.

Our lack of knowledge is partly explained by the difficulty which children have in formulating reasons for their choice. The Schools Council research study concluded that only rarely could a young reader 'be articulate in any very specific way about what he has liked or valued in his reading'.[18] What applies to children may also be fair comment on most adults. Nevertheless as teachers we all too frequently press our students for snap judgements on what has been read (Did you like this? How did it make you feel?), requiring them to offer such sophisticated responses as book reviews and expecting them to acquire the appropriate critical vocabulary for assessing works in examination forms. How far are our expectations realistic? Recent work in the junior forms of some Hull comprehensive schools has begun to consider this problem by examining the ways in which children formulate judgements about their reading at different ages.

When a story is being assessed, even in such simple terms as 'It were rubbish' or 'Smashing', what precisely is happening? As adult readers we know that our judgement of a book and our judgements of the experience we get from it are not necessarily identical. It is possible to admire *Nostromo* or *Middlemarch* greatly and yet to get little pleasure from reading them. Conversely, in certain moods we can enjoy novels that we know are trashy, because they are meeting an immediate need: providing escape or fantasy, bringing back happy memories, sending us to sleep. This sort of separation seems uncommon in younger children. In making value judgements on books they are actually describing their personal feelings about what happens when they read them, as in the examples given at the beginning of chapter one. Their instinctive emotional response to the experience dominates any other kind of verdict on the books *as* books; liking and evaluating are identical. Books are remembered as significant primarily because of the emotional effect which they had. When pupils are asked *why* they recall books which they mention from their past reading, their explanations nearly always involve intense feelings: '*Black Beauty* upset me when the animals were tortured so'; '*Love Story* was so sad'; 'The ghost story was exciting but I had recurring nightmares for weeks'; '*1984* horrified me'; '*Kizzy* made me look differently at new children in school'; 'When I read *Only Time will Tell* I cried my heart out!'

Asking children in this way about their reactions to stories which made a considerable impression on them at earlier ages is one means of discovering at what different levels they evaluate books. The comparison between remembered and current attitudes seems a significant indicator of relative maturity.

Most first year pupils say of their old favourites that they are 'too babyish' (a frequently repeated comment), 'awful', 'stupid', 'silly', 'boring to read', 'daft'. It is as though they feel threatened by the enthusiasm which once they had, and now believe that they have outgrown. One 11-year-old girl says scornfully of an Enid Blyton book that 'even a five year old could read it'. The terms of condemnation which are used of the stories are actually judgements upon the earlier reading experiences. Older pupils do not always roll together in this way the earlier and the later responses; they are more likely to suggest that an immature reaction has been replaced by a more sophisticated one. 'Now I'm older and have different feelings towards a book I read when I was little,' says a boy of 13.

Of course, some books remain favourites and are re-read in the same way and with much the same pleasure as originally. A girl of 14 says of the *Swallows and Amazons* books of Arthur Ransome 'I still enjoy reading these books and they have not lost anything with time.' A boy of 14 writes almost aggressively, 'I do not feel any differently about that story from the time I first read it.' The repeated word *still* is a validation of the earlier experience. 'I still think it is a good story', 'I still enjoy reading it', 'It still makes me cry', they say of *Charlie and the Chocolate Factory*, *The Lion, the Witch and the Wardrobe*, and *The Happy Prince*, for example.

The comments that are perhaps most interesting are those that neither reject the early response nor identify with it, but that balance past and present. One indicator of increasing maturity seems to be an awareness that growing out of a book is not necessarily to invalidate earlier feelings for it. A 14-year-old can look back and say: 'It seems babyish now but that is because I am so much older . . . Nothing really happened in the book now I think back to it, they had a shed which they redecorated . . . It all seems rather boring now. I enjoyed it then though.' In retrospect, another can see that in her early enthusiasm she did not really understand a book, 'because it was written for older girls', but that now she can appreciate it properly. In such cases, children are conscious of reading the book differently from the way in which they had previously done. Acceptance of one's own reactions at an earlier age as valid for oneself *then* is connected with awareness that responses other than one's own are permissible.

Younger children's reading diaries or 'book reviews' imply that only one verdict – their own – is possible: 'It was a super book and when I picked it up I couldn't put it down'; 'I read it from cover to cover in two nights and an afternoon'; 'I enjoyed it so much that I wanted to read it again'.[19] Indeed, that reading behaviour is sometimes advanced as a *reason* for personal feelings about a book in a circular argument: 'I enjoyed the book very much because I have read it three times.'

Examining hundreds of responses made by Hull children to stories which they had just heard suggests that there are three broad stages of development in evaluation, marked off from each other by the relationship that is envisaged between readers and text. At the most elementary level, judgements simply convert personal response into a generalized assertion: if I like a story, it must be good. Novels, pop-groups and football teams are all supported in the same way. There are clear difficulties in discussing opinions with a group divided between those who found the story boring and those who thought it interesting if their valuations go no further than this. At the next level, judgements reveal awareness of the relationship between reader and book; verdicts are based on what effect the story has produced on the individual. This implies some sense that others may react differently. At the third level, there is an awareness that judgements need to be described in terms which other readers can discuss, that there should be some apparently objective justification for the verdict. These three can be briefly illustrated.

At the most elementary stage, most pupils of 11 or 12 who are asked about their reactions to particular stories respond in one of three ways, each of them also common among the seven to nine-year-old children investigated by Vera Southgate and others in their Schools Council survey.[20]

(a) Unqualified assertion, as of a self-evident truth. It seems enough for many children simply to say 'It was good', or 'It was boring', or 'It went on a bit'. Sometimes the comments are personalized rather than being presented as a generalization, but they are still absolute: 'I didn't find it interesting', 'It is not my type of story', 'I only liked it a little because it is not the type of story I like'.

(b) Naming a preferred quality or type of story. The assumption is that an adventure story or a funny story or an exciting story must therefore be good (or not). For example: 'I enjoyed it because it was funny', 'I liked the story because it was exciting', 'There was not a lot of action in it', 'It was an adventure story but it was still quite interesting', 'It was a typical school story', 'It was very old-fashioned'.

(c) Describing the theme or the plot. Children may describe the story at some length or in a single phrase, but they imply that to be 'about' ponies or football or rockets or monsters is an assurance of a book's success. Again, they are operating in the mode of younger children, who – when asked why they liked a book – reply in terms of their interests: 'Because I like dogs' or 'Because I like bears'.[21] Sometimes, indeed, there seems no need to accompany the description with evaluation. Asked about his opinion of one story a boy simply retorted, 'It's about a girl!' Others made remarks like: 'I don't really like stories about bullying and boys', 'I like stories about children more than grown-ups', 'I like it because of the fighting and stealing', 'I liked it when the chickens were going to have their heads cut off', or 'I enjoyed it because it was about fishing'.

At the second and rather more mature level, judgements concentrate more on the relationship betweeen the reader and the book. Particularly in the 12 to 13 age group there is more awareness that personal response is the basis for assessment, and that individuals may not necessarily agree. Two very common reactions are of particular interest.

(d) Specifying a particular effect on the reader. Rather than simply asserting a judgement, children are more likely to ask, 'What effect did reading this have on me?' They say, for example, 'I liked the story because it made me tense and excited', 'I was interested to know what the people would do, what happened to them', 'I liked the story because it makes you realize how cruel you have been and makes you think twice in the future', 'It made me come to feel sorry for such a person as the boy whereas at the beginning I assumed he was just a bully', or 'It justs reminds me of boring days spent with the family'.

(e)   Personal reaction to the 'rightness' of the story. There is increasing concern with links between the story and personal experience. Children sometimes seem to imagine that novels or stories could be different from the way they are: they would be better if they ended in another way, or omitted parts, or if the characters were different. 'I don't like the story much, because I don't like the way the boy was bullied', 'I enjoyed it because it shows you can't go around bullying people', 'I didn't like the way that the boy told the truth and got into trouble because of it', 'I like it apart from the ending, which seemed wrong', 'I liked the way it stopped at the end, because it made you think what would happen next'.

At the third level, particularly from 13 onwards, there are the dawnings of an attempt to find apparently objective reasons for the evaluation. Instead of simply describing the effects of reading on themselves, children seek reasons that will appear valid to others.

(f)   Judgements of credibility. A concern for the 'rightness' of the story is narrowed to concentrate on how far the experiences seem 'real' or 'true'. For example: 'I liked the story because it seemed so real', 'It's good because it explains a possible situation in a child's school life and home life', 'I liked the story a lot because it is something that can happen in everyday life', 'I don't think this would have happened in real life, but it was still interesting', or 'I liked the story a lot because this is what would happen, this is true of life'.

(g)   Attempted technical judgements. Writing with one eye on the teacher, pupils say: 'It had some good words in it', 'There was a lot of descriptive words and I liked the characters', 'I think it was well written . . . it had a good start and ending', 'The characters were too extreme, all good or all evil', 'The plot was original, it was easy to follow, it kept to the point and it had a good ending', 'I liked the story because I think the characters of the people came out effectively', or 'It had a moral behind it, but it disguised it well'.

In general, as would be expected, older pupils expressed the reasons for their judgements more fully and in a more sophisticated way than younger ones. Their replies bear out Applebee's comment that as children grow older the difference between liking and judging becomes clearer.[22] Even at 13–14, though, it is clear that most of the attempted critical judgements are pretty thin and clearly dependent on the teacher's example (vocabulary, plot, character are the instinctive headings). Students are learning that value judgements have to be substantiated by pointing to features in the text that may provide 'objective' evidence. At this key stage of development, students learn (or fail to learn) that reading in a certain way, concentrating on certain elements in the story, is to become a critic. By trying to move them too quickly, however, by presenting texts that are too difficult, by demanding over-sophisticated responses and making them feel that their own are inadequate, or by presenting stories as 'work' rather than a source of enjoyment, we may hamper rather than assist their development.

THE DEVELOPMENT OF RESPONSE TO STORY

It is clear that children's notions of what a story is are built up gradually from many different encounters with words spoken and written by many people. Mother may be the dominant figure, telling the familiar tales to the child in her lap, but other adults, older children, the radio and tele-vision, cassettes in the car, and, later on, teachers, comics, printed books, even advertisements and cereal packets, will contribute to the developing awareness of the conventions of fiction. Early picture books for very young children build up awareness of sequence, repetition and causality, as pic-tures tell elements of the story which children cannot yet read for them-selves. The concept of making meaning, frequently from the 'sub-text', is there in the splendid *Rosie's Walk,* in which the whole plot with the fox is omitted from the one-sentence text and has to be constructed from the illustrations.[23] At a surprisingly sophisticated level, *Peepo* ('Here's a little baby, what does he see?') not only builds up the structure of a day and of a set of family relationships, but also creates the particular feel of a day in war time, though this is never mentioned in the text.[24]

The work of Ames and Applebee has shown just how early children develop awareness of what stories are. According to Ames, when they were asked 'tell me a story', half of the two-year-olds investigated, and the majority of three-year-olds, would do so. Applebee has shown how early in children's own stories such conventions as formal beginnings and end-ings, causality and stock characters begin to appear.[25] How is it, then, that these children are learning to formulate stories, and to explore events which are progressively further removed from their actual experience?

Psychologists have demonstrated that our memories of an event cannot be separated from the way in which we make sense of that event. What is true of real events holds good for fictional ones too. Our sense of pattern, what are sometimes called 'story grammars', dictates the way in which we recall what we have read or seen. Children learn the modes of story that operate in their own society, which will vary in detail from those of other cultures and other periods. By degrees they develop an unspoken aware-ness of what is appropriate in terms of plot structure, of character, of style, and so on for various kinds of narrative.

Very young children have only a limited acquaintance with stories and therefore find them very difficult to repeat. In one set of experiments, young children were asked to re-tell a favourite story which they knew well. Most of them were reluctant and argued that they did not know how to do so. Direct questioning revealed that they knew all the facts of the story, that it was potentially complete in their heads, that if they were given a lead they could say what step followed next. But they could not unreel the whole story: they were unsure where to begin, and how the incidents were linked. They were insufficiently aware of the conventions which dictate how stories work.[26]

As we grow older and experience hundreds of stories heard or read, we subconsciously establish typical schemes or frameworks, which enable us more easily to sort out and understand any new story which we encounter, predicting likely outcomes, assessing the characters and so on. Bower's research in the USA has shown that if a text violates some of the conventional patterns or 'rules' of story grammar, then that story seems less coherent to readers, is harder to understand and to re-tell, and is forgotten more readily.[27] Stein and Glenn showed that children who are familiar with the story grammars of their own culture not only use them to make sense of new stories but also tend to add missing conventional elements when they re-tell those stories.[28]

By the time they enter secondary school, most children are instinctively aware of the 'rules' or conventions that govern different types of story. Few or them will be able to express such concepts coherently, but if asked how a given story is likely to conclude, or how a particular character will probably behave, most of them will give an answer consistent with the mode of the story.[29] This process by which we 'build in' an increasing ability to recognize and interpret narrative conventions and patterns has been termed *naturalization* by structuralist critics.

> To naturalize a narrative convention means not only to understand it, but to 'forget' its conventional character, to absorb it into the reading-out process, to incorporate it into one's interpretative net, giving it no more thought than to the manifestational medium, say the English language or the frame of the proscenium stage.[30]

Secondary teachers are continually made aware of the difficulties which their students have in making an appropriate response, because they have not yet *naturalized* the conventions of a particular form or period. Those who are only familiar with more explicit narration may find it hard to 'fill in' the assumptions of eighteenth and nineteenth century novels, as when we are told that Darcy 'expressed himself on the occasion as sensibly and as warmly as a man violently in love can be supposed to do'.[31] Jane Austen assumes that readers will be able to reconstruct what a man of his class and personality and period would say. Most young twentieth-century readers, however, find the task extremely difficult until they have more experience of other stories set in the period. (It is instructive to ask sixth-formers, here and elsewhere in Jane Austen's work, to write down briefly what they think the actual spoken words might have been.) Their assumptions about what goes on in the carriage between Mr Elton and Emma, when Jane Austen says that he seized her hand and was 'actually making violent love to her', can be summed up by one sixth-former's drawing, which shows a demented clergyman dragging at Emma's décolleté dress and crying 'Geremoff!'[32]

In attempting to chart the difficult area of developing response in terms of increased understanding and sensitivity on the part of Hull children, we have tried to reconcile two quite different sources of insight. Primarily we considered our own direct observations of the ways in which children talked and wrote freely about their reading. We noted the different ways in which they operated when invited simply to 'tell me something about the book', varying from mentioning one episode or giving a narrative summary to a personal reaction or a discussion of the issues raised. We considered the kind of expectations children had about stories, the sorts of outcome they anticipated, and their notions of 'appropriate' conventions. In addition, though, we drew on developmental models of the kind mentioned earlier, and more particularly on the insights of what might be called structuralist critics, like Roland Barthes and Jonathan Culler. The general concept, developed in chapter two, that we all re-create or enact texts by bringing to the words on the page our knowledge from reading, can be sharpened by the notion of artistic and cultural 'codes': systems of conventions which we have assimilated and which make texts readable. Making sense of a story can be seen in terms of the degree to which the reader can 'operate' or 'deploy' the necessary codes or conventions, within which the author also writes. The notion of focusing attention on certain particular aspects of fiction, that might thus be investigated in a number of different texts, seemed a helpful way of examining the different interpretative strategies we employ at different ages. Our developing ability to read fiction, in these terms, is controlled by such elements as our awareness of the way in which actions interrelate and our ability to predict how events will turn out, our discernment of character and the ways in which particular people are likely to behave, and our knowledge of human groups: the ways in which people act in different societies and cultures.

What we were seeking was a group of simple, basic questions that could be asked with only minor alterations of a considerable number of stories across an age range of 11–16, and that might discriminate between different modes and levels of response. Out of a number of questions tried out, four fairly obvious ones seem to have been useful indicators, and have been used with about 1000 children. These, and the abilities they are intended to probe, are as follows:

(A) Theme. Awareness of the essential structure of the narrative. 'In a sentence, what do you think this story is about?' The restriction on length was intended to concentrate attention on what basic narrative or thematic elements seemed most important to the reader. It was hoped that answers would reveal something of how children thought stories worked.

(B) Empathy. Ability to 'read' characters and to enter into their situations. 'Which of the characters do you feel most sympathy for, and why?' The stories chosen were obviously those in which it was possible to feel sympathy for more than one character, but it was the reasons given, not the choice of character, that were significant. This was one of the questions which produced major variations acording to sex. In Dorothy Baker's story, *In the Balance,* for example, four or five times as many girls as boys aged 11–13 said that their sympathies lay with Granny.

(C) Motivation. Ability to understand why people in certain situations act as they do. 'Why do you think X did Y?' Again the incidents chosen ('Why do you think Granny put the coin in the fish's throat?' 'Why do you think Odd stole the brooch?') were ones which could sustain a number of possible interpretations.

(D) Prediction. Ability to comprehend likely outcomes beyond the story in terms of the text. 'What do you think will happen when X takes place?' Predictions asked for here were essentially those needed in order to 'complete' understanding of the story. They could involve not only awareness of character and situation but responses to the tone and mode of the story.

It is important to say that the replies to these questions were classified not according to any pre-arranged coding system but by grouping similar responses and trying to define what marked off one group from another. What follows is therefore not a proof of any hypothesis but a structured set of generalizations about many individual responses. The most hypothetical element is the arrangement under each of the four questions, A to D, of 'stages' or 'levels' of response, to provide a tentative model of development. In general, they suggest a shift away from reacting to isolated, particular details towards more perceptive responses to the total meaning of a text. The fact that a majority of English teachers, given examples of these responses to 'grade' without having seen the model, do, in fact, order them similarly is in no way conclusive. To have any real confidence that children follow a pattern of development through successive stages, it would be necessary to carry out longitudinal studies, following individuals over a number of years.

The model which follows is simply intended to offer a basis for discussing the responses of individual children to stories in a more coherent way than has previously been possible. The so-called stages or levels have no 'real' existence: they are abstractions based on generalizing from many individuals. What they are intended to do is to 'freeze' moments in a con-

tinuing process for our attention, just as naturalists may film a flower at
hourly intervals, to give a clearer impression of what otherwise remains an
imperceptible development. This model, like others, is intended to make
our discussion of growth in response more articulate. In no sense is it
designed as a testing device. It provides a possible framework for considering patterns of literary learning and for comparing reactions of the same
child at different ages. It might serve as a quick way of establishing where
the members of a group are in terms of their capacity to respond to stories,
to help in the selection of books appropriate to their reading abilities and
to establish whether they have reached the stage at which discussion of
response is likely to be fruitful.

Brief notes are given on each of the stages under the four major headings in order to indicate how they are seen as distinct from each other, and
they are accompanied by examples of pupil responses to two stories: *The
Thanksgiving Dinner* by Truman Capote and *In the Balance* by Dorothy
Baker.[33] The age of each respondent is given, and normally the answers
quoted include those of the youngest who give coherent replies at the
stage being illustrated. Thus A1 is the simplest level of response about
Theme, and is illustrated by the answers of 11-year-old pupils; B5 is the
most advanced level concerned with Empathy, and draws on the replies of
pupils aged 13–16.

A   Theme: awareness of how narrative works

Basic question: 'In a sentence, what do you think this story is about?'
A1   One particular character or idea is snatched out of a complex structure and presented as the focus of the whole story. Answers like these
could frequently apply to many stories.

> The story is about Buddy. (11)
> It is about a keen fisherman. (11)
> The story is about friendship. (11)
> It is about fishing. (12)
> The story is about being greedy. (11)
> This story is about relationships. (13)

A2   A fuller but inaccurate attempt to summarize the events or to state
the theme of the story. The mis-reading shows a failure to comprehend
what is actually presented in the story.

> The story is about a little boy whose uncle is a very keen fisherman and is
> always trying to catch the biggest fish. (11)
> It is about a man who enjoys fishing but has no luck at catching them. (12)
> The story is about a boy's opinion of another boy and how he went from enemy
> to friend. (11)
> It is about a bully at school who learns to make friends. (11)

The first two answers misrepresent the facts that the protagonist is a girl and that her uncle is successful in his fishing; the last two substitute a conventional happy ending for the fact that the boys do *not* become friends.

A3 A vague or unfocused statement, accurate as far as it goes in grasping something of the main idea, but so open that again it could be applied to a number of stories.

> It is about a girl who talks about what her grandma and uncle do. (11)
> It is about an uncle who has a picnic with his family. (11)
> It is about something which you shouldn't do. Two wrongs don't make a right. (12)
> I think it's about telling the truth and owning up to things when you know you've done it. (14)

A4 A more accurate narrative or thematic summary, but one which misses an essential detail, because of a failure to distinguish between more and less significant events or because the meaning is reduced to a ready-made moral judgement.

> An uncle goes fishing with a friend, he catches a trout and bets his friend that it weighs a pound. (12)
> It is about a man wanting to get a better fish than anyone else and then giving it away. (13)
> The story is about a schoolboy who is bullied and then waits to get his own back. (12)

Answers like these present the situation but not its resolution, whereas the following present a conclusion without localizing it in terms of the narrative:

> The story demonstrates that cheating to help someone often makes things worse. (13)

> I think this story is about being repayed in one way or another for cheating or selfishness. (14)

A5 More perceptive attempts briefly to convey the essential meaning, showing awareness that the events of the plot arise out of character, motive and situation. Some sense of what is significant, of the implications of events, despite the demand for brevity.

> When a young girl goes with her rich uncle fishing, she is shown by her grandmother that she does not agree with betting, but in the end she tips the scales in weighing a fish, so that her uncle wins. (14)

> This story is about a bully who picks on Buddy and how to get revenge Buddy decides to humiliate Odd in front of everybody by telling that he has stolen Miss Sook's brooch, but he shouldn't have done this because 'two wrongs don't make a right'. (13)

The story is about Buddy who hates Odd but can't really think of a reason why and uses incidents like the stealing to project his hatred. (15)

B   Empathy: ability to 'read' people and their situations
Basic question: 'Which of the characters do you feel most sympathy for, and why?'
B1   Answers that seem incoherent or irrelevant. In some of these cases a genuine explanation is 'buried' but not explicit, and further discussion might elicit it.

The girl, because she makes you feel one of her family. (11)

Granny, because of all the food and betting. (11)

Odd Henderson, because he was so tall. (11)

B2   Responses which abstract one specific, physical detail from the story, often a minor element. Characters are here seen exclusively in terms of action: they are pitied because of what happens to them: losing, being hit, getting into trouble.

The girl, because her granny makes her wear horrible stockings. (11)

Granny because she lost half-a-crown. (12)

Mr Pierce, because he never wins bets. (12)

Buddy, because he keeps getting hit. (11)

Buddy, because he was only getting his own back and was scolded for it. (12)

B3   Entering into an individual's situation at a relatively elementary level, and without relating significantly to any other characters. The focus is on the more obvious, stock implications of a person coming off badly: losing a bet, being cheated, getting shown up.

Mr Pierce, because he lost the bet when he should have won. (11)

Mr Pierce, because he has been cheated out of a pound. (12)

Odd Henderson, because he got shown up at the Thanksgiving. (12)

Odd, because I think he will be poor and in need of money. (12)

Odd Henderson. It was probably his upbringing that was the cause of his temperament. He must have been badly brought up with not much care and attention. (14)

B4   Sympathy grounded in the way a character suffers because of the actions or attitudes of others. The stress is on the feelings aroused in the central situations of the story.

Granny, because Uncle will blame her for cheating and making a fool of him. (12) ·

Uncle, as he is unaware of the cheating going on, and he will be blamed for it by Mr Pierce. (15)

Buddy, because he wanted to get his own back, but Odd was better than him at everything, it must have been frustrating. (13)

Miss Sook, because she was caught up in it all, and wanted the boys to be friends, and it was making her miserable as though she was to blame. (13)

B5   More complex sympathy *with* (rather than pity *for*) the character, relating with some psychological insight to the whole story. Characteristically concerned with the way in which characters view each other, and thus with such themes as lost illusions, vain hopes, sense of betrayal, acting badly with good intentions.

The girl, because she has faith in her granny and uncle, but is shown at the end that they aren't like she thought they were. (13)

Granny, because although she objects to betting she cheats in the weigh-in, which is obviously against her nature, to prevent the whole day being ruined for the girl and for Mr Pierce. (15)

Buddy, as he seems unhappy and afraid . . . he's perhaps shy and doesn't seem to do the right things . . . at the end, when he proves Odd to be a thief, it is Buddy himself that is maybe humiliated and feels the worst. (16)

C   Motivation: ability to understand why people in certain situations act as they do
Questions like: 'Why do you think Granny put the coin in the fish's throat?'
'Why do you think Odd stole the brooch?'

C1   Reasons that cannot be supported from the text, or which depend on a mis-reading.

Because I think she felt for him and he didn't have much money. (11)

To try to teach the uncle a lesson. (12)

Because Uncle couldn't afford to lose a pound note. (13)

So if he got caught he would say Buddy gave it him. (11)

So he could own up to his mistake. (12)

C2   Obvious literal responses that avoid real explanation. These work at the level of 'Ask a daft question and I'll reply in the same way . . .'

To make the fish weigh more. (11)

So the fish would weigh a pound. (11)

Because he wanted it because it looked nice. (12)

C3   Limited perception of the immediate, physical effects: to win, to sell, to give. These operational explanations focus on what the character will do or get physically.

For Uncle to win the bet. (11)

So that Uncle would not lose a pound. (12)

To get his own back on Buddy. (12)

Because he might be able to sell it. (12)

So that he could give it to Anabel. (12)

C4   Reasons grounded in understanding of the character's feelings. Motivation is seen as resulting from or leading to certain emotions, rather than just as a means to physical ends.

Because she couldn't bear the thought of Uncle losing his money. (11)

So that her son wouldn't lose the bet to someone she didn't like. (13)

I think he took it to see what it was like to steal something. He might of thought he was acting big. (13)

Odd took the brooch just for the excitement of it all – after all he was only 12. (14)

C5   More coherent explanation in terms of character relationships within the situation. The reasons seen as appropriate here are those based on the supposed effects of actions on other people.

Because she knew that Uncle didn't like losing, and didn't want him to be disappointed or his pride to be hurt. (12)

Because if her son had lost, the rest of the day would have been worse for everyone. (13)

It sounds as if the family was not well off and . . . he probably takes it to sell for some money for them or perhaps to give to his mother as he could not afford much for her. (15)

He did it on impulse, with doubts in his mind. He felt that Miss Sook was kind, yet he wanted to hurt the family. (15)

D Prediction: ability to comprehend likely outcomes beyond the story in terms of the text.

Questions like: 'What do you think will happen when Mr Pierce gets the fish home?'

D1   Suggestions that are implausible in the light of the text, that are based on faulty assumptions or make unjustified inferences.

He'll eat it with her uncle. (11)

He might think the coin had been put in for him because he lost the bet. (11)

D2   Like C2, a literal response at a superficial level, without considering the implications of what is suggested. There is no awareness of 'and *then* what . . .?'

He will open the fish and find the money. (11)

He will find the half-crown. (12)

D3   Prediction involving some degree of empathy. These responses consider what the character's immediate thoughts and feelings are likely to be, but do not pursue them.

He will find the coin and think he has been cheated. (12)

He will realize what has happened, and think Uncle deceitful. (12)

He will be rather angry. (12)

D4   Moves beyond the stage of D3 to consider what the ensuing action is likely to be. At this stage, children may project their own reactions into the character rather than imagining what that person would be likely to do in the situation.

He will find the coin and keep it. (11)

He will find the coin and try to get his money back. (12)

He will go round and have an argument to get his pound back. (13)

He will start complaining and tell everyone Uncle was a cheat. (13)

D5   Awareness of a range of possible choices, and the selection of one that best seems to fit the character and the situation. Shows more ability to get outside the reader's personal reactions than D4.

He would realize what has happened but I do not think that he would have the courage to tell the girl's uncle. (12)

He will have a joke about it. He will know that Granny was wrong, but he is rich and she is not. (13)

He will not take it to her uncle, because he could not prove it, and he would not want to cause a big row. (13)

When children's answers are classified according to this model, there is a high degree of consistency about them; that is, individuals seem to respond at a similar level to each of the questions A-D. Very few vary by more than one level across their four answers. Here, for example, are the responses of two first-year secondary pupils:

A   It is about fishing.
B   Mr Pierce, because he will find a coin in its throat.
C   To make the fish weigh a pound.
D   He will find a coin in the fish's throat.

A   A man who is very keen on a hobby, and is a show-off who is determined to win his bet.
B   I think Mr Pierce, because when he gets home he will feel cheated and sad.
C   Granny put the coin in the fish's throat so that it would weigh more and therefore Uncle would win the pound note.
D   When Mr Pierce gets the fish home he will feel cheated and very sad.

The first of these answers two questions at the first level and two at the second; the second pupil responds to all four questions at level three. Here are the replies of an able third-year pupil, responding at levels four and five.

A   The story is about a young girl whose uncle makes a bet about a fish and whose Granny cheats so the girl's uncle can win.

B   I feel most sympathy for the girl telling the story because she knows that Granny was wrong and has nothing to comfort her. Mr Pierce would find out he was right, the Uncle would still think he was right, and Granny would have the knowledge that she stopped her son being humiliated and upset.

C   Granny put the coin in the fish's throat because she didn't like to think that the uncle would lose. She didn't want him to lose a pound, and she didn't want him to be upset because he hated being wrong.

D   I think that Mr Pierce will find the coin and when he does he will be displeased but he will not go rushing off to demand his pound back but will think about it and decide that although what Granny did was wrong she did think her causes were good enough for him not to make a fuss about it, and he knew that he was right anyway so he wasn't very bothered.

Although there is a predictable spread of responses in mixed-ability groups, with numbers of pupils at three different levels, the results seem to indicate some sort of developmental pattern. In each successive year of the secondary school up to 14, more children give answers at the higher levels. On the other hand, good readers of 13 or 14 respond as well as readers two years older, and there is not much overall difference between the responses of third-year and fifth-year pupils. There are several possible reasons for this:

(a) there may be a spurt in developing ability to respond to stories between the ages of 10 or 11 and 13 or 14.
(b) the stories chosen, which had to be accessible to pupils of different ages, may have been too easy to demonstrate the additional maturity of pupils of 15 and 16.
(c) the concentration on examination work in years four and five may have inhibited the further development of individual response to stories.

It seems worth pointing out that in different Hull enquiries, 13–14 recurs as a significant stage of development. It is at this age that most pupils have developed a range of modes of reading (see chapter two), that they attempt to ground judgements in apparently 'objective' criteria, and that they become capable of more sophisticated levels of response. These findings would appear to support Peel's generalization that in Western education, 'the ages of 13–14 come up again and again as times of transition from circumstantial to circumspect judgement'.[34]

THE TEACHER'S ROLE IN DEVELOPING RESPONSE

The purpose of the Hull enquiries has been to shift attention from one basic question, 'How do readers *make* meaning?' to an even more fundamental one, 'How do readers *learn* to make meaning?' Critics have considered the question only little. The notion of 'literary competence' is common in Jonathan Culler, indeed it gives the title to one of his essays, but how is that competence achieved? Culler writes defensively that 'the claims of schools and universities to offer literary training cannot lightly be dismissed' as a 'gigantic confidence trick'.

> The time and effort devoted to literary education by generations of students and teachers creates a strong presumption that there is something to be learned, and teachers do not hesitate to judge their pupils' progress towards a general literary competence. Most would claim, no doubt with good reason, that their examinations are designed not simply to determine whether their students have read various set works but to test their acquisition of an ability.[35]

Teachers may, as Culler suggests, test how far their students reveal 'their acquisition of an ability', but this still leaves vital questions unanswered. How far is the ability acquired naturally, as part of the simple process of maturation? How far is it a learned ability, acquired to greater or lesser degree according to the learner's motivation, intelligence and so on? And how far is it an ability or skill that can be imparted, in which the teacher is an essential element?

There are two major problems in discussing the effects of teaching on pupils' responses to literature in general and fiction in particular. First, there is the unreliable nature of the measuring instrument. The useful small book by Alan Purves, *Evaluation of Learning in Literature*,[36] gives some impression of the range of possible measures, and there is evidence that different results can be obtained by applying different kinds of free or controlled test. The second difficulty is to disentangle the effects of teaching from those arising from increased maturity and greater experience of reading.

There is ample evidence that attitudes towards a text will frequently change with repeated readings. Harding, for example, found that after four readings of a number of poems his undergraduate subjects were much less likely to classify them as 'too difficult' and much more likely to say that they found them 'attractive but easy, and unlikely to yield more'. His common-sense assumption was that 'repeated readings of a poem can be viewed as practice at a task'.[37] A small-scale study of the responses of 13-year-olds to short stories suggested that even reading stories of a similar kind, or employing a similar literary device, might increase the chances of the stories being rated favourably. In this sense, reading itself, the simple exposure to text, without specific teaching, is in itself an educational experience.[38] Even here, though, the grouping of the stories was a deliberate teacher's strategy, and so 'teaching' of a kind. Without denying the importance of maturity and practice, there is a good deal of evidence to show that teachers affect the reading of their students.

Experimental evidence about the influence of teaching on pupils' ability to 'appreciate' literature has come largely from America. In a pioneering study of the late 1920s, Broening suggested nine criteria for measuring growth in literary appreciation and devised a corresponding series of tests to assess this growth. She found that her experimental groups, which used materials and activities planned to develop qualities of appreciation, read considerably more, did markedly better in tests of literary appreciation and were better in explaining their preferences than the matched control groups.[39] In a comparative study of three methods of teaching fiction, Dwight Burton found that the methods assessed differed little in effectiveness, but that all but one of the experimental groups gained significantly over the control group in tests of appreciation. He concluded: 'Appreciation of fiction, as measured in this study, can be taught to some degree in a relatively short time.'[40] Later studies have tended to reinforce this impression. Sanders, for example, found significant differences in the pattern and quality of responses of control and experimental students to stories read during the teaching/learning period and subsequently.[41]

Attention has shifted progressively from whether teaching makes a difference, which seems to be agreed, to what it is precisely that teaching does. James Wilson's mid-1960s study of the response modes of college freshmen before and after studying three novels has been influential. Wilson found statistically significant reductions in the proportion of narrational (simple re-telling) and evaluative (direct or implied literary judgements) responses, and a balancing increase in interpretational ones. The implication was that to study and discuss texts changes the nature of response that students make to them.[42] Sanders similarly found that his experimental groups made a higher proportion of interpretational responses than his control groups, who made more literary judgements.[43] By relating changes in students' preferred modes of response to those of their teachers, Michalak not only confirmed the impression that instruction involves a strengthening of interest in interpretation, but also suggested a link between teachers' methods and changes in response: 'There is a direct relationship between the way literature is taught and the way students respond to it.'[44]

What follows in the remaining two sections of this book concentrates on the teacher's intervention in the learning process. They examine the implications for the classroom of those models of the reading process and of developing response to fiction that have been discussed here. In particular they consider how a reader-response or 'transactional' critical stance demands a reassessment of the teacher's role. It is striking that many English teachers who long ago threw off what John Dixon once called the 'heritage' model of English in their general classroom work, continue to operate it when teaching literature. The notion of a particular literary tradition, reinforced by external examination syllabuses, still seems to be associated with particular methods of study. The emphasis is on uncovering an 'authoritative' view of the text, on developing the ability to write critical essays in an accepted style, and on avoiding idiosyncratic responses in favour of agreed ones. The corpus of works and the methods of studying them combine to reinforce certain ways of understanding education and society; they are a form of conditioning to accept particular views of the transmission and use of knowledge. Teachers who have been influenced by the central place given to reader and audience in recent literary criticism must find such a pattern of work unsatisfying. They will be conscious of what takes place during their own acts of reading, their ways of getting at stories, the changes that have taken place in their views, their dependence on certain patterns to structure their interpretation. Consequently they will also be aware of the same processes in their students as *they* make their own meanings with increasing subtlety and precision. To facilitate that learning demands quite different strategies. In the section that follows, therefore, case studies of some successful teachers illustrate the kinds of response made by children of different ages to fiction in situations designed to promote that learning. This in turn is followed by a brief sketch of some of the implications of modern critical theory for the teaching of fiction in schools.

Part Two

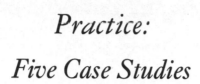

Practice:

Five Case Studies

INTRODUCTION

These studies provide an opportunity to consider some of the approaches that capable and experienced English teachers use when teaching fiction. After being introduced by the editor, each author describes a programme of work, following the same basic format, though with slightly different sub-headings. First there are brief details of the school and class to place the work in context, then reasons for choosing the particular text for that group, and then at greater length an account of what was done, accompanied by examples of children's responses in talk and writing. Finally, some time after each study had been written, each author was asked to evaluate what had been achieved, and point out any significant implications for future practice.

    The first two studies, by John Foggin and Keith Bardgett, are concerned with the use of class readers in the first two years of the secondary school. The next two studies, by Judith Atkinson and Paul Francis, consider different ways of developing pupils' responses in the third and fourth years. The final study, by Mike Town tackles the problem of introducing fiction in the examination year.

4 Building on the class reader

A Wizard of Earthsea and *Earthfasts*

JOHN FOGGIN

1 THE AUTHOR

John Foggin has taught for 17 years, in grammar schools, a 13–18 high school, and a College of Education, and is currently Head of English in a comprehensive school of about 2,000 pupils. As Senior Lecturer at Northern Counties College he was responsible for developing courses on remedial reading and reading development for the high school range. Since moving to his present job he has spent one year's secondment at Bretton Hall College of Higher Education, working with the Bretton Language Development Unit's project team on *Literature and Learning*. This involved working with two middle school classes and their teachers over a year, developing approaches to fiction with 9, 11 and 12-year-olds, and also in monthly workshops with 15 teachers from the complete First – High range. He is also a tutor for the New York University Off-Campus Summer Program for American teachers of English, and has been visiting speaker at a number of NATE branches.

2 BACKGROUND

The school is a purpose built 12 form entry 11–18 comprehensive serving a large rural/suburban catchment area. The area is generally affluent, and there is (by now, but not initially) a lot of parental support for our approach.

English teaching is substantially class-reader based; because we expect books to generate ideas for exploration we try to choose books that will challenge and ask questions of our brightest children and yet provide an accessible experience for the weakest. Teaching groups are mixed ability; remedial readers are not excluded from English lessons.

Books are normally used on a half-term borrowing timetable. In general the aim is to set up a six week programme emphasizing a particular 'activity' which the book should 'naturally' suggest. For instance, books like *The Silver Sword* (or like *The Hobbit*), where the structure depends on a quest/journey lend themselves to the making of board games. A book like *The Splendid Journey* lends itself to diary work and persona or 'in-role' writing. There are three basic assumptions: the work done should not simply start from the book, but should constantly return and refer to it; secondly, much of the work, including writing, should involve small-group work and small-group discussion; third, and most important, is the assumption that books, in Britton's terms, involve us in 'improvising upon representatives of reality'. This improvisation can take the form of 'play' (this would include reorganizing the events and characters of a story into new formats – board games, story-boards, newspaper reports, TV programmes, puppet-plays) in which case the book becomes mainly 'stimulus' or 'data'. On the other hand it may involve demands on empathy, on learning to accommodate to new orders of experience (this would include imaginative exploration in both drama and writing). The first activity takes us away from the book or runs parallel to it; the second should take us deeper into it, and the lives of its characters. Both activities are important, but I assume that 11-year-olds, in general, will find demands on imagination difficult to meet, and that 12–13-year-olds are just beginning to cope with such demands.

3 THE TEXTS

A Wizard of Earthsea by Ursula le Guin (Penguin): used in Year One (11–12).

Whilst I was originally attracted by the book's emphasis on Naming, and 'language' as magical, and also by the dual nature of the hero, Ged, reading and working on the book with several first-year groups has resulted in my focusing first on Ged's education at the School on Roke being echoed by my pupils' experience of a new, very big school, with several teachers instead of their single 'class-teacher' in the Junior School; secondly, the book involves a quest, a complex journey which can be reconstructed as a game of chance and choice – the kind of game the children will naturally play, and which therefore provides them with a structure and 'vocabulary' to deal with Ged's search for his 'dark self'.

Earthfasts by William Mayne (Penguin: but currently out of print): normally used with second-year (12–13)

This beautifully written book offers a lot of possibilities: it is rooted in three (quite slight) folk tales and fables; the two central figures are presented through some splendid dialogue; the story is full of powerful atmospheric moments – the boy emerging, the stones 'walking', the disruption of market day, the emergence of Arthur; all these are open to exploration through 'play'. On the other hand, the Drummer Boy's predicament is traumatic, and one of the central characters has to learn to cope with the death of his friend. These are difficult *imaginative* problems which I hope to bring 12 and 13-year-olds to explore and accommodate too. I suspect the 'fantasy' content of the book would alienate older readers; the writing would be too complex for younger ones!

4   A WIZARD OF EARTHSEA

The notes that follow are in the format used in the department to build up an ideas bank that we all can use.

Year: One   Two   Three
Book Title: *A Wizard of Earthsea*: Ursula le Guin (Penguin)

Details of class	Slightly below average. No high fliers. Three remedial readers. Two very insecure boys and one similar girl all demanding a lot of attention. Class by now entirely used to drafting and rewriting, and to writing for publication or display.
Length of sequence	Half term. Twelve double lessons (70 mins). Two single lessons per week used for other activities.
Emphasis	Reading aloud, inferential comprehension, recall. (This was this group's first sustained close look at one book.) Display work . . . emphasis eventually on improvisation and 'play'.

Lesson sequence

Week One
Told class they were going to write report (like school reports) about a character whom nobody quite understands and who finds it hard to understand himself. They will have to make up their own minds about him.
Introduction to book. I read (part edited) up to Ged's decision to go to the School on Roke. Gentle discussion: what kind of boy is Ged? Why does his father treat him so strictly? Why can't his aunt control him by her

magic? How does he feel about saving the village from the Kargs? Why is he so stung by the challenge from the witch's daughter? What problems will he face at the school?

Gave out reading assignments for *Instant Book* (Appendix 2) . . . I chose to use this because it was essential to get the book 'read' quickly; because the book is so difficult this was meant to make it accessible to the whole class. One week allowed for rehearsal.

Also during the week gave out copies of book and asked class to read chapters three and four up to the celebration of the Long Dance. Arranged for remedial readers to read together with their remedial teacher.

They should find out, alone or in groups, how many teachers Ged had, what they taught, and how he behaved towards his teachers and to other pupils.

Week Two

Discussion. Recap of the guesses we made about Ged last week. Were any of us right? Have we learned anything new about him?

Reminded class they had to write school reports on Ged. We looked at 'Reports on myself' written at start of year, and at copies of old school reports. Talked about which were the most useful to the reader they were intended for.

Writing in groups or pairs. Draw up a list of exactly what each Mage teaches. Reporting back to class. Gradually build up detailed picture of the 'Syllabus' (this is difficult . . . calls for a fair amount of inference, hence need for group work and reporting back).

Homework: write reports on Ged in exercise books . . . try to write as though the teachers had written them.

Second lesson of week. Instant book read. Takes one hour. This badly done so we planned to do it again after proper rehearsal. No discussion of the story possible.

Week Three

Instant book read again . . . successfully this time. Story line and detail remained clear and accessible. Ten minutes discussion. What is the *Shadow*? A lot of uncertainty; gradually a lot of analogues suggested (Incredible Hulk, Jekyll and Hyde . . .). Eventually class decided that the Shadow was Ged's evil self released by the spell of Summoning. (On previous occasions the decision has been that the Shadow is a force from outside the world, so before children couldn't quite see how it could have Ged's name . . . perhaps the Shadow stole the name.) In addition, children can put the problem into their own words but still fail to grasp what it is about:

Mark: 'At the end of the book I didn't quite understand it where the sea turns to sand and the shadow and Ged say each others names to find out the shadow is a part of Ged.'

Next lesson: add to Ged's report. He has to leave Roke. What will the new Archmage and the other masters say about him? Write the Archmage's report and change the others as necessary.

Week Four

A lot of reading reports out aloud in class and in groups, suggesting changes.

Individual assignment: produce a booklet of reports on Ged. Rest of week taken up with individual tutoring, drafting and redrafting of reports.

Also told class that they would go on to make a game based on the book and that they would do this in groups.

Week Five

Opened first lesson with anecdote session about board games they own and play. Kids defended their own favourites. We tried to isolate factors which make some games more successful than others. Agreed on need to be able to make choices and decisions (like Ged). Asked class to think about adapting the story of Ged to a game format.

As groups of kids completed their report booklets, I gave group tutorials on making the game. What sorts of things stop Ged's progress, or help him to catch the Shadow? List of events and characters built up from group's recall of book plus a guide-line sheet written by me. Four groups of 5 to 7 taught in this way; work on games begun.

Week Six

All reports now ready for display; everyone expected to read as many as possible during the week and in the week after the holiday.

Individual and group teaching as the class got down to games making. Most groups asked for materials (card, coloured papers, etc.) to work on games over the holiday.

EVALUATION

Extra time needed after the holiday to allow time to complete the games, and try them out on other first-year groups. Enormous amounts of time put in by more than half the class.

The reports produced some excellent inferential thinking.

Broad aims of this sequence were well met, but at the expense of some aspects of the book. Few children bothered to read the book as a book . . .

this often happens as a result of using Instant Book . . . Many didn't have time, and most used it as a reference text for the game. This doesn't matter too much, I think, provided that there is a lot of private reading time in the next sequence. For this group, I chose to do this, and chose *The Midnight Fox* as the class reader on the grounds that it *should* be a more private read anyway.

WRITING THE MASTER'S REPORT

Despite the shared group work, the reporting back, and the building up of knowledge about The Curriculum of Roke in *class*, there is considerable variation in levels of response, which in turn indicates how *I* need to respond to individual needs. Four brief examples should illustrate what I mean; all of them are attempts at writing the Master Changer's report. These and other examples of children's words are reproduced as written.

Georgina

Master change taught ged to change his ways and to ge good and sencible. He also tells about true spells and explaines How. if a things realley to be changed.

Helen

Sparrowhank learns very well and very quikly. He learnt how to change slones in to diamonds and how to change himself into lots of different thing like birds, lions, and donkeys.

Debbie

When Sparrowhawk is ready to learn changing he must not change I repeat not change a single pebble or grain of sand until he nows what good or bad will follow. It is very dangerous because it can shake the shape of the world. To change somethink you need to change the hole of it even the world and to do this you need to be able to put it back to it normal self. I hope Sparrowhawk continues to produce good work.

Emma
Sparrowhawk has worked extremely well this term, he is quick and eager to learn, a bright boy for just fifteen. I have taught him of the spells of true

shaping and a few of the Great Spells of Change. I found that Sparrowhawk studied hard at his work, he does however find Equilibrium a little difficult to understand, but he still presses me to let him work on quicker when he isn't ready. I think that Sparrowhawk will go far if he keeps his wits about him and is wary of the effects of certain spells.

Comment:
Georgina couldn't quite grasp the notion of 'writing in role'; in addition she blurs her own feeling that Ged should 'change his ways' with the role of the Master Changer. Nevertheless, she picks up the idea of 'true spells' and suggests that there is *real* change (as opposed to illusion) as well as showing *she* has judged Ged's conduct: I wouldn't expect her to 'accommodate' to it. Incidentally, at the end of the booklet she signed off: 'I have inJoyed doing it Hope you Like it.'

My feeling is that the 'game' hasn't hindered her response, and may have helped her to 'frame' it.

Helen copes more successfully with the writing in role, but is actually less responsive to the situation than Georgina. She picks up the point about stones and diamonds almost directly from the text, but misses the *dangers* of change, and the overambition that Sparrowhawk displays in his studies with the Changer. The last detail – 'birds, lions, and donkeys' – illustrates what I mean by 'play'. It's improvising for fun.

Debbie and *Emma* both show a strong, imaginative grasp of the role they have taken up, and both show a subtle understanding of the dangers Sparrowhawk needs to be warned against. Of the two, I'm most impressed by Debbie who is struggling to assimilate, by framing it in her *own* language, the notion of 'Balance' – a finely adjusted 'ecology' which the magician disturbs at his peril.

AN INSTANT BOOK, AND PUPILS' RESPONSES

There's no magic answer to the problem of presenting class readers to mixed ability groups, as these comments from *another* group reading the *Instant Book* reveal!

Helen: 'I liked doing an Instant Book because I got a good idea from the Instant Book because I hadn't read the book before. I suppose you could call it the skeleton of the book (At first I was completely lost until I read the Instant Book).'

Sara: 'I don't like reading out aloud because I am not use to it. I am use to doing it quitely to myself.'

John: 'If I don't have to listen for my cue and worry about my reading aloud things would all fall into place without interruptions or pauses.'

Martin: 'I like reading in a circle but I cannot follow it . . .'
I persevere because enough is picked up of the story and its characters to enable us to talk about Ged's quest together, and to provide a context for any specific sequences we might read together.

Committed readers have often read *the book* before they rehearse their part!

Instant Books [for this teaching game I am indebted to Ann Crocker, formerly of Northern Counties College, Newcastle upon Tyne]
Edit the book of your choice (using as much of the story as you need) down to 30 passages (i.e. 1 passage per pupil in the class), each passage normally no longer than half a page of the text.
Number each passage and allocate them to pupils according to reading ability. Use more than 1 pupil per passage where there are passages of dialogue. The longer the text, the briefer the narrative links should be to fill in gaps; the teacher should take the part of the narrator.
Prepare a script. The format I use is as follows:

NARRATOR. Cues and readers   *Passages and cues*

Ged grew in power and pride;
taunted by Jasper he raised a shade
with the sound of voice, and the
motion of body and hand

1	Reader p. 70	1	CUE: . . . motion of body and hand p. 70 START . . . the other boys stood watching. . . . none saw them. END
2	Reader p. 71	2	CUE: . . . none saw them. p. 71 START . . . the words of the enchantment . . . full of fear. END

The right-hand side of the page is cut out into slips which can be given out to individuals who then find their place in the book. The cue line is the one they listen out for. It's their cue to begin reading.

The teacher keeps the left-hand side of the sheet as a script and a record of who reads what. The slips are collected after a few minutes, and the whole kit can be reused. Each complete kit takes about three hours to prepare.

Reading: Arrange the class in a circle so that every reader is reading to an audience. Emphasize the need for eye contact and so on. Since each passage is short and well-rehearsed, children will normally do justice to the story and to themselves.

Once or twice a year this is an interesting way of sharing the experience of a book that would otherwise be inaccessible to many pupils. Older pupils move on from this to preparing their own instant books to be used by the whole class.

5 EARTHFASTS

Background

The next sequence on work, primarily for 12 to 13-year-olds, is less detailed than the account of the *Earthsea* work, but is intended to illustrate the difference between 'imagination' and 'play'. (Although the work is normally undertaken at my own school, the examples of children's work are drawn from work I did at the invitation of the staff of Cathedral Middle School in Wakefield, while I was seconded to the Advanced Diploma course at Bretton Hall College. A detailed analysis of the writing appears in a forthcoming pamphlet from the Bretton Language Development Unit.) The *work* was primarily 'done' by Joan Foye, the class teacher.

Year: Two
Book Title: *Earthfasts*

Details of class Band One in a 'two-band' year. There were no remedial problems, therefore. All children were independent readers and writers, and well-motivated. All were accustomed to working through drafts to a final version.

Length of sequence Approximately four weeks.

Emphasis Imaginative re-tellings in role; editing and presenting; poetry – using texts as stimulus.

Resources Set of transparencies of skies, water, trees, stones. Display of photographs and illustrated texts on stone circles and standing stones. Four copies of the text (it's *still* out of print. Come on, Puffin Books!).

Lesson sequence

We planned work on *two* of the four unnerving situations the intelligent, independent and rather 'bookish' heroes have to deal with.

The first occurs when a Drummer Boy, lost in the eighteenth century, walks out of a hillside and into their lives. Why and how they will cope with him and his predicament is an education in imagining the boy's plight and how best they can help him.

The second involves a circle of standing stones which move – and return to life as giants: a second eruption into their lives of the archaic and irrational. We felt there could be considerable possibilities in exploring as 'spectators' the rather sombre, eerie or magical world of 'Stones'.

Week One

Read the first section of the book to the class. Reading took an hour or so during one morning, introducing the boys Keith and David, and the Drummer Boy; the Drummer Boy's inability to take in what has happened to him, up to the point where the twentieth century overwhelms him and he runs away into the night.

After talking about the events and the boys we offered the class two opportunities for writing:

1   Re-tell the story so far, but this time from the point of view of the Drummer Boy. Tell it as if you were him OR as a narrator. You can add episodes both before and after the ones you've had read to you.
2   The Drummer Boy has run off . . . what will, or should, the boys do now? Suppose they talk about what's happened and what they should do now. You can write their talk as a script or as a dialogue in a story. You can work in pairs, and rehearse it/try it out with a tape-recorder if you like.

They wrote drafts and I added comments and suggestions before they wrote second, or final versions. They had a lot of opportunity for checking back in the text, and for talking to us.

Week Two

Because we'd concentrated on the moral dilemmas of the characters so far, we went on to put them back in their very atmospheric landscape. We also wanted to get away from writing (or talk and write) as a response to fiction; the fact that Joan Faye is an Art teacher by training isn't insignificant! We also wanted to counter the emphasis on teacher-reading-to-class created by our having so few copies of the book!

Divided the class into four groups. Each group given a copy of the book plus a set of transparencies from Teachers Centre. Each set contained, roughly in equal proportion, shots of sunsets, trees in different seasons, weathered rock outcrops, hillscapes, exposed roots, silhouettes. They reviewed the slides using a projector, then began to rehearse readings of the opening section.

Task They had to produce a slide sequence to accompany their reading. They could edit their reading. They could use each slide more than once. They could also, on Joan's advice, use different coloured gels to change the tone or mood of each image, and soft and hard focus, plus shifts between them. Though A-level English students have terrible problems with this sort of editing job, the children presented four clear, coherent and completely *different* versions of the opening, so we were able to see quite clearly how we may very well be reading quite different *stories* though we read the same book (which is why we read together – to discover what *other* people have 'made' or recreated).

Weeks Three and Four

Joan had continued to read the book to the class as a serial and gone beyond the Drummer Boy's journey into the dale he had known so long ago. The class had written another piece in which they improvised the dialogue between the Drummer Boy and the old man who is actually the boy's great-great-grand-nephew; there's no account of it in the book, but it's clearly a conversation which persuades the boy of a truth he has resisted for too long – that he's found himself 200 years out of time.

Joan had now reached the sequence when the boys investigate a mystery of standing stones which have been moved. It could so easily be a Blyton-ish experience (Five go to look at a stone circle) but we hoped to recover the imaginative power of these strange places, and to get the class working on poetic form.

Working with illustrations in books (slides would have been better!) I talked about stone circles, the isolation of the places they were found in, the experience of 'dowsers', the mystery of their building, and the magic they could contain, and the ceremonial and sacrifice and sun-worship they attached to.

In question and answer session I then built up a 'stone-poem' on the board. Where am I? What time of year? day? weather? What am I doing here? How do I feel? What can I see, hear? What is going to happen? Is anyone else around? The responses to the questions are 'filtered' and edited until there's a poem-shape on the board. The class can then browse through more pictures, and refer back to the Jingle Stones episode in the text.

Task Write your own Stone poems; the class will subsequently design poem posters, and produce a Stone poem anthology using a multi-coloured Banda set of colours. Each member of the class gets a copy.

Evaluation There is a lot of other 'work' in the book – possibilities include a journalistic investigation into David's death, culminating in newspaper production (or a radio or TV programme centring on the paranormal). This is popular with 12 to 14-year-olds, partly because of the opportunity for role-playing in safety! We were happy to leave them alone with this class where we were concentrating on empathy, and sensitivity to 'place'.

Drafts and revisions. Joanne's story.

Joanne
Original version: (this is the very beginning of her story. She wrote about 4 A4 pages).
'I thought you said he was going with you,' (muttered) Keith.
'Well I lost him,' said David disappointed.
'I suppose he's gone back to the castle, to find his friends,' said Keith.
'What are we to do about him?' said David.
*'Well we'll have to help him understand he's lost,' said Keith.
'Where is he going to stay?' said David
'We will have to put him in the barn where no one will see him.'

Written Comment
Have a think about the bit marked *.
It's not only what he's lost but what he's found.
Supposing David asked: 'However are we going to explain it? . . .'
Can you imagine that conversation?

Second version
'Well we'll have to help him understand that he's lost,' said Keith.
'He doesn't even know what year it is,' said David.
'Well we need proof to show him,' said Keith.
'We can't take him to town,' said David.
'We could show him my Grandmother's calendar and tell him it's Autumn and not Spring,' said Keith, getting the calendar out of the drawer.
'He's going to be very confused,' said David.
'I mean, finding yourself in another time,' said David.

**Then Keith realized*:
'We're his only friends as well,' said Keith.
They were silent then David murmured.
'I don't know,' said David, there was a long pause as they stared *into fire*,†
then Keith spoke:
'Well we could follow him and see where he was expecting to see his friends,' said Keith not really believing it.

*† these details added when she re-read the second version.

'Maybe he would understand better that way,' said Keith.
'Where is he going to stay?' said David.
'We will have to put him in the barn . . .'

Joanne had written a long, nicely developed eventful Famous-Five-ish story – the detail about the convenient barn indicates the convention she had assimilated. It's not a convention that is reflective about motive or inner life! It suggests, I think, that she may be taking the *events* from *Earthfasts* (she can assimilate them happily), but not the distinctive 'life' of its characters. On the other hand, her re-write shows that there's more to Joanne than the 'conventional' story format allowed her to express. The changes are dramatic and revealing.

Whereas in the first version the Drummer Boy is effectively a logistic problem, an item to be disposed of, in the second the two boys, and their modes of coping with the problem, are *imagined* quite differently. Keith is all for action, for doing something, for practical solutions (like getting the calendar). David, on the other hand, is quieter, more reflective, and arguably more imaginative about the Drummer Boy's plight. There are silences and no sudden solutions. David's tentativeness is dramatized by the choice of the verb 'murmured'. Keith continues to suggest plans, but having 'realized' the basis of David's uncertainty, no longer 'really believes' in their viability.

This tiny sequence illustrates two points. One: there are moments in fiction which make difficult imaginative demands on the reader, and we need to be careful in our choice of which moments to highlight and to help our pupils towards. Two: *this* writing in role is more difficult than the role-writing in the *Earthsea* reports, because the format of reports is a familiar one, and teachers traditionally report on pupils in a 'distanced' sort of way. It's important, and difficult, to estimate 'imaginative demand' and to gradually *increase* it as pupils grow older. By the time they are 15–16 most should be able to measure their estimation of the characters in fiction against that of the writer.

Standing Stone Poems

These poems illustrate a 'problem' of class-reader based work. I don't know whether they take the writers deeper into the world of the book, or are simply written 'in parallel'. I *hope* that they help the children to realize their own meanings for the stones which they then take back to the book, enriching and dramatizing the text because they have already improvised around the 'setting'. For this reason I offer the same sequence of work to classes reading *Elidor* (another Year Two 12 to 13-year-old text).

Jane picks up a trigger phrase from the text: 'cold hell'. This sets the tone of a poem that also shows a fascination with unusual words.

'One step beyond cold hell it stands
the red sun hangs heavy in the sky,
a lonely figure
unmoving
unheeding
though man may destroy all suffering,
it stays,
waiting,
the noiseless fountain of death spreads
stinking waters on humankind,
Yet it stands
a petrified demon scaled with litchen
dry
ossified
until water touches it,
then the stone sweats
evil black slime,
immobile
until it can reign supreme,
pointing a finger of death
undamaged?
well,
the devil looks after his own.'

Rocky Although he calls his poem '*Stones of evil*', Rocky recovers a different life for the stones and their purpose which is rooted in another part of the text. In *Earthfasts* Jingle Stones come to life as giants that roam the Yorkshire Dale! Where Jane perceives malignancy, Rocky sees stasis, a moment of pure anticipation.

'A ring of standing stone
Desolate, abandoned, lonely
Cold to the touch, a chill in the bone
Quietly overlooking the moor.
Hard as iron, cold as snow
Tall as a giant, quiet as a grave
Kings of the moors that came from nowhere.
Cold hard stone
Tall and thick
A circle of mysteries

From the dawn of time.
A dark mist
Uncovers a puzzle
Standing stones *rising from the ground*
Giants from the days of old.'

Diane comes closer to the way I read the passage in *Earthfasts*, sensing the contrast between the rather innocuous Jingle stones and the chilling fear that the boys reluctantly come to acknowledge.

'Stones are cold and motionless
Covered with dull moss,
Round their weary edge
When the mist leaves the rocks
The stones are covered
Like a grey veil
When you stand next to them
You feel as though
Someone is beside you
But,
It's just the shadow
From the dark.'

5 The Machine Gunners:

A Workshop Approach

KEITH BARDGETT

1 THE AUTHOR

Keith Bardgett is at present Senior Master at Monkseaton High School, Whitley Bay. After doing his degree at Cambridge and his Education Certificate at Oxford, he taught for two years at Redefield School, Oxford, before moving to Denbigh School, Milton Keynes, as Head of the English Department. While at Redefield with his then Head of Department John L. Foster, he co-authored a series of commercially produced Topic Tapes, and a series of Careers programmes which was broadcast by radio Oxford. His first publication, *Skinhead in the Classroom* appeared in *Children's Literature in Education* (1972), and since then he has given many lectures on the relationship between Reluctance and Departmental Organisation to NATE branches, LEA courses, and the Schools Library Association. This work led him to his most recent publication, as contributor of an article on *The Nature of Reluctance* to *Reluctant to Read?* (Ward Lock, 1977). He has been both an O-level Examiner and a CSE Consortium Secretary. He was a member of the Farmington Trust, working on the relationship between Literature and Moral Education. He places fiction firmly at the centre of his teaching, and believes in the necessity of 'starting where the kids are'. He also believes that in many schools, teaching gets in the way of learning. His relationship with his pupils is one of partnership, and they must take responsibility for their own work as quickly as possible. This, linked to a concern for quality of product, leads him inevitably to a workshop approach.

2   THE SCHOOL

The school in which the lessons I am about to describe took place is a 12–13 co-educational comprehensive with 1200 pupils on roll, and a 10 form entry. It is situated on a council house estate, but also draws a smaller number of pupils from surrounding villages, and from a recently developed private estate. It has good social mix and has a high reputation in the area as a genuine comprehensive school.

3   THE DEPARTMENT

English is taught in mixed-ability groups, in half year blocks, throughout the school, with all pupils taking the school's own CSE Mode 3 Examination, which makes no distinction between Language and Literature. In addition, many pupils take O-level Language and Literature. Numerically, A-level English is one of the most popular subjects. All English work in the first two years can be seen in some ways as a preparation for the autonomy required for the independent study of Literature in the Upper School. Individual teachers have a great deal of freedom in what and how they teach, but most work ought to fit in with the broad 'Rationale for the Curriculum' which was agreed after many hours of departmental meetings. This rationale provides a theoretical basis for all work in the English department, along with specific suggestions as to the kinds of activity which should be taking place with each year group. The direction is that which is reflected in a theoretical shift of attention from the subjective (the pupil's emotions, thoughts, experiences, reading) to the objective (how are these things focused in texts – all kinds of fiction, including their own?), and a practical shift from the concrete (this phrase, sentence, paragraph, book) to the formal (what kind of book is this, what techniques does the author use?). By the start of the third year it is hoped that pupils will have experienced a wide range of fictional material of all kinds and standards (for how can we know the good if we cannot distinguish it from the bad?), and will have acquired sufficient technical knowledge, and the confidence this brings, to be able to work independently, or in small groups, on texts of their own choosing.

4   THE BOOK

My reasons for choosing *The Machine Gunners* by Robert Westall are straightforward. Ever since its publication in 1975 it has proved to be enormously successful, one of those rare books which is bought not only by English teachers for use as a set, but by individual children in book-shops. Its merits were recognized at once. In 1975 it received the Carnegie Medal, and was also runner-up for the Guardian Award.

Its qualities as a book are obvious. The subject is intrinsically interesting to young adolescents. Many of the themes – gangs, school, authority, danger, bullies – are those which strike a familiar chord in every reader, and the characters are clearly delineated in such a way as to present the necessary paradox: they are recognizably individual and can therefore be readily identified with, as to some extent representational.

As a book for teaching, other qualities quickly become apparent. The story line itself is very strong, the pace never flags, the pupils always want to know what will happen next, and they are never kept waiting for long. Because of this there are plenty of places where a teacher can break off at a crucial point, certain of a groan from his audience (I use that word deliberately), and equally certain of instant receptivity at the beginning of the next lesson.

5   THE CLASSES

The book was taught to two classes, a first form (12+) and a second form (13+). I will identify each piece of work accordingly. My aims for each class were the same – enjoyment, discussion, identification, leading to first an exploration of their responses to the text, and then and only then to the text itself. This article concentrates entirely on the first of these, because for me this has to be the basis of the kind of textual criticism required at more advanced stages. To jump straight into 'study' is to remove the possibility of reading in its deepest sense. If the pupils are ever to understand and appreciate the unique appeal of fiction, it is necessary that they experience it, and make it their own.

6   THE LESSONS

For the first form, *The Machine Gunners* was their first experience, with me, of a full length novel, so I read the whole book to them out loud, with them following in their copies. I make no apologies for this traditional approach. It provides a valuable shared experience, ensures that the poorer readers' enjoyment of the story is not hampered by technical difficulties, and most important of all, I am able to transmit my own enthusiasm. It needs to be done well, with careful pacing at the pre-planning stage so as to end each lesson at a high point in the action, and with consistent but different voices for each of the characters. Before embarking on these lessons, I had done detailed sketches of my own for each of

the characters, and had tape-recorded passages of dialogue to be sure
that, aurally, the characters could be differentiated. For me, as Hamlet
almost said

'the book's the thing
wherein we'll catch the conscience of the kids'

So I tend not to stop for general discussions on War, the meaning of Existence or whatever, but only for specifically textual reasons, such as to
focus on a particularly effective piece of writing, or mood-setting, or moti-
vations. Even these I like to keep to an absolute minimum, and the work
is intense. During this period, every English lesson is devoted to reading,
with the aim of getting straight through the story as quickly as possible. To
punctuate it with language lessons or whatever is to destroy any semblance
of continuity and momentum (and therefore interest) can be quickly lost.
Other, more general, responses are better recollected in tranquillity.
Analysis of any kind is an activity which comes after experience, not during it, and this would be my main criticism of any kind of chapter-by-
chapter approach.

This overall strategy was the same for the second year, except that after
reading the first four chapters to establish the characters, I told them to
read the rest of the book themselves, with very tight deadlines, and, again,
every lesson was devoted to USSR (uninterrupted sustained silent
reading).

After the reading, the physical layout of the room becomes important.
Pupils must be able to sit anywhere, with different areas of the room
designed for particular purposes. Some desks were paired, others in
groups of four, one large group of desks together at the back for art-work
(although, as the work progressed, some of the 'professionals' negotiated
access to the art rooms for the production of the final masterpiece). And,
of course, some single desks for those ready to ooze creativity! Obviously,
pupils moved about within lessons, and between lessons, according to
what they were doing. Although we had all shared a common experience,
the follow-up activities were entirely individualized, although temporary
groupings were formed for specific group tasks.

Discussion took several forms, starting with the obvious 'which bits did
you like best and why?' and moving on to whether or not the story was
plausible, and whether or not they had clear pictures of the characters.
Two of the first-year girls, Freda and Catherine, asked if they could tape
an interview about the book. Here is a transcript of part of what they produced:

C   What age do you think this book was suitable for?
F   It depends really on the reader. I think it was really suitable for the
     ages of 11 to 14-years-old. What do you think?

C   I enjoyed it so I really agree with you. Next question. Do you think the
     children react to this kind of life well?

F   Well, I don't think I would have acted like that but I would have
     expected them to. I'm not really sure.

C   Let's move on. Would you like to be in Chas' gang?

F   Eh . . . yes, I think I would want to but not everyone would want to. I
     think older girls would be occupied with their boyfriends and things
     like that.

C   Also, how would you react to Rudi or any other German?

F   I don't know but I expect I would hate Germans because they were on
     the enemy side.

C   What did you think of the language?

F   I think it was a bit far-fetched for younger children but for older chil-
     dren it was more up to date.

C   Do you think Audrey was really a tomboy inside?

F   I don't really think so but she preferred to be with the boys.

C   What did you think of Nicky? Was he too weak to be in the gang?

F   Y . . . Yes, he was really too weak but it was the gang and all the rest
     that wanted him so that he didn't have to go into a home.

C   Was it too boyish for girls?

F   No, not really – you see it wasn't actually about the boys themselves
     was it?

C   No, not really. I don't think so either. Did you ever feel sorry for
     Boddser Brown?

F   No, not really. I think he was a bully and most people were on his . . .
     Chas' side. I think he deserved what he got.

C   Do you think the story was too unreal?

F   N . . . Yes, it was.

C   (Emphatically) Well I don't think so. I think it could happen to chil-
     dren who were that determined.

F   I don't think so.

C   I do.

F   Well, I suppose so.

C   (Triumphantly) Yes. What would you have done if you were the chil-
     dren's parents?

F   Well I would have been very angry and cross and I think I would have
     sent them away to Approved School. Would you?

C   Yes, I should think so. Would you recommend this book to any other
     children?

F   Yes. I enjoyed reading it. It was a good book. Yes, I would.

There are a number of things which interest me in this tape.
Catherine's first real question is very difficult and badly phrased. She is

stretching towards a concept she does not yet possess, yet Freda picks up what she means, and shows that simple identification is an inadequate response. She points to the book's internal coherence, and has obviously developed from the response common to her age group, that if she wouldn't behave like that, it is therefore unreal. I think she is perceptive in recognizing that, through her experience, Audrey ceases to be a tomboy and plays a crucial feminine role in handling Nicky, and she goes on to identify very clearly the protective role which the rest of the gang adopts towards him.

The next question strikes right at the heart of a traditional complaint, 'This is a boy's book'. It is a pity that Freda does not expand on her answer, but she seems to be pointing to the crucial fact that books have a 'meaning' and that that meaning is at levels beneath the plot. I don't think it reasonable to expect pupils of this age to have anything more than this vague awareness, yet without it true critical development is impossible. The response to the question about Boddser Brown is stereotypical yet it is followed immediately by the dynamic intervention of Catherine, who, like Freda earlier, draws attention to the fact that it is the internal coherence which makes the novel work. True, they lapse back immediately to the trite level on which they began, but I would argue that, on the occasions selected above, the girls were genuinely grappling with the text at a critical level.

The written work asked for from the pupils in both forms was superficially unstructured. A list of possible activities was placed on the blackboard, many of the suggestions coming from the pupils themselves. Each one was carefully explained. Perhaps a crucial factor was the wall display. I cleared the walls in my room, and said that I would put up a wall display which would represent all aspects of their response to the book. This provided a reinforcement to their already strong motivation. Here is our list, though it is by no means exhaustive:

Character Studies.
Book review.
An alternative ending.
Additional adventures using the same characters.
Taped interviews.
Drawings.
Copies of war poems from anthologies.
Structured poems of various kinds.
Unstructured poems.
Playscripts for radio of parts of the book.
A reunion of the characters 10 years on, showing how they have changed.
Rudi telling his life story up to the point of his capture.
The trial of Chas and his friends. What do their parents and teachers say about them?

Alternative rules for Fortress Caparetto.
Diagrams and Plans of Fortress Caparetto.

What did this produce? Lots of drawings, some of a very high quality, a copy of Churchill's famous exhortation, copies of poems culled from anthologies placed around the room, extracts from the book they had found particularly effective, or horrific, or humorous, rules for the Fortress, rules for other gangs, copies of contemporary newspaper cartoons, illustrated extracts from weapons catalogues and, slowly at first but steadily gaining momentum, work showing genuine signs of real engagement and creativity.

It is perhaps worth pointing out at this point that both classes had, before beginning the book, done a considerable amount of poetry work, based on the excellent book *English Through Poetry Writing* by Brian Powell (Heinemann, 1968). They were therefore all accustomed to the idea of the importance of form, of the shaping of their experience, of the importance of the right word in the right place. Just as the aim of the production of autonomous readers requires a structured approach to the experiencing of fiction, so the aim of the production of autonomous writers, if their writing is to have intrinsic quality, requires an awareness of the forms of writing leading to the discovery of the true freedom which comes from writing within externally defined constraints.

Here, then is some of their work. I make no greater claims for it as poetry, but hope that the range of response will encourage other teachers to adopt a similar approach, in which the emphasis is taken away from teaching, and placed very firmly on learning through structured exploration of individual response.

David (13+) chose to do a haiku sequence called *'Life on a Destroyer'*

Rocking up and down
water sprays across the deck
the wind echoes through

the empty turrets
creaking as the waves crash down
nothing stirs on deck.

The storm is over.
Figures begin to appear
manning their stations

standing on the bridge
peering round looking for life,
a sub breaks surface.

Battle stations sound
not a second can be lost
men's lives are at stake.

The guns are loaded
accuracy is needed
As the sub descends.

The ship moves slowly
over the top of the sub.
Depth charges are dropped.

The depth charge goes down
an explosion can be heard
as the sea sprays out.

Yet another drops
the sea bed seems to rumble
debris is sighted.

The sub has been sunk
Lives have been pointlessly lost
but the war goes on.

The choice of the haiku form has resulted in a very concise narrative. He has a storm, a calm, a fight and a moral conclusion (inevitably the weakest part of the poem) in 10 stanzas. He links each stanza satisfactorily, and the strict syllable count has produced some effective lines.

Keith (13+) chose the same form for his poem '*Air Raid*'.

The drone of engines
high above in the night sky
seems to get nearer.

The searchlights are on.
White beams cover the dark sky
A plane is spotted.

The guns have started
white blobs light up the darkness
tracers dot the sky.

The bombs start to drop
the city glows a dull red
houses disappear.

A plane struggles back.
Silence falls on the city
The siren screams out.

Darkness has vanished
the sun is rising again
light reveals the death.

Men sigh with the relief,
their families are living

others stay silent.

Like David's, this has a recognizable narrative and poetic structure. The spacing of the last stanza is his, not mine, and I find it interesting that he feels himself sufficiently in control of the verse form to experiment, with such obvious success.

Philip (13+) chose as his model Louis MacNeice's poem '*Under the Mountain*', and has obviously attempted to produce the same kind of effect by looking at the same scene from two different perspectives:

Seen from above
the searchlight beams shoot up
out of the blackness into the blackness.

Seen from above
the ack-ack gun is like a firework display

Seen from above
London is a forest fire.

When you get down
there is panic because the searchlight is stuck
and the bombs are crashing nearby.

When you get down
the gunners are rushing about loading and unloading
firing, but only hitting anything with luck.

> When you get down
> the fire is a raging inferno
> with charred bodies lying on the ground
> and firemen finding fresh corpses everywhere.

Although the stanza lengths vary, he has nevertheless kept to a basic format, stanzas one and four, two and five, and three and six being thematically linked.

Sarah (12+) used the same idea of contrast, but her poem is less formal:

> Inside was the snugness of love
> the shelter was filled with smiling faces
> but with fears inside their bodies,
> The peaceful sound of people sleeping
> and the noise of boiling tea.

> Outside was the chaos of war,
> the screaming of people caught in a fire,
> the confusion of which way to go,
> which way to turn.
> The bombs going off in every direction

> the terrifying explosions in the street,
> people running into the shelters,
> hoping that the air raid would soon be over.
> Then, as if by magic, all was quiet.
> The raid was over 'til the next time.

Matthew (12+) sticks to rhyme, and this produces obvious weaknesses. On the other hand, he does seem to capture Chas' ambivalent feelings about the pleasure and security which mingle with the dangers of war:

> War has broken out
> the gang are getting together,
> they're going to build a hide-out
> that will stand all weather.

> Sitting in the hole
> with sandbags, lamp and bunk,
> the hide-out is really made
> of any old junk.

The shelter is nearly finished,
the hole in the roof we'll mend
we've worked so hard on the shelter
we hope the war won't end.

We've survived the air attacks
and a great big German bomb
the war was going to be such fun
it's a shame the Germans have gone.

The war is over now
the world we rule
but there's one thing I don't want to do
and that's go back to school.

As was to be expected, some of the work was sentimental, but this one by Gaynor (12+) is not without charm:

Under one demolished house there lies a little girl
cuddling her little teddy. She's in another world
her soul in Heaven
her body lying still
a pretty bloodstained nightie
blowing in the breeze.

A tear would trickle down your cheek
if you saw this bloody sight
it's happening somewhere else right now
'cos the bombers are in flight.
The little girl, no care in the world
is lying quite undazed
her eyelids shut, her teddy smiles
he's not at all amazed.

His stuffing pokes out of his head
his seams are splitting wide,
his little paw is clenched so tight
as he lies there on his side.

Whoever guessed this sweet girl's life
would suddenly come to a halt
the furry teddy is now on his own
It's really no one's fault.

Some pupils (not necessarily the most able) produced work which I think shows real potential. David (12+) took a 'before and after' approach in one of his poems:

Before the war the world was calm
no fighter bombers guns or tanks
the air was filled only with bird song
not the humming of endless swarms of planes.
Every meadow was green, a doormouses city
not a soldiers muddy grave.
That was before the war.

During the war, the world was ablaze
the towns bellowed smoke like angry dragons.
Families crouched in small tin huts
like insects in a matchbox
and when the bombing had stopped
who had survived?
only the lucky ones.

Who were the safest, the soldiers fighting
or the families left behind,
defenceless to the heartless bomber pilots
during the war?

After the war the cities were rebuilt,
the rubble cleared away,
the victims brought home, wounded or dead.
The reunited families rejoiced while the widows wept.
The war had brought together neighbours
but separated families.

Paul (13+) created a moving word-picture:

The lonely black shapes
loaded with death
are high in the sky
as the deadly cargo
is unleashed on the city
the sky gets brighter
ambulances, fire engines, people causing confusion

the people run for cover
the children wail and scream for their mothers
the sirens sound the all clear
as the sun rises majestically over the city.

A few hours later
children would be playing
where people had died.

Finally, a poem by Elaine (13+) which I think needs no comment. Classroom creativity is a pyramid. The higher the base, the higher the apex will be. I would like to think that this one poem justifies the approach outlined above in a way that I could never hope to do. It was produced in exactly one hour, and is called, quite simply

The Machine Gunners

Once it was still,
the back yards unmarred
then the extasy of gazing
into cool green leaves and hard bark.

Sitting with the lights on
without fear,
knowing the night would bring nothing
but another day, another year.

What is Life
they must have thought
as they forced forward
its dark and twisted termination
and what is it, to be caught
between the horror hammering of the skies
and holding only memories in my mind?

Oil lamps, sandbags, worry.
Haunted are these crazed
but strangely magnetic hours.
Brazenly life continues secretly dazed
flying back strongly against its fate.

The obsession of survival,
Rest Centre teas
anchored trees obliviously sway
until, late on, the darkness seizes,
the confusion resumes.

Once, in this now stark, cold world,
without warmth and glow,
where tranquility overflowed into peace
I ran with understanding on the grass below.

A mind seared with frustration
inevitably runs blindly,
without understanding, it is strained
and suddenly it snaps,
it drifts away like a day long ago.

Once, during the understanding,
I would play, fully sane
and run through summer fields
until winter shook its cold mane,
but still I roamed safely
in this normal happy world.

Yet now I sit below
these illuminated stranger skies,
thinking of them retaliating
and not being able to hear their painful cries.

Who knows what might happen
after these twisted years,
death is common,
so are tears.

Who will come through
with nothing but memories scathed
by destruction of friends and family
in which their minds are bathed,
the heartache, will it ever fade?

The desolation did not drain all human will
rebuilding with anything spare
and wondering about the enemy
did they really care?
The same pattern all over
Germany. England.

7 CONCLUSIONS

What conclusions can be drawn from this approach? The first and most important is that it provides a theoretically acceptable bridge betwen advocates of the traditional and progressive approaches. This is crucial if the approach is to be department-wide. Every teacher must find something there with which he is familiar, and on which he can build. The extremes of both approaches are eliminated. Although the book is taught in a traditional way, so as to preserve the sense of a shared experience so easily lost when reading becomes totally individualized, the work which arises from it is progressive in the sense that it acknowledges, and makes room for, the vast range of individual responses to the shared experience. It is also progressive, I would suggest, in the sense that the pupils genuinely progress from the experience of the book to an understanding, and then an articulating, of that experience. They do this, though, within parameters which, though broad, are clearly defined. All follow-up activities are task-specific, and of limited duration. Momentum, so important in the reading, is equally important in the written work .

The second conclusion I would want to draw is the inevitability of the workshop approach. If one is concerned with the quality of response, then an atmosphere of experiment is necessary. Although the examples I have quoted are in a sense finished products, in another and more important sense the cut-off point was arbitrary, and based on an intuitive sensing that they had had enough. The rough drafts, the constant re-writings, the use of the same themes in different forms, these were the really important things which were happening. This was where growth through learning was taking place.

What, more basically, made these lessons successful? The choice of a book to which pupils could respond enthusiastically, and, equally important, one which I could teach enthusiastically. Careful preparation not only of the text, but of the class, so that they knew what was expected of them. The provision of a pattern of working in the classroom which implied that the teacher had faith in and trusted his pupils. Finally, a belief stated explicitly and implicit in the whole approach, that learning is more important than teaching, and that self-motivation (ultimately the only kind) comes to pupils when they take responsibility for their own work, because they realize they are doing it for themselves.

6 Three Short Stories with a Common Theme

JUDITH ATKINSON

1 THE AUTHOR

Judith Atkinson graduated in English at Bristol University, where she also trained for teaching. After six years in two Midlands grammar schools, she became second in the department at Shenley Court, a large comprehensive school on the outskirts of Birmingham. She was subsequently appointed Head of Department at a 13–18 High School in Hull, and is now Head of Department at Wolfreton School, an 11–18 comprehensive near Hull, with some 2,000 pupils and 16 English teachers. She is at present completing her studies for an M.Ed. degree at Hull University, writing a dissertation on the responses to poetry of children aged 11–15. She contributed a chapter on *Theme and Topic Work* to the volume *Teaching English Across Ability Range*. Judith has been active for some years in NATE and currently chairs the North Humberside Branch.

2 BACKGROUND TO THE WORK

I read and worked on the three short stories *The Lion* by Walter Macken in *Storymakers 2* (Harrap), *Adolf* by D. H. Lawrence in *Thoughtshapes* (OUP) and *Jamie* by Jack Bennett in *Escapades* (Arnold) as the core of half a term's work on the subject of humans' relationship with animals.

The class were a mixed ability group of 13-year-olds in their first year of a Senior High School. The school is a large comprehensive on the outskirts of Hull, which has an intake of children from both inner city and suburban neighbourhoods. The children came to the school from Junior Highs with very different experiences and expectations of English lessons, and the kind of structured thematic and reading work that I shall be describing was chosen deliberately to introduce the class in their first term to the different ways of working I would expect them to be familiar with later in the year.

3 CHOOSING THE STORIES

When planning the six week block of work I knew that I wanted the group to read a work of fiction which would present the pleasures and responsibilities of living with animals. A reading of a novel like *The Red Pony* by J. Steinbeck would have suited my aim well, as I was at first mainly concerned with the relevance of the subject matter rather than the form of the work chosen. Finally I decided that the three short stories seemed more approachable for a group new to me and they also offered opportunities for comparing different writers' treatment of a similar theme. I hoped to provoke the group's interest and involvement in the different problems and dilemmas described in the stories, and to make them aware of the contrast between children's and adults' attitudes to animals, which was a common theme in each story, and to help them towards some awareness of the way the stories differed in their handling of narrative and in the viewpoint of the narrator.

It was also important to me, when deciding how the stories should be presented, to prepare follow-up work which would introduce the children to a varied range of activities in response to reading. Many of them seemed to have come from their Junior Highs with the 'read round the class then write a book review' pattern firmly established.

4 LESSON SEQUENCE

In the two weeks preceding the reading of the stories the group experimented with different ways of describing animals' movements. They read and wrote poems about animals in the wild, usually animals of prey. After looking at photographs of animals in zoos they worked for a double period in pairs on planning a perfect zoo.

This led well into reading *The Lion* in a single period at the beginning of the following week. In the story Tim, a small boy, takes pity on a docile old lion caged up in a run-down touring menagerie. He visits the lion every day and watches in disgust as the keeper, nicknamed by him Putrid, taunts and ill-treats the animal. Aware that the lion is probably ill, Tim decides that setting it free in the wild will cure it, and he frees the animal and walks with it, in innocence, through the crowded town centre. When the police and keepers catch the lion and return it, a compassionate Inspector orders it to be killed by the local vet and reassures Tim.

' "Samson is gone back to the woods, Tim," he said. "You watch. One time maybe when you are playing in that wood, you might see Samson standing in the sunlight."

"Resting on the soft leaves," said Tim eagerly.

"That's right," said the Inspector.'

The story is written from Tim's point of view and in the simple language of a child. What interested me was the way the story implied the cruelty of the adults and their complete lack of understanding of Tim's compassion and action in freeing the lion, and the way the Inspector is presented as the adult capable of understanding and delicately handling the child's feelings. I hoped the group would be aware of this. The story is also enjoyable for its characterization of the adults, particularly Putrid, the keeper.

As with the other two stories, I read *The Lion* aloud to the class. The reading took most of a 40 minute period but left time for me to ask the whole class some questions which would establish that they had grasped some of the essential elements in the story – for instance, how old they thought Tim would be and why; why he would have nicknamed the keeper Putrid and why the Inspector needed to send a note to the local JP. Their answers, particularly about Tim's age, were perceptive. The following lesson was a double period. I planned work that I hoped would give the children the opportunity to express their understanding of the different characters' reactions to Tim and the lion. I gave each of the 25 children in the class a part, either as a character in the story or as 'extras' such as other children, shoppers, Putrid's fellow keepers and Tim's mother. I asked them to note down what they had seen and felt on the day of the lion's escape and their opinion of the event. For the rest of the lesson I taped a local radio news programme about the incident consisting of interviews, conducted by me, with most of the people concerned. I worked out beforehand the order in which I would question people so that 'both sides' of the controversial incident would emerge in a balanced way during the tape.

The group obviously enjoyed the taping, but, more importantly, their answers often showed a grasp both of their assumed character and of feelings and attitudes implied in the story which we had not discussed as a class. Tim's mother said of her quiet, independent son, 'He usually keeps himself to himself, doesn't talk to people.' The boy playing Tim showed that he understood how young and trusting the child was when he answered that the lion at the end 'was let free in the forest'. The Inspector, played by a boy whose written work had so far given little evidence of quickness and perception, answered about his actions at the end of the incident, 'I knew he'd be put down. We told Tim that he'd gone into the jungle so he wouldn't be sad, so that he wouldn't feel that all his efforts had been wasted.' The zoo keeper emerged rightly as a pugnacious character: 'Well, we ain't done 'owt wrong to it. It's been tret well for its age. I don't see what I've done wrong. I can't keep my eye on all the animals can I?' The keeper also lived up to the nickname given him by Tim: 'Well, it's not true, is it? It got the best meat; everything. Give it the best cushions to sleep on, best bales of straw. I was mainly thinking about Samson.'

On the following day I played back extracts from the tape and then introduced another activity which would require the children to see Tim's childlike actions from an adult standpoint. After some discussion of the style and format of a front-page news story, each child reported on the lion incident as though it were the lead story in the local newspaper. These are extracts from three reports, all ambitious in different ways. They are reproduced as written by the children.

BOY ATTEMPTS TO SAVE LION

A young boy caused chaos in the streets yesterday when he led a lion through the busy shopping streets in Withernsea town.

Tim Kay felt sorry for a lion at Mr Cobby's circus and took it into his head to take the lion and set it free in the woods. Tim led the lion through the busy streets causing a terrible commotion. People dropped their possessions and darted into the shops. Within seconds the whole street was deserted. People were worried about what might happen to Tim but he didn't seem to notice anything was wrong and that this wild animal could turn and savage him any moment.

Inspector Butler fearlessly approached Tim and the lion. He coaxed Tim away from the beast whilst the circus people stepped in and captured it.

Later the vet came to see the lion. He immediately saw that the lion had already been living for much too long and he put it down. Tim was not told of the lion's death.

Inspector Butler had strong words with Alphonsus and Mr Cobby. Cobby apparently did not know of how the lion was treat and did not seem to care very much anyway.

LION IN THE STREETS

Yesterday school Boy let lion in to the main streets of Withernsea

Chaos in the streets when school Boy walked Down main street yesterday afternoon. When Tim Kay took lion in the street police and circus men captured the lion with nets Tim Kay said I was not afraid of the lion I felt sorry for him so I LET HIM OUT MR COBBY, the mannager of the Circus said the lion was harmless He said the lion was well looked after Joe Fennigan vet said the animal sould not have bean left in a pen of a small size the animal shoud have been killed year ago it was cruel to let it live like this. The police are going to Fine Cobby and Co for £5,000 and the circus it to be disbanded.

COBBY'S CIRCUS SCANDAL!

An eight year old boy caused havoc in the streets, by walking a lion through the main shopping precinct.

Tim Kay showed courage and faith as he freed a savage, but peaceful creature out to his freedom.

The traumatic experience caused chaos and dismay in the street. Here we have Inspector Butler's account. 'I was called into a case, a strange one at that. Reports had said a lion was roaming the streets. When I arrived at the scene I calmly walked up to Tim (for I knew the lion was harmless).'

After consulting the vet the lion had to be put down. Mr Cobby's Circus is a dismal place for animals.

I was pleased that this had succeeded both as language work, as it was the first time the group had been asked to write in a journalistic style, and also as a means of expressing their understanding of the excitement of the climax of the story and the personalities of the three main characters. Tim, for instance, had been seen by the first writer as a child unaware of the adults' fears, by the second writer, with his deliberate use of capitals for Tim's words, as an independent, determined boy, and the third had seen his 'courage' and 'faith'.

Adolf, which I read to the class in the first lesson of the following week, is the story of a family's attempts to keep a wild rabbit as a pet. Told by an adult narrator looking back to his childhood, it describes how their father comes back from a night shift down the pit with a baby rabbit deserted by its mother. The children's mother, remembering trouble and sadness brought by previous attempts to tame wild creatures, objects to its being kept, but the children and their father persuade her and the rabbit is christened Adolf. As it grows it becomes both more exciting and more troublesome until eventually the mother insists that it must go and the miner returns it to the wild where it promptly hops away 'with utmost indifference'.

Of the three stories, this was the one which provoked most 'audience response'. The class were obviously amused by Lawrence's descriptions of the rabbit's behaviour, and the girls in particular were righteously indignant about the family's indulgent treatment of Adolf.

As an immediate response to the story I wanted to provide the children with a means of expressing their involvement with the characters and their feelings about the rabbbit. After briefly establishing the different attitudes of the mother and father, I asked all of the class to spend the last ten minutes of the lesson writing about their view of Adolf, as though they were one of the members of the family. As I had misjudged the time the story would take to read, there was insufficient time for this work to be done in detail but, at the least, each child spent a few minutes identifying with their chosen character and looking back reflectively at the story. These are two views of how the mother and father felt:

(i)   One day my husband brought home, from his night shift a little rabbit. As soon as I saw it, I didn't want anything to do with it, for every other animal my husband had brought home it had ended in dismay and sadness. But I felt sorry for it but I felt sorry for all the animals but at the same time I hated it. When my husband took it back I was sorry to see it go but for the things it did, went in the sugar, butter etc. I was also glad to see it go because it would be in the woods where it should be.

(ii)   When I first found Adolf he was lost and bewildered his family was all dead, I felt sorry for him. After a while he became mischievous and crafty. My wife thought it wrong for a rabbit to be in the house. He got up to some tricks but it was all part of growing up.

I thought it sad, that he had to return to the woods. When a rabbit comes of age its no use keeping it in the house, it has a mind of its own.

In the following double period I wanted the class to look in more detail at the story, particularly at Lawrence's vivid descriptions of the animal and its behaviour. I hoped they would discover passages such as:

'He would sit on the table humping his back, sipping his milk, shaking his whiskers and his tender ears, hopping off and hobbling back to his saucer, with an air of supreme unconcern.

'Suddenly he was alert. He hobbled a few tiny paces, and reared himself up inquisitively at the sugar basin. He fluttered his tiny fore paws, and then reached and laid them on the edge of the basin whilst he craned his thin neck and peeped in.'

I asked them to work in pairs and to make lists from the story under three headings: *Write down words and phrases which describe what Adolf looked like and how he moved*, *Make a list of his habits and adventures*, and *Discuss and write down your impressions of Adolf's character*. This lasted for 20 minutes and was followed by the class sharing their lists. I wrote some of the offered words and ideas on the board and encouraged some of the children to comment on the success of Lawrence's language as it appeared in their examples.

It seemed important for the children to make use of the insights they had gained from studying the story. I had already discovered that each of the class owned a pet, so I set them to write portraits of animals well known to them, including the aspects Lawrence had introduced into the story. I hoped their writing on a familiar topic would be enriched by their reading of *Adolf*. In most cases the portraits had more than usual detail and vigour, and one girl's writing in particular had obviously been influenced by Lawrence's narrative style and his picture of an animal as part of a family.

Portrait of my Rabbits
One morning when my dad had finished his night shift, he came and told my little brother that he had got us a rabbit. My little brother woke everybody up shouting that we had got a rabbit. At first I was not really bothered about the rabbit because although I always wanted a pet when I was younger I was not at all enthusiastic about having an animal now.

The rabbit had to be put in the shed for the first day because even my dad had no idea that we would get a rabbit. A man at work had just offered him it and my dad took it. He went to the shop in the afternoon and brought everything which we would need for it.

Before the hutch was ready we tried to see the rabbit but we daren't open the shed door in case the rabbit escaped. We tried to look through the windows at the rabbit. We didn't see it very well through the windows because it kept getting hidden under boxes and buckets.

My dad had made a nice hutch and run at the bottom of the garden by the time we got home from school. We soon found out that the rabbit hated being picked up. My father and I were the only people who could pick it up. If my sisters or brother tried, it would give nasty kicks and scratches with its back feet. My mother daren't pick it up anyway.

The rabbit kept digging holes all over its run. It kept disappearing down one of its holes and my dad was constantly filling them in. Once it dug a very deep burrow straight into the next door garden. When we saw it had gone my dad put his arm down into the burrow which he thought was just a small hole and found that even with his arm outstretched he could not find the end of it. When we saw that the rabbit was definately gone my sisters and brother were all crying and panicking. They went into our neighbour's garden to see if they could find it. There was a hole in the middle of a flower bed which my sister had to fill in. After a lot of searching we found that it had been hiding in the burrow and had run from the middle back into its run.

After we had had it about a month my father discovered that it had had babies. They were so small that he could not see them until he pulled back the straw in one corner. From then on me and my sisters would spend hours hoping to get a quick glimpse of one of them.

We saw that there were three of them, one white and two black. The two black ones didn't seem very active but the white one always seemed to push itself forwards. They always stayed together. They slept cuddled up to each other whilst the white rabbit tried to push himself in between them to sleep.

Now the rabbits are quite old. The white one stays with his mother and is much more adventurous than the black ones who will stay together.

Jamie is a South African story in which a boy, anxious to enjoy a swim in the reservoir on a friend's farm, sends his dog Majoor home by himself. The dog strays into another farm and kills several precious Leghorn hens. When Jamie returns home his father orders him to kill the dog himself, despite the mother's protests. Accompanied by his friend from the native village Jamie takes the dog and shoots him and the two boys sadly bury the body. Jamie is filled with anger against his father, and then, gradually, against himself.

I hoped the story would raise questions in the children's minds about responsibility for animals, and, by implication, for other areas of experience. The relationship between Jamie and his parents could arouse some controversy particularly when the father orders the killing of the dog. Jamie's confused reactions to the experience are honestly explored at the end of the story and I hoped some children would identify with them.

During the 10 minutes which remained after reading the story I could have found out children's opinions about the killing of the dog through class questioning but I preferred them to share their reactions in groups. To give this a structure I asked two groups of six to prepare arguments to defend the father's decision and another two groups to 'prosecute' him. In the following lesson spokesmen from the various groups introduced their various arguments and a general discussion followed. The incident in the story had obviously involved most of the class strongly. As the discussion developed it was clear that several children had made the link across to their own houses, families and pets. For example, one girl said, 'It'll be on the boy's mind for ever. I know it would be on mine.' As a balance to this another girl pointed out the difference a farming community would make, with the danger of dogs savaging stock. There was strong feeling against the father, most children saying that he should have killed the dog himself and, as one child suggested, 'should have said he'd run it over by mistake.' Only a few children saw why the father had acted with such apparent harshness: as one girl said, 'It taught Jamie a lesson. It was his dog and he ought to have kept the responsibility.'

I wanted to bring the class back to the story, and see how the narration, which sees everything through Jamie's experience, helps to make the father seem a less sympathetic character than his son. After the discussion had ended with a resounding vote against the father's handling of the situation, I asked the class to re-read to themselves the short scene in the story between Jamie's parents and the farmer who returns the dog. I asked them to think about the characters of the three adults and then each of them wrote a longer version of this scene, as a script. Some of the completed work showed a good understanding of the parents' different attitudes to Jamie and through the character of Mr Buchner, the other farmer, a grasp of the setting of the story and the significance of what Jamie had allowed the dog to do.

In the last two lessons of the week, I gave the class some work to do which would require them to look back and see the story as a whole. I asked them each to present the story in a comic strip version, as though for a children's comic. They were to use eight 'frames' on a piece of plain foolscap paper. This is an activity I often use as a follow-up to reading. It seems a valuable exercise for looking at the narrative 'shape' of a story, for presenting it in a different medium and for demonstrating understanding. The children have to begin by mapping out exactly what takes places in each 'frame'. Where this story was concerned there were decisions to be made about how best to follow up the different strands and how to conclude it. Would the original ending with Jamie lying sullenly in his bed fighting his feelings be the most dramatic way of finishing a comic strip version?

I was very pleased with the lively and inventive work this produced, and interested too in the different emphasis given to the story by individual children's selection of incidents. Here, for instance, are three different endings, shown in each one's last two 'frames'. Janine, in her first frame had Jamie, with his gun, and Kiewet, his friend, both looking down at a grave decorated with flowers and a named cross; there is no dialogue. Her last frame has Jamie spread-eagled on his bed, drumming his heels and fists and shouting, 'Hate Jo, hate Dad, hate Buchner.' Andrew shows Mr Carson speaking to his son about the dog. Jamie says, 'Shoot him! w-w-what for?' as his stern father replies, 'For killing the stock.' The final 'frame' has no dialogue, but a drawing of Majoor's grave under a tree and the words above it: 'Jamie didn't want to kill Majoor but he knew he'd have to. A shot is heard and everything is silent except for a boy shedding tears.' In Claire's highly detailed first 'frame' Jamie sits next to Kiewet under a tree with the gun propped up between them. Jamie's horse crops the grass behind them and Majoor sits on his haunches with his eyes on Jamie and his tongue lolling out. Jamie says, 'So that's it Kiewet. Oom Kooma insists that Majoor be done away with.' Kiewet replies mournfully, 'Ah Baas

Jamie. Ah Majoor. And now Baas Jamie?' In the final 'frame' there is no dialogue; Jamie and Kiewet kneel on either side of a rough patch of soil, the gun is on the ground and the horse is looking up from its eating. The comment reads, 'A shot was fired and a lively unexpecting dog slumped to the ground. They buried him under the boerboon tree.'

Before moving on to a last, more general group activity to bring the block of work about animals to a close, I wanted to bring the three stories together for comparison and discussion. I divided the class into four groups, gave each a tape recorder and sheet with three questions. The questions were intended to structure and give purpose to the groups' discussions, but I made the mistake of asking the groups to write down their findings at the end of the discussion. For two groups this became the most important activity and the discussions were very limited. Some points are worth recording, though, from the tapes of the other two groups. The three questions were: a) In all three stories the adults and children have attitudes to animals which are different from each other. Take each story in turn and discuss how i) the adults, ii) the children acted towards the animals. b) Do you think the child in each story learnt anything from what happened? If so, what? c) which story did each of you in the group enjoy most, and why?

In discussing a) the children were united in their condemnation of the zookeeper in *The Lion*.'Alphonsus was a little Hitler', 'it's wicked, really cruel.' Tim was seen as lacking in common sense – 'he should have told his Mum' – although one girl felt that 'he got the right thing in the end'. The parents in *Adolf* were criticized chiefly for their indulgence towards the animal: 'they were daft about it', 'not strict', 'they treated it like one of the family'. The father was praised by one boy for his sensitivity to the animal and his common sense in returning it to the wild. In response to b) most of the children felt that Tim had learnt nothing from his experience in *The Lion*: 'he was too young to understand'. The children in *Adolf* had learnt not to put rabbits on the tea table but also 'not to get too attached to an animal' and that 'the rabbit was happier in the wild'. Most felt that Jamie had learnt a lot, 'not to be careless, stupid', 'he'd learnt to train the dog better', 'to take his responsibilities', 'the father punished Jamie by making him kill the dog'.

All three stories were given as first choice by someone. *The Lion*: 'I liked it because it showed how much he liked the lion and loved it a lot,' 'the boy was nice' and it was 'more interesting then the others', *Adolf*: 'it weren't as sad', 'it had a nice ending', 'I like rabbits and it was about a rabbit'. *Jamie*: 'it would teach people that they have to take more care with their animals', 'I didn't like it much at first but when I'd done the cartoon it brought a new light on the story'. *The Lion* was criticized by one boy because 'it was too far fetched, the others could have happened'.

5   EVALUATING THE WORK

In looking back over this block of work I felt that certain aspects of it had been successful but that in retrospect there were things I would have done differently.

Choosing fiction to read with mixed ability groups is sometimes difficult, but it seemed that these three stories had 'worked' well. Their language made them immediately graspable (for children of all abilities), whilst at the same time each one raised issues for thought. They also seemed right for the difficult age of 13, as all three stories invited the readers to see events both from children's and adults' points of view. It was clear from the atmosphere in the classroom as I read and from the activities which followed that these were stories which were enjoyed.

I was pleased with the variety of the 'follow-up' activities I evolved to help the class channel and express their responses to the stories. As I indicated in the description of the background to the work, I wanted to introduce the class in their first term with me to different possibilities of what to do after reading. I also wanted the activities to be appropriate to the distinct character of each story, and I felt that they were.

These, summarized, are the activities I planned and the aims behind them.

1 *Role play* – the interview programme from *The Lion* – to explore characters and their reactions and relationships.
2 *Writing accounts of the events in the story in a different form* – newspaper reports of incidents in *The Lion* – to see the story from a different perspective.
3 *Writing and talking briefly about the viewpoints of different characters* – the parents' reactions to Adolf – to share the main characters' feelings and thoughts about the central issue in the story.
4 *Modelling writing on the original story* – accounts of owning pets after reading *Adolf* – to show awareness of the writer's characteristic use of language and narrative structure.
5 *Debating the issues raised by the story* – arguments about Jamie's father – to express the readers' reactions to the controversy raised by the author.
6 *Presenting the narrative in a different form* – comic strip version of *Jamie* – to examine the authors' narrative method in adapting it to a different medium.
7 *Comparing different authors' handling of a similar theme through discussion* – final group-work on tape – to return to the stories and see them in perspective.

The work which involved children in exploring character and discussing the issues raised was productive. I was less happy about the ways in which I had invited children to look at the stories as stories. Only the writing 'modelled' on Lawrence's story and the comic strip version of *Jamie* gave children the opportunity to show how they had responded to the language and shape of the stories. I could have included, for instance, as one of the final activities a discussion of the three very different but equally effective conclusions to the stories.

In looking back at the organization of the block of work as a whole I felt that I had structured it too tightly. In keeping relentlessly to my 'plan', I had moved everything on too quickly and had not allowed time either for enough individual reflection on the stories or for longer-lasting and more open-ended activities. Also what was missing from my tight schedule was the opportunity for children to return to what they had enjoyed reading and to relish their favourite moments. It would, for instance, have been more valuable in the final group discussion questions to have substituted for (c) 'Which story did each of you in the group enjoy most and why?', an instruction such as 'Take it in turns to re-tell to the rest of the group the parts of the stories which you enjoyed most.'

In relation to the rest of my teaching and thinking about helping children to respond to their reading, this block of work has several implications.

It confirms my conviction that teachers need to find a variety of ways to help children to give expression to their responses. When I began teaching in a grammar school, I inherited from my own experience, from my training and from my colleagues the 'standard' forms of expressing response to reading. When a work of fiction had been read, children wrote character studies or formal essays about issues arising from their reading. In my first post in a comprehensive school the now commonplace kind of writing assignment often given to children reading fiction as part of a CSE course came as a revelation. Children were given assignments such as, 'Now that you have finished reading *Of Mice and Men*, imagine that you are George and write your account of the last part of Lennie's life.' I was frequently delighted by the perceptions children expressed through more open-ended writing of this kind. I have been encouraged by this to experiment with different kinds of channels for response and to think continually about the activities which best suit individual books. I have also become more aware, and this was confirmed by children's work on the three stories, that activities need to suit individual children. It proves impossible to predict which activities will work with which children. This implies that whenever possible children should be provided with alternative activities so that they can choose the ones which will serve them best. With the class described in the case study I was consciously introducing them to a range of follow-up activities so that they would be able to make informed choices about ways of working later in the year.

A further implication of the work was that I was reminded for future practice about the gap between children's evaluation of what they read and their responses to reading. When I asked the class as part of the final discussion of the three stories, which one they had enjoyed most and for what reasons, I was not surprised by the tepid and teacher-pleasing answers. These contrasted with the lively involvement with reading shown in the activities. I was not surprised, as this is nearly always what happens, yet, as a teacher I continue to ask children whether they like what they read. In future I would hope to act on the realization that evaluation and active reading are two parallel but different activities; in addition, to accept that the expression of evaluation is difficult and that many A-level students still find it taxing to articulate reasons for their likes and dislikes.

Finally, in my future practice I would want to concentrate on what was significantly missing from this block of work. I mentioned earlier that I felt I had failed to provide enough time for individual reflection on the stories. Immediately after each story was read I steered the class as a whole into activities chosen and evolved by me. At no time did I allow each individual in the group a space, after or during reading, for the private relationship between reader and text to grow. Now, and in the future, I would want to remedy this. I would pause during reading, if this was appropriate to the particular narrative, or after reading, and ask each child to write down in any form, however fragmentary, the thoughts and feelings associated with the experience of reading or listening to the story. It would be valuable for children just to sit and think about their reading, but writing is, I think, more valuable because through it children crystallize their responses. Once a child has come to terms with the story for herself, other activities, often shared with others, can explore those first immediate reactions. I forgot, in planning for a class to have their reading enriched through shared experience, that the first act of reading and responding is shared between the individual reader and the story.

7 Emphasizing the Author

Barry Hines and Kes

PAUL FRANCIS

1 THE AUTHOR

Paul Francis has been teaching English in comprehensive schools since 1967 and enjoys working in schools which try to cater for all the educational needs of all their pupils. *Beyond Control*, his study of discipline in the comprehensive school, was based on his early teaching and written for student and probationer teachers (Allen and Unwin, 1975). From 1973–81 he was Head of English at Belper High School, a purpose-built, eight-form entry comprehensive catering for all pupils aged 13–18 in a small Derbyshire town. Since 1981 he has been a Deputy Head of Madeley Court School, Telford, where his main interest is in developing interesting materials and varied ways of working for pupils aged 14–16, in an area where social deprivation and unemployment challenge many of the conventional motives for work in school. In his own teaching, Paul Francis has pursued a number of enthusiasms at various times, in pursuit of the complete English teaching grail which he defines as 'Renaissance Man plus punctuation'. Particular interests have included spelling confusions, transactional reading, play-writing by pupils and discursive essays (of which one example is his case study in *Coursework Assessment in English*, edited by Patrick Scott for NATE, 1983). He has also written and produced a number of plays for pupils, five of which were published as *Power Plays* (Edward Arnold, 1981).

2 BACKGROUND

Belper High School, a 13–18 comprehensive, had no caning, streaming or uniform, and put a strong emphasis on individual tutorial attention and close links with parents. Parental occupations covered a wide variety of light industries, shops and farming, and the mixed ability groups in which English was taught contained a full spread of ability and motivation. The English department was built on the assumption that materials, problems and insights would be shared communally, while teachers were also encouraged to develop their own ideas and teaching interests. (This is more fully outlined in *An Introduction to Blob Theory*, in *English in Education*, Vol. 15, No. 2, Summer 1981.) The Belper department valued individual reading based on class libraries (as outlined in *Towards a Fiction Policy*, in *English in Education*, Vol. 13, No. 1, Spring 1979), but also worked to make a small number of texts into viable units of work for each member of a mixed ability group. It was from this work that the current case study arose.

3   CHOICE AND APPROACH

Kes for the fourth year? It sounds like a pushover, one of the few safe bets in teaching, but it may not be that easy. There is teacher fatigue to contend with, since I know it backwards and can't really believe that there are pupils who haven't read it. Then again, the book isn't non-stop action, and does present some problems for slow readers eager for thrills. On top of that there's the tendency for some teachers to settle for 'realistic' working-class fiction as lowest common denominator; as a result, the pupil who's just done Stan Barstow's *Joby*, Sillitoe's *Short Stories*, *Timothy Winters* and Bill Naughton's *Spring and Port Wine* may not see *Kes* as a revolutionary breakthrough. Finally, I have reservations about glorifying individuals as the victims of nasty institutions. It's a powerful, emotional appeal, but it doesn't help us to do the difficult, necessary thinking about living together in large numbers. So, there's a lot going for it, but a lot of potential snags too.

There is a wide range of teaching opportunities with *Kes*, but for this particular fourth-year mixed ability group I narrowed down to the specific target of Barry Hines as author; my slogan, to adapt the commercial, was 'Kes Means Hines.'

I was also interested in exploring the different media of books and films, and was able to make use of the film of *Kes*, a full set of books, a VCR recording of the *English Programme* about Barry Hines, and four sets of duplicated sheets, as follows:

(a) notes on, and quotes from, the Barry Hines *English Programme*
(b) six short extracts from the book, for analysis and discussion
(c) a list of eight possible purposes an author might have
(d) an outline for the final essay

The work was spread over a five-week period, although other English work unrelated to the book also took place in that time. The plan of campaign was as follows:

Week One: Read first few pages aloud; issue copies, allow some reading time
Week Two: Show Barry Hines VCR; take notes, some discussion
Week Three: Discussion of own passages; group discussion of sheets (b), (c)
Week Four: See film of *Kes*, take some notes; brief discussion
Week Five: Write essay

In closer detail, it worked out like this:

4   READING

There probably are teachers who set reading homeworks and know that everybody does them, but I don't share their confidence. Reading a book is a solitary, silent activity, best carried out in large chunks of time, so that makes it difficult to do in school. We should set aside a regular minimum period of time for silent reading, but even on a sacred 40 minutes a week some pupils won't get through the whole of *Kes* in less than a term, even if they can remember where they'd got to last week.

On the other hand, if you send copies home how do you know they get read? Weekly tests, random spot checks in front of the class ('When did you last read your novel?'), routine filling-in of record cards with summary of the plot so far – all these seem a long way from the kind of reading most teachers want to encourage, and if you're not careful you've lost more time in checking up on homework than you've actually gained from setting homework at all.

And then there is the problem of different reading speeds. Give a class *Kes* and some of them will have finished it that night, while others won't actually read all the way through it even if you allow them a year. The only sure way you can control progress is to have one copy, from which the teacher reads aloud in carefully selected chunks, lesson by lesson. That can be a nice group experience, and can ensure that the less able can follow the story; it makes use of the teacher's dramatic talents, and it can lead to all sorts of fruitful follow-up work. The only snag is, for pupils it has very little to do with reading.

My solution for *Kes* was to bank a lot on the basic appeal of the book, and to encourage pupils to read it at home as far as possible. I set certain times for reading in class (when I checked individually on the progress of known slow or reluctant readers) but I made it clear that the books would only be available for six weeks and would have to be handed in at the end of that time. I also told myself quietly that I didn't mind if everyone didn't finish it, which was just as well.

I used lessons to provide encouragement, starting off with my public reading of the first few pages. I established that Billy was the central character, drew attention to a few early clues to his personality and background, and gave warning of the possible problems created by the book's manipulation of time-sequence – skipping briefly ahead to pages 21, 44 and 48 (Penguin edition). Later on I did a brief outline on the board of Billy's school day, to give some sort of shape to the book in case anyone was drifting in a mass of detail. Generally, though, I wanted a reading arrangement that was as close as possible to the adult one of reading for pleasure, with motivation provided by the book rather than by fear of retribution. That might not always be my approach, but it was with this book and this class.

5 DISCUSSION

It's a book that engages strong sympathies and stimulates contrary opinions, so there ought to be ample opportunity for talking about it. With this class I may not have made the most of this, and shortage of time prevented me from using a device that has been very fruitful before. Small groups are each fed an extreme statement about the book:

'Billy's mum is not to blame.'
'Billy deserves all he gets.'
'The school does all it can for Billy Casper.'
'Billy is a thoughtful lad who's just unlucky.'

The groups have to think and talk about their statement, and gather relevant evidence from the book both for and against; they then have to try to reach some kind of overall conclusion, and report back their findings to the rest of the class. Provided groups are given time in which to carry out their researches properly, this can be very useful.

With this particular group I angled discussion rather differently, because I wanted to place the emphasis on the writing of the book, the intentions and tactics of the author, rather than on what happened and the people in it. I was lucky to have as a starting point the English Programme which shows Barry Hines talking to some school pupils about his work, his experience of reading, his motives for writing and his present work habits. After watching this and briefly discussing it (mainly to draw out pupils' reactions to him as a person, likes and dislikes, surprising or unusual features that interested them), I asked them to think about the way the book was written.

All pupils had to prepare a short passage from the book that they were ready to read aloud, and briefly comment on what was good about it. The brief was almost as crude as that, and predictably I got a wide range of responses ('it's good description because it uses clever words . . . it's funny . . . that's an important bit of the story . . . you can really feel as though you're him . . . they talk just like real people . . . I felt sorry for Billy . . .' and so on). The range of answers, though, allowed me to make a few passing points on details, but also to establish the key fact that there were different kinds of writing involved.

I then formed the class into small groups which cut directly across their normal friendship patterns. No group had more than four members, and nobody worked with anyone they normally worked with. This rescued quite a number of pupils from the expectations normally placed upon them (to lead the group, or be silly, or do nothing, or so on) and focused much more concentration on the task in hand. In this case, they needed all the concentration they could get.

They all had sheets containing six extracts from the book:

(a) part of the opening description of Jud's and Billy's bedroom
(b) an argument between Billy and his mum
(c) the end of the description of the caning
(d) Billy's 'Tall Story' that he writes in English
(e) part of the commentary on the football game
(f) part of the cinema sequence at the end of the book.

They also had a smaller sheet which outlined eight possible aims that a writer might have in any part of a novel:

(1) to tell the story
(2) to describe a place
(3) to build up an atmosphere – the 'feel' of a place or event
(4) to describe a character
(5) to show people together, in interaction (arguments, love, contrasts . . .)
(6) to show a person's thoughts and feelings
(7) to explore important ideas, like love, money, power . . .
(8) to make the reader react in a particular way (feel sorry, be amused, get angry . . .).

The groups had to try to allocate numbers to each passage. They could use any number of aims for one passage, and could add new ones if required. They could use a number more than once, and some they might not use at all (with this particular book (7) is difficult, because although central themes of class, conflict, love and so on are dealt with, there's hardly any direct generalization of them by the author). The aim was not so much to reach right answers as to grasp the differences between various passages. The caning was obviously more powerful and serious than the football match; the argument between Billy and his mum was simpler to

follow than Billy's thoughts at the end; the detail of Jud coughing into
Billy's neck, like the mis-spelling in Billy's essay, invited the reader's sympathy – but the two passages work in a very different way.

For the purposes of this article it would have been nice to tape all the
groups, but that was not practicable. My subjective judgement, though, is
that the groups were usefully busy, actively engaged in what they were
meant to be doing, and that by the end of the session some pupils had
thought a lot more about the business of writing than they had at the
beginning.

6   WATCHING AND LISTENING

A key part of this process involved careful attention to TV and film, and
that does need thinking about. It is not the same as sitting at home, switching off or chattering if you get bored, but on the other hand the teacher
need not require every minute of attention to film to be 'paid for' with
hours of written answers to comprehension questions.

I tried to compromise. I frequently told the class that there would be
one big piece of work at the end of all this, but deliberately did not give
them a clear outline of it in advance. I wanted them to take some notes, but
also wanted them to select what they saw as most important and interesting. On the Barry Hines interview I in fact already had sheet (a) ready
printed but I did not allow the class to use it until two weeks after the programme. I wanted them to take their own notes, but also needed some
kind of insurance for those who were away or those who hadn't managed
the note-taking very competently (and the time gap gave me the chance to
look at their notes in some detail). If I provided my notes every time, of
course, the clever crooks would see it coming and not bother to take their
own notes, but I make a point of not doing things exactly the same way
every time ('Think BIG – keep them *b*usy, keep them *i*nterested, keep
them *g*uessing').

With the film I wanted to concentrate on watching, and did not want
conscientious pupils scribbling hastily as they tried to summarize every
piece of action. I already had a synopsis of the main events of the film and
made that available for anyone who wanted it, but asked the class to concentrate on looking for differences between the book and the film, and
ways in which the film added to the book. In whole-class discussion, fairly
clearly directed by me, we looked at the addition of the club scene, the
amount of comedy, the changed order of the school day, the endings, and
so on. I also invited them to look at technical points about the film – settings, sound effects and music, actors who convinced them, good
moments and possible criticisms. Here again, I encouraged the taking of

some personal notes which might be useful later, but I didn't set specific
tasks or demand set quantities of work.

7   WRITING

At the end of the half-term I set aside all of the week's lessons for one
piece of written work. It took Barry Hines as the starting point, and I
wanted the class to make use of all their notes, impressions, ideas and
opinions. I gave them an outline sheet which suggested a plan of action,
but they were encouraged to treat it flexibly – and they did. The main
headings went as follows:

Barry Hines
His way of writing
The book
The film
Differences
Your own reactions

'The book' section had subsidiary suggestions, but I deliberately didn't
ask for any plot summary or character analysis. I was aiming primarily at
the author's purpose and means, and didn't want description of Billy
Casper getting in the way: 'Barry, not Billy', to adapt a phrase used by one
of the class.

This may horrify some as a waste. Billy Casper is an interesting, convincing character, well worth describing. Lots of pupils will respond to
him more fully than to, say, Ralph, Joby, Snowball, Kino, George or Lennie (to pick at random from some of the stock titles studied by this age
group). On the other hand, there must be a limit to what you can do with
any one book, and every time you do a book you must – for the pupils' san-
ity as well as your own – exclude a whole number of interesting possibilities. With this class I had just done a series of character studies on a
play, and we all needed a break. Variety, as ever, is the spice of life and the
staple diet of happy teachers.

The positive gains of author study are substantial. We have worked on
this as a department, right across the ability range, and have achieved
enough success to convince ourselves at least that this is not only of value
to potential 'A' level candidates. Barry Hines' natural articulateness,
nearness to the world of many pupils and explicit social comment make
him a particularly promising candidate, but it's quite possible to use a
similar approach with (at least) Lawrence, Orwell, Steinbeck, Ray Bradbury, Arthur Miller, Wilfred Owen, Charles Causley or Ted Hughes.
Each of these can be appreciated as a distinct character, with recognizable

background and personality. All have clear, powerful attitudes to their subject matter, and have written or spoken in an accessible way about their work. Nor is it essential to have a VCR tape of an interview with the author; it should not be beyond the wit of a couple of English teachers to devise a dialogue involving an author. All it needs is the will, some basic information and a little bit of nerve.

The gain is that it presents a book as something with purpose – a human being is involved in writing the thing, rather than just teaching it. It incidentally offers some good preliminary training for advanced students in looking beyond the characters at the author in action in the novel, a difficult art they often need help with. There are also possible gains for pupils as writers which comes from the chance to identify more closely with writers' choices – now why on earth did he do *that*?

8   RESPONSES

My own evidence for any kind of evaluation consists of my own subjective reactions, blurred in the memory, and the essays the class wrote in the last week of the half-term. I gave them all the week's lessons if they needed them (with possible extras for those who got stuck or finished early), because I wanted detailed, thorough pieces of work, and the maximum chance of consultation for those who got into difficulties.

So far as quantity was concerned, that worked well. There were a lot of very good, long pieces of work (nearly all between two and eight sides of A4, with a steady average at over three), most of which tackled the kinds of questions I'd asked them to look at. There were disappointments – a couple of idlers I should have got to sooner in the week, some who didn't make use of the material offered, some mindless plot summary (but less than usual) and a few individuals who simply didn't do enough thinking.

On the other hand, there was no clear pattern of failure, no one obviously identifiable group who missed out (girls, boys, bright pupils, slow readers, less able, anti-fiction brigade). And there were a number of pleasing successes, cases where I was convinced that someone had got more than usual out of reading or writing or both.

The close attention to extracts bore fruit:
'Barry Hines describes things in great detail, and seems to make big things out of little things. When Billy was delivering papers, he goes to a big house and the door is open. Billy notices small things – "The hall and stairs were carpeted". In Billy's house the hall and stairs aren't carpeted and to Billy this is obviously a sign of luxury.' (Katharine)

Some pupils, predictably, note the fact of comparisons or descriptive detail but don't add any comment on them, but that's not a disaster.

Acquiring confidence in analysis is a gradual process. First you get the habit of specific quotation, then you go for increasingly substantial comment. Overall I was pleased that a number of pupils produced evidence in this way, either recalled from previous discussion or chosen by themselves.

The dialogue obviously struck a lot of them as important, in a way I hadn't expected and certainly hadn't consciously 'taught': 'Barry Hines wrote the book to show that life is like that and you have to take it as it comes. In the book Barry Hines gives his people an accent. He writes like this all the way through and in some places where people speak it's quite difficult to read – for example:

"Tha' what? He's t'cock o' t' estate, that's all."

His way of writing brings to the reader a reality. He doesn't put a frill on it really, or make the book have a happy ending so it's nice, but he makes it seem real.' (Beverley)

For my money the stress on Barry Hines as author worked well.

'It started at PE college when the teacher gave them some writing to do. Barry seemed to enjoy it – "I had this romantic idea to be a writer – it was crazy." He started to write small stories in his spare time, and they got larger and larger!' (Rachel)

The assumed intimacy of 'Barry' seems to me harmless, part of an infectious enthusiasm. This needn't imply any lack of intelligence or precision, as Rachel's selection of quotations elsewhere in her essay amply demonstrates:

'I write about coal miners, steel workers and people who live in council houses. You've got to write about what you're close to . . . I write about my own backyard.'

Or again:

'It seemed that there hadn't been any books about the Billy Caspers of this world – the failures . . . I wanted to redress the balance.'

Anyone who's bright enough to see these points as central to this essay shouldn't be worrying about whether to refer to the author as 'Barry' or 'Mr Hines'; she's already doing the important job, thinking about what he writes.

There are dangers, though, and enthusiasm can lead to a rather hasty self-confidence:

'He has his own individual way of writing, quite different from any other author. He describes his characters very well, and the way that the scenery is and what sort of feelings the person is having.' (Robert)

This claim for Barry Hines' uniqueness isn't substantiated, and rests more on Robert's enthusiasm for the book than on a close comparative reading of other novelists. On the other hand, there are worse faults, and in going for an ambitious goal you're liable to get some misses – just as students in the early stages of an A-level course will often come up with pretentious nonsense in their struggle to find a suitably academic voice.

What really cheered me was the willingness of some pupils at the very bottom of the ability range to tackle the business of writing about Barry Hines: 'Barry is an honest man he talks a lot about Billy in Kes it is a fabulus book . . .' (Simon); or 'I started laughing at most parts in the book because as well as being a good story it is very comical. I felt sad for Billy when Jud killed he's hawk . . . Barry Hines was brought up near a mining village. He was clever but he acted daft at school. Barry wrote about the Caspers bacause they had never been mentioned in books before so thats why he wrote about them.' (Richard)

Later Richard would get a grade five CSE, but in this piece of work his response justifies the gamble of asking all pupils to think about authorship. Far from this being a sophisticated branch of study accessible only to experts, it may well be one of the few approaches which could render literature intelligible to those readers who currently don't know where books come from and who don't care how and why they come to be written.

Attention to detail need not inhibit personal response. Penny provides a nice example of this, as she illustrates the way in which Barry Hines portrays the insensitivity of some teachers:
"Liar."
"I have, Sir. I was first through. Ask anybody." He stroked his cheek, his eyes brimming.
"Right, I will."
'It goes further but I'll stop there. That showed an example of picking on a pupil. As I read Kes I don't know how I reacted because I get really involved, as though it's me.' (Penny)

That is only one of a number of tributes to the compulsive power of the book for a wide range of readers.

It is not universal, though, and part of the justification for my rather technical, neutral approach to this book stemmed from my own unease about insisting on particular reactions to working-class deprivation, divorced parents, impersonal schools and so on. A bright child from a genuinely caring middle-class home isn't under any obligation to feel sorry for Billy Casper. It is all the more impressive then, that Michael writes as follows about Billy's 'Tall Story':

'It is written as though it was spelt by Billy, for example "sentrall eeting" for "central heating". This is to get across the idea that it is Billy, not Barry, writing. I think this gets the idea across very well. It made me think, as I suspect it was intended to, how lucky I was compared to Billy Casper's life. We take carpets, central heating, ice-cream, fish and chips etc. for granted, but for Billy it is just a Tall Story.' (Michael)

This is a full, intelligent response. That superbly poised 'as I suspect it was intended to', the gradual building up of a key thematic point out of one small detail, a real maturity and compassion – and all the stronger, I feel, because there was no explicit demand for it from me.

Perhaps though, as Nicola suggests, it is 'a good book, but more for boys.' Or perhaps not:

'I enjoyed the book and got very engrossed in it. Once I started to read, I didn't want to put it down. I felt sorry for Billy all the way through the book, and I sometimes felt sorry for his mum having to cope with Billy and Jud on her own. I came to hate the teachers at the school, except Mr Farthing. He was the only one to understand Billy. The ending of the book brought tears to my eyes. I could imagine Billy running across the fields and shouting for Kes, and crying when he found his dead body in the dustbin.' (Diane)

Denis is a renowned scatterbrain and compulsive 'thinker'; ask Denis why he's gazing out of the window, at the ceiling or drumming a pen and he's 'thinking'. Yet he too testifies to the book's power:

'I liked reading the book it was very interesting.
It is one of those books that when you start reading you have to finish it. The book keeps you interested all the time and does not allow your mind to wander on to a different subject.' (Denis)

Philip speaks for a lot of his contemporaries when he sums up:

'I think that Barry Hines did do exactly what he set out to do, and very well, because when I saw him talking about his background I could see the similarity between him as a child and Billy Casper, and the life of both people. It's an original idea, and that is why it's good, and I like it.'

9 EVALUATION

In retrospect, I feel a similar sense of satisfaction with this course of work. There are always some pupils you could do better with – that's one of the reasons for going back next Monday morning to try to do better. And there were some regrets: that either CSE requirements or my lack of nerve didn't allow a larger share of the final product to be oral, or that not using the *Kes* film might have led to an even more demanding piece of literary study (bringing in *The Blinder* and 'Billy's Last Stand', and extracts from *The Gamekeeper* – which has a very different mixture of detailed observations and social purpose). Nonetheless, overall I was happy.

I was glad that I'd set only one piece of written work, glad I'd tried to exclude from that a lot of the conventional space-filling, glad that I'd set aside a lot of time for the actual writing. I was pleased that I'd encouraged pupils of all abilities to think about the author in action, and that I'd persuaded so many of them to embark on some detailed technical analysis within what they did.

The mixture of media worked well, and for many pupils the encouragement to read in their own way and at their own pace gave them an independent satisfaction I couldn't have got from a more closely monitored approach. I was especially glad that I hadn't tried to force particular views of Billy Casper or of the book's success; personal judgement does seem to me to be one of the tasks that all our pupils should attempt, and while that may well need structuring so far as presentation goes it doesn't require dictation. That's why I like what Karen wrote:

'I didn't find the book or the film very interesting, however I think I preferred the film. It was easier to follow, but I don't think that the film managed to do what Barry Hines had set out to do, that is write about something that happens in our society and that many people don't realize about. The film was more of a comedy; it should have emphasized Billy's feelings, showing how he really felt. The film should have had a different ending, including Billy's dad. The conclusion of the book gives the reader a good explanation of why Billy acted as he did, instead the film didn't really answer this question. The spectator would go away feeling sorry for him, but not knowing why. 'I didn't like the book, because there were too many descriptions that were not interesting.' (Karen)

She may or may not be right; what matters is that she is thinking, clearly and hard, and caring sufficiently to put over what she thinks with intelligence and feeling. And it is that process, surely, that we are after, rather than a particular view of *Kes* or Barry Hines.

8 Keeping the Set Book Alive:

Great Expectations

MIKE TOWN

1 THE AUTHOR

Mike Town was born and educated in South Yorkshire before studying for a degree in English and Politics at Keele University. After graduating Mike settled in North Staffordshire, where he has taught in three local mixed secondary schools in both urban and rural areas. The particular work for this book was accomplished while he taught at Cheadle High School, an 11–18 comprehensive. He is now Head of English at Biddulph High, a 13–18 comprehensive, just north of Stoke-on-Trent. As most of Mike's experience has been with older secondary school pupils, he is particularly interested in the problem of teaching 'literature' to young people who are growing sceptical of its value in education and who are becoming more reluctant to work at understanding any writing that is not immediately accessible. Mike has recently gained an MA at Keele for a thesis about the teaching of poetry in secondary schools. This general survey and analysis included classroom research that compared different approaches to teaching poetry. At the moment he is working on a book that set out in detail a series of poetry lessons for school children. Mike is also an examiner of GCE and CSE English Literature and an active member of the Staffordshire branch of NATE.

2 BACKGROUND

Every year when I study the list of set book options, I am bedevilled by the same fundamental doubt: should young people be subjected to an examination in English Literature? I worry because I wonder what effect the stringencies of the examination course will have on the pupils' attitude towards literature. I have the awful fear that I may smother the very spark of interest that I have been working so hard to rekindle in reluctant readers and douse the fired imagination of the enthusiastic.

'Discuss the significance of . . .'
'Comment on the effectiveness of . . .'
'Criticize, with close reference to the text . . .'

The lengthy critical analysis demanded by such exam questions must put many pupils off reading for life. Indeed modern authors such as William Golding and Laurie Lee publicly mourn the inclusion of their stories on the set books lists. How can 16-year-olds be expected to appreciate Lawrence or Hardy when they have not the emotional maturity even to understand the relationships described? How can they be expected to analyse the complexities of style of Dickens or Conrad when their writing is at best little more than clear? Someone once said that any fool can criticize, and many do. Am I making fools of my pupils by demanding detailed literacy analysis? They say, 'I enjoyed that book', or, 'I found that story interesting'. I demand to know why. And more. I demand to know why other more knowledgeable critics like the book and how the author managed to create such valuable prose. For many pupils, the step from reading a book purely for enjoyment, to studying it for public examination is immense; for some it is impossible.

Like everyone who has such doubts I am constantly searching for better ways of studying set books – ways that are both effective and interesting. What follows is just one idea for studying stories. In analytical terms it is a way of examining plot. As the plot, or story line, is probably the most accessible element of literary analysis, it may be a valuable introductory approach to studying prose. More generally, this method provides an approach from which pupils can study most stories and, at the same time, compare them. However, most importantly, it is a way of demonstrating to the pupils just how much they already know about a book simply from reading it and therefore giving them confidence in their own opinions and abilities.

3   THE PUPILS

I was teaching at Cheadle High School, an 11–18 mixed comprehensive serving a small town situated about 10 miles east of Stoke-on-Trent. Each year-group was divided into Upper and Lower halves. The class I chose was of fifth-year pupils of mixed ability within the Upper (academically most able) band. Remembering that 'O' level exams are designed for the most able fifth of each year group, it meant over half of the class would be studying the set books with little chance of gaining a good 'O' level pass grade. I had taught this class for well over a year and knew them well.

4   THE STORIES

I chose three stories, to be studied in separate 70 minute lessons, in the following order:

The Parachutist by D'Arcy Niland (published as a short story in a teaching anthology *Story Lines*, by Arnold Thompson, EUP.) Length: five pages
The Secret Sharer by Joseph Conrad. Length: over 50 pages
Great Expectations by Charles Dickens. Length: 450 pages

The last two titles were chosen because they were set texts on the O-level literature syllabus and were found particularly difficult by the pupils on first reading. I chose *The Parachutist* because it has a simple narrative structure with beginning, climax and end clearly defined, and it was a suitable comparison with the other longer texts. Consequently I hoped that the pupils would enjoy studying *The Parachutist* and then apply the same critical techniques to the other, more complex stories.

5   LESSON PREPARATION

The Parachutist and *The Secret Sharer* were read by the pupils the evening before the lessons. *Great Expectations* had been read over the previous few weeks.

I asked the class to divide into five groups of their own making and to select for themselves a chairman for each. The groups were made up of five or six pupils, each with a copy of the appropriate text, and seated round a table on which was placed a portable cassette recorder to record the discussions. They all had writing materials.

6   LESSON PLAN

(i) *Study of the beginning of the story*. The pupils first copied the following questions from the blackboard:
(1)   How does the opening passage prepare us for the rest of the story?
(2)   What does it tell us about the relationship between the characters and the atmosphere of the story?
I then read the opening passage (about half a page) of *The Parachutist* to the class. They followed the passage in their books. I asked the pupils to

answer the questions as fully as possible, first by discussing each other's views, and then by writing down any points from the discussions that they thought answered the questions. The discussions were recorded.

I went round the groups, sometimes listening, sometimes joining in by provoking argument if the discussion was flagging.

After about 10 minutes, I stopped the discussions and asked the chairmen to report their conclusions, one point per group, in turn, each of which I repeated and opened to comment from the rest of the class. I also encouraged the pupils to supplement their written answers with points from this reporting session.

(ii) *Study of the end of the story.* At the end of the reporting session, the pupils copied the following questions:
(1)   How is the concluding passage different from the opening one?
(2)   Explain how it completes the events and relationships developed in the story.

I then read the final half page of the story to the class.

The pupils discussed and answered the questions as before, including the reporting sesssion.

(iii) *Study of the climax.* After the reporting session, the pupils copied the following questions:
(1)   Compare the climax with the opening passage; what is common to both and what has changed?
(2)   How does the climax determine the course of the rest of the story?

I then asked which part of the story the pupils thought was the climax – i.e. the passage during which something happened that determined the course of the rest of the story. After deciding this, I read the passage to the class.

The pupils again discussed and answered the questions as before, including the final reporting session.

The same lesson plan was followed, with minor modifications, for the other two stories. For *The Secret Sharer* the passage used as the 'opening' of the story was, in fact, several pages into the text, and the climax immediately preceded the end. Such modifications are discussed later. Also, as *Great Expectations* has several climaxes, the selection of the most important one took longer. Otherwise, despite the difference in length and complexity of the stories, the procedure was the same.

7   THE DISCUSSIONS

To suggest that the teacher should encourage pupils to talk about what they have read in order to verbalize their experiences of it – whether comprehension or the lack of it – is not a new idea. I felt that, because of the difficulty of the set books, the pupils could easily have become disenchanted with serious literature had they not been able to share their experiences as they read. I wanted them to develop a positive, thoughtful response to fiction. As can be seen from the following transcripts of the discussions, the element of negative, thoughtless criticism (e.g. 'I don't think it's interesting') was quickly overcome. The transcripts cover the opening passage of *Great Expectations* as discussed by two of the groups.

Ian	How does the opening passage prepare us for the rest of the story?
Neil	It's all bleak isn't it, and barren?
Stephen	It's all, like, marshes.
Nick	Bleak, in other words.
Stephen	It starts off exciting, doesn't it? It's like, dead quiet, and this bloke jumps out on him; well, sort of jumps out on him – he wouldn't be able to run if he'd got a great iron on his leg, would he?
Nick	He did jump out on him, didn't he? He grabbed hold of him and turned him upside down, frightening him to death.
Stephen	Sounds exciting, doesn't it?
Neil	Interesting, straight away.
Nick	I don't think it's interesting ...
Stephen	Well, he thinks the reader's interested but ...
Nick	No, it isn't interesting at the start when it's going on about his parents.
Stephen	Yes, but it's interesting when the man gets him.
Ian	It's a morbid story.
Stephen	Morbid? ... Yes, because everyone's dead.
Trevor	It doesn't give us a fair reflection of the rest of the the story though, does it?
Nick	Yes, because that's all been completely morbid and ...
Trevor	It isn't.
Stephen	Yes, well, most of the story's, like, whatsit, isn't it ... morbid.
Trevor	It's like life. Well, it starts like that so you can keep reading it. If it had started boring you would have put it down, wouldn't you?
Ian	How is it connected to what follows?
Nick	Well, it's completely morbid all the way through.
Trevor	It isn't though ... it finishes happy, doesn't it?
Nick	I don't think it does.
Trevor	He becomes rich and pompous. That isn't morbid, is it?
Nick	I think it's morbid all the way through.
Stephen	Why?

Nick	Because it is.
Stephen	Why?
Nick	Well, first his sister dies . . .
Ian	Then he goes to Miss Havisham's house.
Nick	Yes, and then Miss Havisham dies . . .
Stephen	And the house is knocked down . . .
Nick	And then he can't have Estella.
Stephen	Yes, but he's got her in the end though, hasn't he? . . . He has a good go at being a gentleman.
Nick	Oh yes, only in the end.
Trevor	He always has expectations though, hasn't he? You think something's going to happen good, then it doesn't, does it?
Nick	He still hasn't got her in the end because he isn't exactly married to her.
Stephen	He wanted to marry Biddy but he couldn't.
Nick	You see, he can't have anything . . . so it gives a completely morbid outlook. He keeps getting frightened like when that bloke's on the marshes.
Stephen	It's the same all the way through.
Nick	Mm . . . you think Pip's weak for a start and Magwitch's strong and frightening.
Neil	Pip changes, doesn't he? Through the story and Magwitch changes; like Pip gets harder and Magwitch, like, stronger.
Stephen	Pip might get stronger but in the end he loses all his money and whatnot. He's ruined.
Nick	Yes – what was the question? How is it related to the rest of the story?
Ian	Well, you have Magwitch as Pip's benefactor. Then two characters are in the first . . . on the marshes.
Trevor	No, you don't expect it's going to be him though?
Nick	Yes.
Neil	I did.
Ian	I did as well.
Trevor	Did you? I thought he'd just die away. I thought it was just to make a good start.
Nick	I thought it was him. I didn't think it was going to be Miss Havisham. That was too obvious.

Clearly, this was lively and useful discussion. New ideas tended to be introduced tentatively, often in the form of rhetorical questions which asked for support from the other contributors; this support was usually given when the point was repeated and developed. However, in such a co-operative and relaxed atmosphere, there was freedom to disagree. Nick quickly contradicted Neil in a thoughtless way in which many teachers will recognize; but as the discussion developed and Nick accepted the constructive tone of the other contributions, he replaced his dismissive approach with reasoned argument that demanded close reference to the text.

Although very few substantial points were made, the pupils explored the opening scenes at their own level of interest and understanding, and, almost in passing, began to relate these scenes to the rest of the story. Finally, they returned to the initial question to refocus their talk. Their concluding remarks are, I think, the most impressive because they are implicitly analytical. First, Ian spoke in terms of 'characters'. Then they consider how they expected the plot to develop on first reading. Trevor spoke in terms of 'a good start' to the story. Finally, Nick criticized Dickens's 'red herring' (that Pip's expectations were due to Miss Havisham) as being 'too obvious'. By drawing the evidence for their assertions from the story as a whole, the pupils were implicitly describing the importance and function of the the opening passage.

The second transcript covers discussion of exactly the same question and story, but by a different group of pupils.

Ian	How far does this opening passage prepare us for the rest of the story?
Mark	It's surprising, isn't it?
Ian	It introduces Pip, doesn't it? (agreement)
Mark	It says where he lives . . .
Ian	And people he knows like Mrs Joe, Joe . . . and it shows he was an orphan.
Warren	It's full of action at the beginning . . .
Ian	And it shows you somewhere bleak and desolate.
Warren	It shows the story's interesting . . . It starts off exciting and surprising.
Mark	It sets the scene.
Warren	It captures your interest.
Tim	It introduces the convict as well.
Ian	It introduces everybody and it introduces the scene, where he is, near the sea.
Tim	And it gets on with the story and makes it interesting.
Peter	It doesn't introduce all the characters.
Warren	. . . like Jaggers.
Ian	It starts to introduce the most important characters though, doesn't it? I mean, Pip's one of the most important, and Magwitch.
Tim	Yes, Magwitch is most important.
Ian	How is it connected to what follows? . . . Well, it shows he's near the hulks, doesn't it? Near the prison ships.

Warren	It's supposed to be on the marshes. Is it supposed to be on the Fens?
Tim	And that's why he gets his great expectations in the first place: because he helped that bloke.
Warren	It helped Magwitch . . . he's evil, isn't he?
Peter	He doesn't really know what's happening.
Warren	There he's naïve though.
Ian	Yes, he's got a vivid imagination, hasn't he ? . . . But the main point is meeting Magwitch, isn't it, because that's the whole point of the story really.

(The discussion ended here temporarily so that the pupils could write down the points made so far.)

The discussion in the first transcript is expansive and rambling. The set question was merely a starting point, to be departed from and returned to depending on chance turns in the discussion. The second example is much more controlled and succinct. It seems that the first group felt that if they kept talking about the opening of the book in general, they would eventually cover the main points. The second group seem to have learned from their previous discussions and reporting sessions (*Great Expectations* was the last of the stories to be studied) that similar questions could be asked of each of the stories. Consequently their discusssion was more pointed, as though pupils were accumulating relevant points, one leading to another, in answer to the set question. They had learned to think of the opening scene as an introduction to the characters, setting and story. Warren also considered the author's appreciation of audience, interpreting the exciting action as a device to capture the readers' interest. Finally, and crucially, they recognized how the opening passage introduced the central theme of the novel; as Tim said, 'that's why he (Pip) gets his great expectations in the first place; because he helped that bloke (Magwitch)'; and Ian agreed, 'that's the whole point of the story really' – and it is; the whole plot turns on these great expectations. Although this may seem an obvious point, it is the key to the plot and the teacher should not take for granted that the pupils recognize this.

8   THE ROLE AND INFLUENCE OF THE TEACHER

While the groups were discussing the questions, I experimented with different roles. Sometimes I sat studying the text or leaned against a wall watching the groups from a distance. At other times I stood on the edge of groups, obviously listening and occasionally commenting or asking provocative questions. Generally the pupils were relaxed and keen to discuss the stories. Of course there were occasional giggles from the girls and facetious banter from the boys, e.g. when one wag suggested that the ambiguous ending of *Great Expectations* was designed for a sequel, and others had fun imagining Pip and Estella's love life. Although such thoughts might appear irrelevant, they were also creative and imaginative, and I wanted the pupils to feel in control. I expected my occasional participation to provoke and stimulate. Indeed, until I transcribed the recordings and studied the effect of my intrusion, I thought I had succeeded. My participation was useful when a group was unsure of exactly what was wanted from the question or could not agree; then they either called to me or drew me to them because of their silence. However, on almost every other occasion, my interference was destructive or inhibiting. The style of the discussion changed completely. The previous line of argument ended immediately. If I stood near to them, listening in, they expected me to take over – and I always did. Sometimes my interruptions were quite rude; I simply overrode what was being said. And my provocative questions stimulated no more than the briefest answers, not discussion, from those with enough confidence to speak. I was compromising the freedom and responsibility I had given to the pupils. It may be that a more sensitive teacher could have intervened more discreetly and more helpfully. But I thought that I was being and had been discreet and helpful at the time . . . .

9   THE WRITTEN ANSWERS

I did not prescribe what form the pupils' answers should take. I considered it was the learning that was the most important, not the written record of that learning. Why, then, did I ask for written answers? I knew that written answers would make the pupils clarify and summarize the points made in the discussions. I knew that some pupils would not contribute to the discussions but would communicate in writing. I hoped that the written work would focus everyone's attention on answering the questions and resolving the arguments. Finally, I wanted to be able to assess how much the pupils – including those who did not speak – had understood and learned.

I marked the written answers according to an open-ended scheme so that pupils gained credit for any relevant points that showed some understanding. I then compared the performances according to the written answers with my expectations according to my knowledge of the pupils' ability.

From these comparisons it was clear that the pupils did learn from each other. Although there was no evidence of copying, there were certain

points that, although expressed differently, were common to each group.
They were usually points that had been discussed at length. The recordings showed that these points tended to be repeated several times at different stages of the discussions and usually in several different ways.
Often, when the discussion was flagging, one of these generally agreed
points was re-stated. This had the effect of re-focusing the discussion and
making the point so clear that even the slowest members of the group
could understand it.

It was interesting to note that, although the pupils generally performed
on paper according to my expectations, the individuals who assumed the
leader's role in the discussions did not write answers that were any better
than those of their more taciturn friends. Also, there was much less difference between the most able and the average pupils that I would have predicted. It certainly seemed as though the pupils were learning from each
other, particularly the average from the most able and articulate group
leaders.

10   THE REPORTING SESSIONS

It might have been predicted that the average pupils could benefit most,
especially as the most dominant pupils were dispersed among the different groups. Hence the need for the reporting session.

The reporting session at the end of each discussion allowed an open
forum for the exchange of points. The idea was that each chairman summarized the findings of his group so that every pupil could learn from all
of the points put forward in the different discussions. In practice the sessions went much further. Pupils other than the chairmen offered points,
and lively arguments sometimes developed. At the time I felt that the
reporting sessions were the most lively and valuable parts of the lesson.

What follows is an example of part of one of the reporting sessions. I
have chosen the session that immediately followed, and therefore summarized, the discussions of the opening passage from *Great Expectations*.
Thus the transcripts of the discussions and of the reporting session can be
compared.

Teacher	Well, how does this opening passage prepare us for the rest of the story? . . . Loretta?
Loretta	The paragraphs started dramatically.
Teacher	Explain what you mean.
Loretta	Well, the start of the the story is dramatic and full of action.
Teacher	How does that prepare us?
Loretta	Because what follows is dramatic . . . and this is connected to it.

Teacher	Good. What is dramatic about the opening?
Nick	Well, the beginning is morbid and you feel sorry for Pip. Then a man jumps out and frightens him which you don't expect.
Warren	Yes, it begins all desolate and miserable with graves and . . . and fog and all that, which makes you think the story is going to be all bleak and desolate . . . but then it changes . . .
Nick	Yes, with Magwitch. It introduces Magwitch who is all scaring, when you think Pip is all . . . you feel sorry for him because he's small and helpless . . . then Magwitch . . .
Teacher	Why is this dramatic?
Loretta	Because it's different to what you'd expect and the horrible convict is different to Pip who's poor and pathetic.
Teacher	How is this connected to the rest of the story?
Stephen	Well, Pip and Magwitch are the main ones . . .
Ian	It introduces the main characters and tells you what they are going to be like.
Teacher	Yes . . . Janet?
Janet	It's intriguing because of Magwitch. You wonder what will happen.
Teacher	Yes.
Janet	And it starts with mystery and action which shows the story will be full of mystery and drama.
Several	But it's not . . . some of it is . . . some's boring.
Kay	Yes, but some of it's action . . . the best bits . . . the important bits.
Teacher	Yes, I think you're right. Last point: how does the setting fit in with this? Warren?
Warren	It's a mysterious setting, with the fog and the graveyard; and it shows there could be violent scenes.
Kay	Yes, it's bleak and spooky, like the story all the way through: violence, some death, mystery . . .
Teacher	Mm . . .
Kay	The setting's gloomy, like the book (laughter and light-hearted agreement) . . . showing that something nasty is going to happen. (Here the teacher summarized the points made so far and then continued the discussion.)

The next extract is from the same lesson, but the discussion took place about 20 minutes later, after the end of the story had been discussed in groups.

Teacher	Remembering what we said about the opening paragraphs, how do you think the last page or so completes the story?

	How is it connected with what has gone before? . . . Remember what the start was like. What happened? Lesley?
Lesley	Well, the ending is different from the beginning because there's optimism instead of the gloomy outlook.
Teacher	What do you mean? . . . Go on, Lesley, explain what you mean in more detail. I'm sure you're right.
Nick	I don't think it is particularly optimistic because it's still bleak and foggy and all that.
Loretta	Yes, but they're together, now. Pip and Estella are together because they aren't going to part.
Teacher	Warren?
Warren	Yes, they're going to get married.
Ian	No, they're not.
Warren	They're not going to separate, they're . . .
Ian	Yes, but it doesn't say they'll get married, does it?
Teacher	Angela?
Angela	They're different now, aren't they?
Teacher	How?
Angela	Well, they were childish at the start . . . and Estella was nasty . . . yes a bitch.
Teacher	And what are they like at the end? . . . Stephen?
Stephen	They've learned from what's happened. Estella wants to be friends. Yes, it's fate that they came together at the end.
Loretta	Estella can talk maturely now to Pip whereas she couldn't before.
Teacher	Yes, things have changed, but aren't there any similarities? Janet?
Janet	They're both surprise meetings and there's the same mist hanging over the marshes and there was mist at the end.
Teacher	What does the mist show? . . . You said it suggested mystery and the unknown at the beginning.
Janet	It sort of . . . ends the story, as though it was the end of the day, and the story.
Teacher	Like cowboys riding off into the sunset at the end of Sunday afternoon films . . . yes . . . Stephen?
Stephen	It's ambiguous . . . You're not sure what is happening.
Nick	Yes, you are . . .

The discussion continued like this with the pupils usually supporting each other and building on each other's ideas. Comparing the transcripts with the two earlier ones, it is noticeable that some of the points that successfully survived the criticism of the group discussions were proudly repeated by the original contributor. It is also noticeable that there was still disagreement, even at this stage, and that arguments were often left unresolved, so that individual pupils were forced to decide for themselves. However, several points were completely new and had obviously arisen during the reporting session, inspired by other contributors.

I think the most successful feature of the reporting sessions was the way the pupils were so keen to continue, with only minimal direction from the teacher. Probably the written notes helped because all pupils had an answer in front of them which they could offer confidently in the knowledge that their own group supported them at least. Indeed, the reporting sessions were so lively that it was impossible for anyone to note the contributions verbatim, and many pupils forsook supplementing their written answers to enjoy the discussion better. It did not matter whether the verbalizing of thoughts was written or spoken, as long as the effort was made.

11   WERE THE LESSONS SUCCESSFUL?

The overt purpose of the lessons was to study plot; in fact this conceals their true value. To separate plot from characters, diction, style and meaning is to create artificial and unhelpful distinctions. In studying the three passages crucial to the development of the plot of each story, the pupils inevitably discussed whatever seemed to them to be relevant to the questions. The few brief questions asked stimulated extensive discussion which went far beyond the plot. In fact the points made were evidence of the beginnings of a general but sometimes profound understanding of the stories. With a little guidance, the pupils had climbed into the stories to explore them for themselves. The exact form of questions I posed was relatively unimportant. The terms opening, end and climax should not be taken too literally. As an alternative to the prescribed lesson, it might be just as instructive to allow the pupils to choose their own three passages and ask them to justify their choices in the discussion groups.

Although there was no basis for quantitative measurement of improvement over the three lessons, notions of comparison and learning are relevant. One reason for studying three stories in a series was so that they could be compared; and they were compared directly: 'It's like *Great Expectations*' was said more than once. Other comparisons were less explicit. Most groups soon realized that the setting of *The Parachutist* and the description of it were closely related to the meaning of the story because of the atmosphere they created. Remembering this, the pupils examined the other two stories in the same way. Thus by starting with a short, accessible story, the pupils learned what to look for in the other more complex ones.

Probably such comparisons are more successful when the stories are thematically related. Here, all three stories contained lonely main characters isolated in bleak, unsympathetic worlds: the hawk, stricken with hunger and hunting in a barren, flooded landscape (*The Parachutist*); the Captain, desperately lonely on a new ship, with a unsympathetic crew and thousands of miles from home (*The Secret Sharer*); and Pip, 'all alone', trying to survive in a cruel world which abuses him mercilessly with its false expectations (*Great Expectations*): all three are changed by their experiences.

12   CONCLUSION

Finally, it might be appropriate to introduce a note of scepticism. In some ways the de-mystification of literature is sad. The 'suspension of disbelief' is shattered. The marvellous becomes commonplace. The literary analysis demanded by external examinations may be sterile and destructive. But it need not be so. Imaginative analysis in small-group discussion, carefully organized, can be interesting exploration in which pupils marvel at their discoveries; what they find should deepen their appreciation and enrich their enjoyment. It should encourage the pupil to read the book again because the discussion may provoke new questions in the reader's mind. From the evidence of even these few lessons, I hope that it is clear that pupils can learn from each other, collectively increasing understanding and appreciation. I am convinced that the pupils know enough about a story from a single reading to make such lessons a success, at least as introductory studies.

The crucial element when teaching literature, especially to cynical 16-year-olds, is to stimulate and retain the pupils' interest. This approach – which is by no means original or unique – stimulates that interest, if only because it encourages pupils to talk about and try to make sense of what they are reading; it encourages them to ask questions of the story and, most importantly, it does not attempt to answer all of the questions left unresolved in the pupils' discussions. Developing a response to fiction, even with modern teenagers, demands that the teacher's participation is seminal, that the pupils' own judgements are uninhibited, and that the story is left alive and mysterious.

Part Three

Programme

9 Fiction in Schools

Part one of this book attempted to summarize current ideas about the nature of response, the ways in which we read fiction, and the processes by which these develop. Part two consisted of case studies in which five teachers described their practices in working with fiction in schools. This third part draws on their experiences and on the evidence of research to propose a practical programme for fiction in schools. It asks how the responses of children – during reading as well as after it – can be made central to the teaching/learning process, There is no great shortage of ideas, materials and resources for work with fiction, but they can too easily tempt us into concentrating on ourselves teaching instead of on the readers reading, and what is happening to them. Awareness of reader-response processes should underlie planning, choice and classroom strategies.

WHAT DOES RESPONSE-CENTRED FICTION TEACHING INVOLVE?

All five case studies show teachers, with commendable tentativeness, reflecting on their own practice and drawing conclusions from it. There is a striking correlation between those principles which seem to emerge from the record of research and theorizing in part one and those which come directly from the classrooms of part two. Crudely summarized, the common emphasis can be reduced to a list of points like these:

1 The aim of any programme of fiction reading – as all five teachers make plain – is to help students to develop and refine the responses which they make, to find satisfaction in an extending variety of works and to cope with more demanding and complex ones. There is no sense in ignoring the satisfactions which children find in what may seem to the teacher third-rate material if the pleasures are the same as those prompted at a higher level by the first-rate. The teacher's task is to lead on to the better.

2 Successful work with fiction therefore involves the teacher's developing awareness, manifested in the case studies, of what pupils

read and enjoy, outside school as well as in, 'of all kinds and standards' (Keith Bardgett). Unlike most other forms of study, the
experience of fiction is an activity that is only to a limited extent
under teacher control. Most children will have had long and formative experience of stories before entering secondary school, and their
freely-chosen reading may well be more important to them than
classroom books. Teachers need to establish links with these other
reading experiences and with film and television fiction, as Judith
Atkinson, Keith Bardgett and Paul Francis have done. In practical
terms, this monitoring may involve recording the use of class libraries, encouraging the keeping of reading journals or simple lists of
books read, regular discussions about reading with individuals or
small groups, availability to talk about books in the library, systematic
recommendations of particular novels, and sometimes a willingness
to be 'sidetracked' into discussion of last night's TV serial.

3   Dealing with fiction in schools forces the teacher inevitably into a
relationship with students as people. Successful work implies that
the teacher, in Keith Bardgett's phrase, has 'had faith in and trusted
his pupils', that here is a desire, as Mike Town says, for 'the pupils
to feel in control'. Together they are thrust inexorably into areas that
are not always seen as part of the English curriculum: sociology,
psychology, morality, history. Reading fiction together involves
assessing ideas about human nature, moral choices, social and political change, personal and group relationships, and so on. Whether or
not they wish to do so, teachers teach themselves when teaching
fiction: they cannot avoid revealing their personal views about man
and society in their choices of books, their attitudes to them and the
structure of activities related to them.

4   There are inevitable problems, as Keith Bardgett and Paul Francis
suggest, in getting any group of individuals to read the same text.
Choosing a novel for a group is a hit-or-miss affair at best, and may
produce a wide range of individual reactions. When stories are read
together, the emphasis should be on an enjoyable form of presentation that makes it as much as possible like the reading on their own
that most children prefer. In other words, the reading should not
normally be held up for questions, explanations or teaching points
(however well meant); it should be as dramatically effective as possible; and children should be allowed to listen or follow in the style that
best suits them, so long as they do not interfere with the listening or
reading of others.

5   When a text has been read, the first essential is to leave space for
individual responses to develop and be formulated as they would be
in private reading, with the 'tentativeness' praised by Mike Town.

The teacher has to hold back for a while from the instructor's natural instinct to lead a class to the truth by posing keen questions or imparting desirable information. The encouragement of fumbling reactions, links with personal experience and savouring of particular moments has to come first. Judith Atkinson's chief criticism of her own work was that it was 'structured too tightly' and 'failed to provide enough time for individual reflection'. It may be necessary to tolerate rambling talk and views that we may find inappropriate or even silly until discussion has reached a more advanced stage. Pushing students too fast is only likely to drive them into silence or into mouthing insincere, second-hand ideas. Tolerance also has to extend to the decision of some pupils *not* to respond – or rather to repress response.

6   Teachers have to struggle against handing down ready-made judgements, values and interpretations. It is dauntingly easy to impose, even indirectly, our own views about just how pupils should react, about the 'meaning' of the text or the way in which it should be discussed. Mike Town has recorded how his intervention in group discussion seems in retrospect 'destructive or inhibiting', and Paul Francis expresses a general uneasiness about 'insisting on particular reactions'. Because we already *know* how the book turns out, we are often tempted to stress important clues, to point towards the ending, or to feed information we feel will be useful. The problem is how to come fresh to a familiar story, focusing on how the students respond, how they build up and remake their interpretations, rather than on our own knowledge and our planned awareness of what we hope to 'do' with the book.

7   The first sharing of responses may be better undertaken in pairs or small groups, when tentative ideas can be exchanged without fear of a larger audience. In general, the teacher has to work to create an atmosphere in which open exchanges of ideas and attitudes can flourish, and in which genuineness of reaction is the chief criterion. This may be helped by the workshop approach of Keith Bardgett, or the pair and small groups work of the other four case studies. Students should then be better able to avoid the twin pitfalls of looking for some authoritative 'right' interpretation or of refusing to consider questions of value because 'it's all a matter of taste'.

8   It is desirable to build on the 'vast range of individual responses' (Keith Bardgett) which appear, the way in which, for example, John Foggin's children produced 'quite different stories' from the same text. In some classrooms, different judgements or interpretations are seen as presenting a 'problem' to be solved. In fact, the variety of responses and preferences offers an excellent opportunity for learn-

ing as Judith Atkinson indicates: the chance to consider *why* there are these differences. In general, evaluation should be seen as a late stage in the discussion of a story. The temptation to begin by asking 'Did you like that?' needs to be resisted.

9   The response-centred classroom exists in 'an atmosphere of experiment' (Keith Bardgett), with 'open-ended activities' (Judith Atkinson) which are not too closely monitored (Paul Francis). This depends on a trusting relationship in which teachers are also seen as developing responses through interaction, rather than appearing to be coolly objective or the resident expert (though obviously possessing greater maturity and literary experience than the pupils). This can be helped if the teacher poses open questions which reveal uncertainties and variations, and if the teacher's own views are sometimes modified in discussion.

10   Some model of how abilities in fiction reading develop has to underlie any programme of reading. John Foggin considers the growth of ability to cope with the imaginative demands of fiction; Keith Bardgett's department works within a specific rationale for development; Judith Atkinson discusses growth in power to evaluate and is 'consciously introducing' activities to be used again later in the school at a more complex level. Books and stories, that is, should be introduced with an idea – however tentative – of what they might achieve for pupils in the context of what has already been read and will later be encountered. On the other hand, the curriculum does not have to be so rigid that it cannot accommodate the varying needs of individuals or the new interests and opportunities that arise.

What do these 10 points imply, then, for our teaching of fiction in schools? Before discussing questions of choice, organization and presentation, it is necessary to consider what marks off studying a presented novel as one of a group from reading a novel of our own choice when we are alone. The case studies show that what happens to fiction in school is dominated by three overlapping factors: constraints on what and how children read, the direct effects of teaching and the demands of examination study. Each of these can be briefly considered.

CONSTRAINTS ON SCHOOL READING

How do children feel about the stories they encounter in schools? Despite the popularity of fiction (over 90 per cent of 11-year-olds express a liking for reading stories), the setting for that reading makes a significant difference. When they were asked where they preferred to be when reading, 80 per cent of 11-year-olds and 84 per cent of the 15-year-olds chose somewhere at home, in contrast to eight and seven per cent respectively who preferred to read in school. These results reinforce the findings that more than four out of five pupils of 11 and 15 prefer going off and reading on their own rather than in a group, and that 90 per cent prefer reading silently to themselves rather than reading aloud. Seventy five per cent chose to emphasize the differences between what they read at home and what they read in school, whereas only 14 per cent discussed similarities.[1]

What underlies the strong preference which children express for their own choice of books, as opposed to class readers, and the generalization that nearly three out of ten feel that 'some of the books we use at school are too difficult for me'? The responses of younger secondary pupils suggest that their difficulties are not with any particular features (demanding language, complex ideas, unfamiliar conventions) but are global. Learning how to *switch into* a new fictional world is an ability about which we know little. One of the reasons that children choose to follow one Mallory Towers book with another is that no adjustment is demanded of the reader: the expectations remain constant. On the other hand, a novel presented in class may require 'realizing' in a quite unfamiliar way; there may be new rules for the reading game.

We have become alerted to some of the problems of Reading Across the Curriculum – the difficulties caused by having to switch abruptly from the registers and styles of history to those of science, from geography to RE. As yet we are too often insensitive to the difficulties that some young readers face in coping with a range of fiction and in switching from one text to another. We frequently treat novels as somehow easy by definition, and as virtually interchangeable: one can be substituted for another with no shift of presentation. Consider for a moment, though, the brief openings of eight novels popular in schools for use with children of 11 and 12.

They were flitting the Allmans. Joseph sat at the top of Leah's Bank and watched.

The horse and cart stood outside the house, by the field gate. Elijah Allman lifted the dolly tub onto the cart first and set it in the middle. Then Alice and Amelia climbed into the dolly tub, and Elijah packed them round with bedding. Young Herbert was carrying chairs.

Alan Garner, *Granny Reardun*

Mrs Frisby, the head of a family of field mice, lived in an underground house in the vegetable garden of a farmer named Mr Fitzgibbon. It was a winter house, such as some field mice move to when food becomes too scarce, and the living too hard in the woods and pastures. In the soft earth of a bean, potato, pea and asparagus patch there is plenty of food left over for mice after the human crop has been gathered.

R. O'Brien, *Mrs Frisby and the Rats of NIMH*

The island of Gont, a single mountain that lifts its peak a mile above the storm-racked Northeast Sea, is a land famous for wizards. From the towns in its high valleys and the ports on its dark narrow bays many a Gontishman has gone forth to serve the Lords of the Archipelago in their cities as wizard or mage, or, looking for adventure, to wander working magic from isle to isle of all Earthsea.

Ursula Le Guin, *A Wizard of Earthsea*

We'd gone right through the school collecting the teachers' tea money and had got to the canteen door when Danny waved the ten-pound note at me. It took me a couple of minutes to realize what it was, 'cos it looked highly unlikely in Danny's grimy mitt. Then I pushed him into the canteen, sure to be empty on a Friday afternoon at five to three. The pandemonium of a wet school playtime died away, and we could hear the rain drumming on the roof instead.

'Where dija get that, you nutter?'

Gene Kemp, *The Turbulent Term of Tyke Tiler*

It happened many years ago, before the traders and missionaries first came into the South Seas, while the Polynesians were still great in numbers and fierce of heart. But even today the people of Hikueru sing this story in their chants and tell it over the evening fires. It is the story of Mafatu, the Boy Who Was Afraid.

A. Sperry, *The Boy Who Was Afraid*

Where's Papa going with that axe? said Fern to her mother as they were setting the table for breakfast.

'Out to the hoghouse,' replied Mrs Arable. 'Some pigs were born last night.'

'I don't see why he needs an axe,' continue Fern, who was only eight.

'Well,' said mother, 'one of the pigs is a runt. It's very small and weak, and it will never amount to anything. So your father has decided to do away with it.'

'Do *away* with it?' shrieked Fern. 'You mean *kill* it? Just because it's smaller than the others?'

E. B. White, *Charlotte's Web*

There are many queer ways of earning a living; but none so quaint as Mrs Gorgandy's. She was a Tyburn widow. Early and black on a Monday morning, she was up at the Tree, all in a tragical flutter, waiting to be bereaved.

Sometimes, it's true, she was forestalled by a wife or mother; then Mrs Gorgandy curtsied and withdrew – not wanting to come between flesh and flesh.

But, in general, she knew her business and picked on those that were alone in the world – the real villainous outcasts such as everyone was glad to see hanged . . .

Leon Garfield, *Black Jack*

Marty had to go all the way across the Bubble every morning, since school
and his parents' apartment were both on the perimeter but almost exactly
opposite. This did not present much of a problem: he only had to walk a
hundred yards to pick up an autocabin. After that he punched his destina-
tion on the dial and the robots took over, swinging the cabin out on to the
overhead cable and plotting the course which would take him most directly
to the school depot.

John Christopher, The Lotus Caves

Even the swiftest reading of these very brief extracts shows not only that
they present very different story worlds, but also that they make very different demands upon the reader. To perform each of these texts into
meaning requires a particular set of adjustments to the author's assumed
voice or persona, to the strangeness or familiarity of the implied setting,
to the predicted mode of the narrative and to the conventions that govern
the story telling. To jump from one story and to switch into another, to
read *across* such a range, demands a flexibility which many children find
difficult. Consider some of the variations that mark off these quoted
openings from each other.

The story may be set in the past, and we may be told this directly ('It
happened many years ago . . .') or be left to gather it by hints and allusions
(the gallows at Tyburn or the dollytub) or the feel of the language. It may
be in the future of autocabins and robots, or in the present of teachers'
tea-money and £10 notes, or in a less defined period (do *Papa* and
hoghouse suggest past time or a different locality?). That setting for the
story may be conveyed through firm, physical detail (like piling the
Allmans' belongings into the cart, or the feelings of a wet school playtime),
or it may be implied (like the farm of *Charlotte's Web* or the London low-
life of *Black Jack*), or it may be presented at a more conceptual level (as
in *A Wizard of Earthsea* or *The Boy Who Was Afraid*). The place may be
imaginary (the island of Gont, the science fiction world of *The Lotus
Caves*), or remote (the South Seas), or more familiarly English (though
even here there can be major differences between city and country settings, different regions and class backgrounds).

The characters on whom attention immediately centres may be children, with whom child readers can identify (like Danny or Fern) or adolescents (like Marty) or adults (like the Allmans and Mrs Gorgandy).
They may even be animals, like Mrs Frisby, the field mouse. Equally, the
events into which we enter may be familiar to children (collecting the tea-
money, setting the breakfast table) or very remote (working as wizards,
chanting round the evening fires) or something between these extremes.
We may be plunged directly into the action ('They were flitting the
Allmans') or there may be a much lengthier preparation, as in *A Wizard of*

Earthsea or *The Boy Who Was Afraid*. The viewpoint may be the first person narrative of a child narrator ('We'd gone right through the school . . .') or dramatic (like the opening dialogue of *Charlotte's Web*) or implied (like Mrs Frisby's mouse viewpoint of houses or food, or watching the Allmans through Joseph's eyes) or detached and impersonal (as in *Black Jack* or *The Boy Who Was Afraid*).

The mode of the story may be established as firmly realistic (*Granny Reardun* or *Tyke Tiler*) or appear more stylized and mannered (*Black Jack* and *The Boy Who Was Afraid*) or it may indicate that the novel is to be read as fantasy (about a world of mice, or magic). Of course, first impressions can be wrong. *Charlotte's Web* seems to be set in the wholly naturalistic mode, but we later discover that there is a parallel, and more important, fantasy narrative. The style may be conversational and idiomatic, like Gene Kemp's; or deliberately plain, like Alan Garner's; or ingeniously mannered, like Leon Garfield's; or deliberately stylized like Ursula Le Guin's.

In terms of the experiences and concepts conveyed, the opening of the story may appear essentially simple (like *Tyke Tiler*), or it may pose questions to which the reader will have to bring answers. These may be simple problems of vocabulary (what do words like *dollytub, perimeter, archipelago* mean?) or be concerned with the allusions (what is a *Tyburn widow*? why does the *Tree* have a capital letter? what is a *flitting*?) or with the cultural assumptions (what is it necessary to know about Polynesian culture?) or with story conventions themselves (how does this opening pre-empt future developments?). Emotionally, the opening may give little away, or it can be apparently dispassionate (like John Christopher's), or it can introduce a more loaded topic (the theft of a note, the hanging of criminals), or the emotional temperature may be raised at once (Fern's horror that her father is going to kill the weak piglet).

Each of these texts, then, promises its own pleasures and raises its own difficulties. If the first page seems too hard and insufficiently rewarding, then less able readers may feel too discouraged to make further attempts. How far can teaching enhance the pleasures and diminish the difficulties?

WHAT IS 'TEACHING' A NOVEL?

When we talk – in that convenient teachers' shorthand – about 'teaching' a book, we rarely consider what underlies the term. In the interaction between children and text, what is being learned, and what is the teacher's role?

The novel seems eminently teachable, and that is one of its great dangers. We find it 'easy' to teach for two reasons. First, we are likely to be experienced novel readers ourselves; we find novels simple and pleasurable; we are familiar with the classic examples and have been taught the conventional ways of describing and analysing them. We may be tempted to think that we can transfer our own enthusiasm and understanding directly to our students, forgetting that other readers' responses are only significant insofar as they can become part of our own. James Britton had a vivid image for the effects of this kind of didactic teaching:

> To have children take over from their teachers an analysis of a work of literature which their teachers in turn have taken over from the critics or their English professors – this is not a short cut to literary sophistication; it is a short circuit that destroys the whole system.[2]

Second, we can see a great deal to 'do' with novels; summarizing them and making character dossiers at examination level, building them into thematic projects lower down the school, using them as a basis for writing, talking, drawing, acting . . . Each of these has its danger in thrusting us away from the children's response and towards our own activity, losing sight of that central purpose, 'not to try to teach literature, but to try to teach a neglected, almost forgotten, skill – reading'.

Teaching styles convey hidden messages about the reading of fiction. For example, all that information about the author's life, the social background, the meaning of 'satire' that is sometimes presented as an essential preliminary to the text implies that the reader's personal response is relatively unimportant. The text is approached in a particular way and with certain assumptions that preclude free reactions. Equally, to treat all stories at all levels in a very similar way (the read, ask, discuss, write sequence) implies to children that stories are all the same – a string of incidents – because they are approached in the same way and the focus is on what happens in the story rather than what happens to the readers and why.

By contrast, response-centred fiction work demands a teacher who has understanding of different kinds – about texts and literary criticism, about curriculum methodology and the purposes of literary study, and about children and ways they learn to read – and an ability to see how these relate. Alan Howes has argued that theoretical structures for analysing narrative are only helpful for the teacher when set in the context of these other kinds of awareness. Such frameworks, he writes,

> will have value for the teacher only if he can translate theory into classroom practices that will make students more discerning readers. If the teacher is to help his students become better readers, he must make choices about what students should read as well as choices about how to guide students in their reading. He must have a philosophy about curriculum and an understanding of the reading process.[3]

If teachers are skilful and experienced readers themselves, their task is to provide children in a helpful way with some of that experience – *not* by describing it, but by organizing the programme and giving them practice so that they come to understand through structured examples what makes for mature reading. This understanding we draw largely from seeing how others read. It is particularly in small-group discussion (and later through the words of teachers and critics) that we learn how others respond, what questions they pose, what approaches to the text they employ. Through these exchanges we come to understand why there are variations in response and valuation, and by what conventions we may accept some and reject others. If students are to be introduced to terms like *tone* or *viewpoint* or *climax*, then it must be by applying them to stories already read and enjoyed. Looking back, for example, at texts that are playful or serious, ironic or straightforward, formal or intimate, should help to establish what *tone* is. The teacher's role is not primarily to define the concept but to help students say what they already know in terms of what they are capable of reading. The importance of participating in meaning-making comes across clearly in surveys of pupils' attitudes.

The situation in any classroom grows out of the interlocking perceptions which teacher and taught have of each other and of the task on which they are engaged. Books about teaching sometimes imply an impersonal activity that can be carried out in virtually identical ways by any individual. What is the reality of the classroom situation, though? We enter it with a whole set of feelings already active in us. Our mood, the stage of the day and the term, relationships with colleagues, the recent news, our previous experiences with the group, our attitudes towards the work planned, our relationship with individuals in the class, our own reactions to the text about to be 'taught' – these combine to create a complex pattern of feelings in us. We may believe that it is our professional duty to conceal these feelings: that the teacher role should swallow up the personal.

However, once we begin to focus on personal response to story as central, then we have to acknowledge that each pupil in the class will be approaching the lesson with the same complex mixture of emotions and thoughts that we ourselves experience. If that is true, then how far need we, *should* we, refuse to admit the reality of our own feelings? Our prejudices, tastes, difficulties and assumptions are a significant part of the literary encounter we are setting up, and we should not fool ourselves that we are offering a neutral, value-free experience.

Because response is so personal, the teaching style and interpretative stance that may best suit one student will not necessarily be congenial to another. Just as there in no one 'right' critical position, so there is no single teaching method for all teachers and all students. The sometimes undervalued teaching ability is responsiveness: reacting to pupils' responses to the text as well as to the text itself, seeing the text as an experience to be shared not as an inert object to be imparted, in a threefold relationship. Barbara Hardy has described this stance as it affects university teachers of literature, but in a way that is equally applicable to work in school:

> . . . the university teacher of literature will *as a teacher* be interested not chiefly in his own relation to his subject but in his pupils' relation to the subject . . . the teacher may be so exclusively occupied with details of technique, ideas or background that he can drown the author's voice. The teacher's voice can be the only one. Indeed, the teacher's voice may speak so impersonally, or so technically, and may get the priorities of literary response so wrong that we may get a teaching situation, where there ought to be three voices, but are none at all.[4]

Such a responsiveness means that however imaginative our ideas for activities centred on a book may be, they also have to be susceptible of reshaping. Sometimes the activities themselves can become habitual and divorced from the particular nature of the text ('We've given up *cloze* in favour of *sequencing* this term'). The real problem lies in establishing a rationale for all activity. *Why* are we using this approach and not another? How far should the work be planned beforehand? Are there desirable sequences of work? What does our understanding of the nature of response suggest about how we 'teach' a book? In particular, we need to ask:

> How can this story or novel be presented at a level appropriate to the maturity and abilities of our students without distorting the text?

> How can individual responses be given space to develop, without remaining permanently untouched by contact with the varying responses of others?

> How can these responses be most usefully supplemented and developed by activities the teacher chooses and directs?

David Jackson has vividly caught the crucial weakness of any pre-packaged approach to teaching fiction in his shrewd and sensitive analysis of using *The Midnight Fox* by Betsy Byars with a first-year group.[5] He chose the book because he thought it would appeal to the interest in animals of 11 to 12-year-olds, and because he thought the clash between the real pastoral world and TV-land an important topic. In fact, his major assumptions about the book were undermined by the children's reactions both to the story and to the programme of work he had prepared. Instead of seeing the asides and reminiscences as an irritating interruption to the main story, they found them the chief interest. The work they produced on the basis of interviews about people's views of fox-hunting was 'thin and inadequate'. What interested them, and produced their best and most involved work, were the ideas like giving experiences banner headlines, the Doomsday prediction game, describing great eating experiences and the selecting of contents to be buried in a 'time capsule'. Jackson describes vividly how he was forced to reconsider whether his 'own frameworks for looking at the book were more obstacles than helps'. The reading experiences that were most significant for these young children were those where they were bringing their own experiences to the book and relating the two worlds in both directions: making sense of *The Midnight Fox* and simultaneously using it to organize and structure their own lives.

The problem for the teacher is to allow time and space for this process (by which, in Jackson's words, 'the bond between author's and reader's worlds is cemented') to take place without being either unprepared or directionless.

STUDYING FICTION FOR EXAMINATIONS

Studying is a dangerous word. To *study* a novel may sound a quite distinct activity from simply reading and enjoying it. *Studying* can suggest a need to acquire facts about novels, their authors and backgrounds, or to make generalizations about style and agreed judgements. When teachers talk of *studying* fiction, their subconscious model may be drawn from memories of undergraduate work, with a strong emphasis on learning about literary criticism. Indeed, with the best of intentions they sometimes stress how different work in the fifth or sixth form will be from what has preceded it.

It seems necessary to question some of these associations that have clustered around ideas of studying fiction in the examination years. What do the the attitudes of pupils and teachers tell us about the relationship between examinations and the preparatory work in school? What models of reading underpin the notions of critical activity in the sixth form?

The most striking feature of the 'broken-backed curriculum', in Hull schools and in national surveys, is the way in which a general liking for fiction diminishes once it becomes the subject of an examination at 16. Less than half of the 15-year-olds in the APU sample felt that studying novels in school helped them towards greater enjoyment of reading. Those who were more specific about their reasons for not enjoying reading in English lessons commented on the selection of texts and the methods of study. The books for reading were not their choice, they were too difficult, or they were 'old fashioned'. There was too much concentration on set texts, they were analysed in too much detail, and they became boring because they were studied for too long.[6] The HMI paper *Bullock Revisited* sketches in a picture of unsuccessful schools as ones where examination work was dominated by exposition and summarizing, where little or no time was given to private reading, and where comprehension exercises pushed out any kind of group involvement with novels.[7]

The serious reservations about the examining of English literature, and particularly about its effects on teaching, made to the Newbolt Committee in 1921, have never been convincingly countered.[8] Scepticism about what formal examinations are assessing has led many English teachers to abandon O-level Literature and to seek for alternative syllabuses at A-level, which permit the presentation of course work and dissertations, and open-book tests on a wider range of subject matter.[9]

One study of 100 English graduates training to become teachers found that their memories of English in the sixth form correlated with their views of the A-level examination. Those students who had been unhappy with their sixth form teaching repeatedly described it as 'traditional' or as 'formal' or 'spoon-feeding': a pattern of line-by-line study of the minimum number of texts, dictated notes and a great deal of teacher talk. Such graduates describe the examination as 'a fair test', a process for which their teachers have 'geared' them, 'tuned them up', 'drilled' them, prepared them to 'perform'. The books had become exam fodder: they were 'bored with them', 'glad to see the end of them'. A contrasting group of students, who enjoyed their time in the sixth, described their work most frequently as 'informal': it involved a great deal of discussion, wide reading, imaginative writing, contacts with other arts, theatre-going, and elements of student choice and decision making. By contrast with those in the other group, these student-teachers were much more likely to be critical of the A-level examination. They commonly described it as 'superficial' or 'irrelevant', emphasizing low-level abilities like re-telling and encouraging insincerity.[10]

Both these groups had been 'successful' as students, but it is not difficult to see why those in the second group were dismissive of a test at which they still did well. In different ways they record that their responses, their range of interests, their depth of understanding and the sincerity of their judgements remained largely unexamined. Any consideration of current A-level papers will show that although the questions may be 'fair', they are almost all cramping in their form. They seem designed to discover whether candidates can rehearse specific details to be found 'in' the text rather than in the less controlled and predictable quality of an individual's responses to it. Typically they impose a particular view of a novel which has to be considered ('*The Spire* has been called "a conflict between Faith and Reason". Discuss the book in these terms.' London, 1980), or assume that it is to be read as an illustration of some general truth (' "A nation torn between cultures." To what extent does *A Passage to India* illustrate this theme?' JMB, 1981), or force a dubious choice between options that are not true alternatives (' "Less a satire than a romance." Discuss this view of *Brideshead Revisited* with detailed illustrations from the novel.' JMB, 1981). The point at issue is not whether questions like these are good or bad of their kind, but whether they form an adequate test of response to the novels in question.

There is something deeply disturbing if well-taught candidates who enjoy their reading are dismissive of the examination, and if those who were unimaginatively taught and were bored by their set books approve of it. The chief skills that seem to be tested are acquired technique in answering questions against the clock and the ability to memorise and to deploy relevant arguments and quotations. These are not unimportant abilities, and any examination of the writing of a sixth-form group over a period of 18 months shows how swiftly most students acquire them to some degree. It is what has to be sacrificed in genuine response that is most worrying. Tentativeness must give way to assertion, personal feelings to agreed opinions, enthusiasm to wariness.

There is nothing original in the suggestion that the aims and practices of fiction teaching after the age of 16 should not be dominated by the perceived needs of future undergraduates in university English departments. In fact, there is considerable doubt whether the real needs of even these students are being met by the present system. The question is surely: what kind of reading and response should we expect and hope for from students of 16 to 18?

The pressures of the A-level examination are of two kinds: the direct influence on students (manifested in the form of questions asked) and the indirect effect on teachers (conveyed through implied models of writing about a literary work). Consider the direct pressure first, which is even more marked in practical criticism papers and questions than in those on set texts. How are students encouraged to approach passages of prose? The instruction was formulated in a variety of ways by a single examinations syndicate in 1981: 'Write a critical appraisal', 'Write a critical analysis', 'Write a critical appreciation ' (Cambridge, 1981). Are the terms meaningless variations, or do they demand different activities? If so, how does the syndicate make clear the distinction between appreciating, analysing and appraising?

The impression that is given of what criticism is 'about' and of the kind of reading that is appropriate is frequently open to objection. In the 1960s, for example, one board repeatedly used variations of the same formulation:

Compare the following passages of prose with respect to
(i)   the intentions of the authors in composing them, and
(ii)   the methods by which those intentions are put into effect. (Cambridge, 1963)

> Do you think that the writer had any other purpose in mind when he wrote
> that passage to describe the sun? (Cambridge, 1964)
> Do you think that the narrator had any other intention in addition to nar-
> rating the details of the incident? (Cambridge, 1965)

What of the student who had been convinced by the New Critics that the
author's design or purpose cannot be known and that it is undesirable that
it should be considered? The questions were framed in such a way that
this position simply could not be held. A particular critical stance was
being imposed on the students who sat that examination. Significantly,
'intention' has now virtually disappeared from rubrics, though the
author's 'attitude' and 'purpose' may still be proposed as subjects for discussion.

It remains not uncommon to find that damaging distinction between
content and style being propounded in the rubric under the guise of 'helping' the student:

> Write a critical appreciation of the following prose passage, paying close
> attention to the content and the way in which the writer has handled it.
> (AEB, 1982)

This notion that the authors find their content, like bricks, ready-made
and then 'handle' it invites a quite inappropriate response to the question,
and raises doubts about how students will be assessed. Even more bewil-
dering was this instruction, used for a number of years in the 1970s:

> Comment on *one* of the following. Comment on such things as subject-
> matter, meaning, and the features of style which contribute to its full effect.
> (Oxford, 1975, 1976, 1977)

How is *meaning* here to be separated from subject-matter and style? In
what sense can *meaning* be called a *thing*? Does the reader's notion of the
full effect have to coincide with the examiner's? Are the *features of style*
somehow separate from it, since the implication is that not all the features
do contribute to that full effect? The overall impression is that certain
qualities, effects, techniques are arguably, objectively 'there', to be picked
out and discussed. It is no real surprise then, that examiners' reports so
frequently complain of candidates' listing of figures of speech, engaging
in irrelevant technical analysis, or low-level labelling of effects, divorced
from critical understanding. Their implied model is one of critical dissec-
tion to be *followed* by personal response in the form of evaluation. The
argument of this book, however, is that this is *not* the way in which we normally read or criticize.

The indirect pressure on students, through teachers' sometimes faulty
notions of the kind of writing that will be acceptable to examiners, is more
subtle. In some sixth forms, the main thrust of the work is to eliminate

those personal and subjective responses that have arisen in reading and to establish an 'agreed' pseudo-objective norm of interpretation that the teacher believes will be 'successful'. It is still not unknown for students to be told, 'You may feel like that, but it's not safe to put it in an answer.' In such cases, the teacher presents a model of what response 'ought' to be like, drawn from a selective acquaintance with established critics, and the students are expected to mimic it. Louise Rosenblatt has commented that all too much traditional literature teaching is like spectator sport: 'the students sit on the sidelines watching the instructor or professor react to works of art'.[11]

Unfortunately, the problem with such modelling is that academic critics frequently advance their judgements in an apparently impersonal and 'objective' way which is actually a poor example for fifth and sixth form students to imitate. Ingarden has pointed out that critics who are extremely familiar with works of art can come to judge them as a purely intellectual experience, without being aesthetically moved at all. It is dangerous for students to try to operate in such a way, forgetting that it is 'the *experience* which alone, and in an essential way, makes this judgement valid'.[12]

Academics can be too easily shocked by what seem to them young students' limited or idiosyncratic reactions to a novel. Certainly all kinds of subtleties and felicities may be missed by children. But the responses of academics can be equally blinkered, as any examination of the correspondence in critical journals will demonstrate. Each new feminist or Marxist or structuralist reading of a novel is an assertion of what has previously been ignored. If we believed that there was some absolute, 'ideal' reading, then compared with that all readings are failures. In fact, though, we need to assert that children and their teachers are engaged in precisely the same kind of creative response to the novel as the scholars and critics, though the level and forms of the activity may be different.

Teachers sometimes ask whether response-centred teaching at sixth form level means accepting *any* view of a text that pupils put forward. The simple response to doubts about student autonomy is to examine the alternative. If students *really* hold a view, then what are we asking them to do? To pretend *not* to believe it, and to parrot an interpretation they do not actually hold? The problem is only real if we believe that interpretations are absolute and unchanging, and literary history or our memories should disabuse us of this. Nevertheless, although we are not asking them insincerely to take on board judgements or readings that they do not share, we are not suggesting to them that meanings are purely subjective. The very fact that there are variant readings makes it essential for them to be compared and examined. What is missing or misconceived in any interpretation is likely to be shown up by considering others. It is frequently helpful to look at cruxes where there is no agreement between scholars and critics: a signal that readers simply *must* decide for themselves. Sharing and evaluating are essential elements in literary learning. By organizing these activities appropriately, the teacher is teaching criticism. That simply means helping children, by establishing points of comparison and contrast, to give some shape and structure to their reading experiences, to make sense of the text, to be able to talk sensibly about it.

It is certainly helpful that students should be introduced to what others have written about the novels they are studying. What matters is *when* and *how* this is done. Although the reading of criticism needs at least as much help as the reading of fiction, students are often expected to engage with difficult material quite unprepared. Some of the simple activities that might be practised to introduce them to ways of approaching the critics are:

(i)   Take a brief critical interpretation of one of the stories or novels that is being studied. Ask students to consider how far the critic is revealed as a reader and how far the interpretation is presented impersonally as 'objective'. Ask them to distinguish the facts from the opinions. How far is an interpretation 'a matter of opinion'? How can readers set about deciding how far an interpretation is 'true'?

(ii)   Provide two different interpretations of the story, which vary markedly. Ask the students to identify the points of difference, and then to discuss *how* they would propose to choose between them in each case. If there are issues which cannot be decided, then why is this? What does it suggest about interpretation?

(iii)   Duplicate several descriptions of what the story 'means' according to different critics. Suggest that students, working individually, mark those with which they agree with a tick, and those with which they disagree with a cross. Then ask them to compare their reactions, and to discuss particularly where there are differences. Go on to discuss whether there is a meaning 'in' the story or whether readers 'find' or 'make' meanings. What would their *own* statement of the meaning be?

(iv)   Give everyone a copy of a brief critical account of the story, either written by the teacher or taken from a critic. Ask them to consider carefully where they agree and disagree. Then ask them to identify any points where they feel that their own responses or opinions have been affected by what they have just read. Get them to discuss their reactions with one another. When the members of the group have completed this discussion, ask them whether their responses have been *further* influenced by hearing people's views. Were there any conclusions with which everybody agreed? Were there any issues which divided the class into opposed groups?

(v)   When the class has written a critical essay on the story, extract responses from a number of students and duplicate them or read

them to the group. Ask them to discuss the points of difference. Are
they anxious to know who the authors were? If so, what does this
suggest about literary judgements?

What approaches like these have in common is that they are all centred on
response – to the critics as well as to the text – rather than on uncritically
adopting or rejecting ready-made opinions.

What is involved, then, in 'criticizing' a novel? When we start reading
Emma or *Jane Eyre* or *A Passage to India*, we bring to it not only our
accumulated past experiences of life and of reading, and the models or
'codes' by which we make sense of them, but the immediate set of concerns, worries and fears that are besetting us at the actual moment of
reading. In reading a novel, we are simultaneously 'understanding' it in
the light of our structures of experience, and being freed from the limitations of those experiences by entering imaginatively into another world
(not, as is sometimes suggested, 'the world of the novel' but a space in
which we are constructing a world *from* the novel). If that 'understanding'
of a novel is to be more than superficial, then we have to become conscious
of our own activity, of how far our experience, attitudes, values and
assumptions are influencing our reading of the text. Reflecting on our role
as readers can both aid our self-understanding and help us to understand
in what respects we have found it easy or difficult to experience the novel.

Such insights are made easier for most of us by talking about the experience, clarifying our sense of the novel, hearing other people's views, trying
to establish why other responses and valuations are so different. Our
reading may be strengthened as others point out to us episodes or aspects
of character that we have missed, or suggest alternative meanings for
words and images, or attach different significance or motivation to
speeches and actions. These 'others' may include teachers or critics.
Although they may be professionals and experts, with much to tell us
about *Emma* or *A Passage to India*, they are not authorities in the sense that
they can tell us how we *should* respond, how we should read the novel.
They are telling us how *they* read it. Our reading of the critics is in many
ways like our reading of the novel: we make sense of their words in the
light of our knowledge. If there is no engagement between a critic's argument and our own experience of the text, then that critic is saying nothing
to us. The justification for our feeling that pupils must read the novel
before they read the critics is that to learn another reader's interpretation
in advance is to limit and inhibit our own response.

A teacher who introduces criticism into the classroom is endeavouring
to influence the way in which students respond to a text (or, indeed, to
texts in general). Their experiences of the book may be affected by the
information they are given (about conditions in Jane Austen's England) or

by the critical skills that are practised (examining syntactical and image patterns in the opening of *Bleak House*) or by the commentary or interpretation that is offered (paralysis is the theme of *Dubliners*) or by the questions that are posed (what is the name of the governess in *A Turn of the Screw?*). Any of these will be genuinely influential only to the extent that students can assimilate them into their own readings of the novels. To present *un*assimilable critical information is triply dangerous. It encourages students to copy what is neither felt nor understood. It makes them lose trust in their own responses. It increases the likelihood that they will express inconsistent or even contradictory ideas in their attempts to incorporate the new material into their existing interpretation. In addition, and at a deeper level, it may encourage resistance not only to criticism but to the literature itself. We have seen that even highly successful students record that they have become 'sick' of certain novels, unable to read them with pleasure because of the inappropriate critical study they have had to make of them.

The sixth form is just one more stage in the continuous process of learning to read. To separate out the critical study of set texts as a distinct activity is simply to emphasize the damaging dichotomy, discussed in the first chapter, between reading for pleasure and studying literature. Forty years ago F. R. Leavis, with his customary cogency, made clear the foolishness of any such distinction. The central concern of advanced literary studies, he wrote, was essentially nothing more than to equip men and women to read: 'It is plain that in the work of a properly ordered English School . . . the training of reading capacity has first place.'[13] The shared study of literature is simply defined as 'finding out how to talk to the point about poems, novels and plays, and how to promote intelligent and profitable discussion of them'.[14] By contrast, the acquiring of knowledge *about* literature is futile:

> If literature is worth study, then the test of its having been so will be the ability to read literature intelligently, and apart from this ability an accumulation of knowledge is so much lumber.[15]

Leavis's direct concern was with English studies in the university, and only on the final page does he turn directly to the situation in schools. Here, however, he indicates his awareness that the process described – in one of his repeated phrases – as 'training in sensibility' is a continuous and indivisible one that 'might profitably begin at early age'.[16] The earliest engagements with story begin a child's acquaintance with the 'literary-critical discipline' (though we may not choose to call it that), just as the most advanced postgraduate studies are still concerned with 'learning to read'. The emphasis is on 'collaboration' and 'demonstration', not on 'the elaboration of technical apparatus and drill'.[17]

CONCLUSION

Teachers tend to see the role of fiction in school and the pleasures it offers differently from the majority of their pupils. The evidence seems clear that for most children the school is not a favoured place for reading, that books encountered there are less popular than their own choices, and that the methods commonly practised do little or nothing to arrest the decline of fiction reading among teenagers. The examination study of novels frequently has a deadening effect, and the washback influence on teaching methods can be damaging. Restricting students to the minimum number of books, taking them line-by-line through the texts and basing all their work on previous examination questions, may not only cripple their literary development but also may be ineffective in obtaining good grades for them.

We do not have to assume fatalistically that it is impossible to change the situation, though, or that we can escape responsibility by blaming it on the system. There are certainly schools where the majority of children do get great enjoyment from stories, where reading abilities are helped to develop and where examination courses have led to a deeper and lasting enjoyment of books. What makes the difference? What can we learn from the responses of children and from observations of successful teachers about the use of fiction in the classroom? The remaining chapters offer a range of practical possibilities on which teachers can draw in their own way.

10 Choosing the Books

PROBLEMS OF CHOICE

If, as has been argued, access to appropriate and satisfying fiction is a dominant factor in the making of readers and is related to their personal development, then the choice of that fiction and the range from which it is selected are clearly vital. Although we know a good deal about children's preferences, we know much less about what it is that draws them to certain books or what keeps them reading some and turns them off others.[1] The more we discover about variations in response, the more we realize how difficult it is to predict accurately which stories and books will be the valuable ones that will become a significant experience for certain children and affect their ways of looking at the world. For many – perhaps most – children, any impression of what 'literature' is, or what is involved in literary studies, will be dependent on the limited number of texts encountered in school.

There are reasons to be pessimistic about the way in which the selection process is carried out in schools.

(i)   Evidence suggests that busy teachers find it difficult to give enough time to assessing books and that they feel they have been inadequately trained in the principles involved. A recent study concluded:

> Few teachers were aware of the difficulties of skilful book selection or adopted a methodical approach to the problem, so that their choice of sources was often a haphazard or arbitrary one.[2]

(ii)   There is no longer any shared common conviction about what books should automatically form part of an English curriculum. The frequent disagreements between critics and teachers about whether certain popular authors are beneficial or dangerous for study increases the bewilderment that some teachers feel.

(iii)   In a time of stringent economies, some reading programmes are determined by no more profound principle than what is already in the stock-room. Reports from schools, publishers and the SLA give a frightening picture of diminishing buying of fiction, of virtually the whole of a capitation allowance being spent on set books, of stocks fossilizing.[3]

(iv)   Ironically the shrinking of funds for book purchase coincides with a continuing extension of the range of books available. Not only are there more aimed increasingly precisely at specific ages and reading abilities, but they also represent an ever-widening range of topics, appealing to particular interests, and dealing with a changing series of social attitudes and problems. In all but the best of these books that pride themselves on 'immediacy' and 're-levance', the 'contemporary' language and references to fashions in clothes, popular music and amusements date very quickly, and the books frequently have a limited useful life in school.

(v)   We cannot necessarily assume that teachers are themselves keen and informed fiction readers. In one survey in two urban com-prehensive schools, Bob Bibby concluded that, if anything, teachers read rather less fiction than their pupils and made less use of public libraries. Using the categories which the Whitehead team applied to children's reading, 65 per cent of the teachers' recently chosen novels were 'non-quality', and the most popular books were ones like Frederick Forsyth's *The Devil's Alternative* and Colleen McCullough's *The Thorn Birds*.[4]

The general problems of choice, which parents and friends may also experience, are intensified for teachers by the school context itself and by the number of criteria for deciding which books shall be read by whom and how. We immediately detect this variety when we consider why the authors of the first four case studies say they chose particular novels and stories. Their reasons – literary, social or pedagogic – are advanced as if in reply to quite different unasked questions. When John Foggin says that *Earthfasts* is 'beautifully written' with splendid dialogue and powerful atmosphere, or Keith Bardgett praises such merits as story-line and pace of *The Machine Gunners*, recognized by the award of literary prizes, they are implicitly responding to the question: 'How well-written is this book?' When Paul Francis discusses the basic appeal of *Kes* or Keith Bardgett says how 'enormously successful' Westall's novel has proved to be, it is as if they had been asked: 'How popular will this book be?' To say that the experiences of the protagonist will be close to those of first-formers or to young adolescents (as most of the case studies do) or to argue that the text will 'challenge' the brightest but still be 'accessible' to the weakest, is to reply to the question: 'How suitable will the book be for those readers?' To argue as Judith Atkinson does that the texts offer opportunities for comparing different treatments of a theme, for provoking interest in par-ticular problems and for engaging in a wide range of follow-up activities, is to respond to the question: 'How useful will this book be in my English teaching?' Unfortunately, the answers we give to these questions may tug us in different directions. The verdict may be: popular but meretricious, or excellent but too difficult for many. It may be helpful, then, to separate out some of the issues which are involved in choosing a book, especially if it is to be used with a whole class.

IS THE BOOK WORTH READING?

Selection has to begin with the teacher as critic, a role which many find uncongenial. When David Holbrook asked the awkward question, 'What of the critical capacities of the teacher? Does he know what is worth reading or not?', he gloomily answered that all too many teachers only had a 'rudimentary sense of the criteria by which one may try to establish what was good about a work of literature, how one chooses good literature for children or why one chooses good literature to teach'.[5]

In what sense is assessing children's literature different from criticizing adult works? The lengthy arguments of recent years cannot be rehearsed here, but it should be clear that the distinction lies not in the nature of the critical activity but in the envisaged purpose and readership for it. Garner's *Stone Book* quartet or Nina Bawden's *Carrie's War* are to be criticized by the same criteria and methods that we should bring to *Little Dorrit* or *The Rainbow*. The judgements, though, are being made on behalf of a particular audience. Reviewers of adult books are writing for readers like themselves, whereas – as Peter Hollindale has pointed out – the reviewer of children's books is hardly ever read by the potential readers, the children themselves.[6] The reviews are intended to be *used* by librarians, teachers and parents who will be buying the books not for themselves but for children to read. The critical judgements have to be more complex, because they draw not only on literary experience and critical ability but on knowledge of children, their tastes and responses.

Like reviewers of children's books, teachers have to reconcile their own judgements of a new novel with their imaginative anticipations of how readers of 12 or 13, say, will respond. This involves framing some of the basic critical questions in a rather different way. For example, we may ask:

> Does the book offer a major character with whom young readers can readily identify?
> Does the plot get under way swiftly and appeal to children's curiosity and sense of anticipation?
> Is the motivation of characters apprehensible at child level?

The major practical problem arises when the prediction of response and the personal critical judgement tug in different directions. How do you balance the expected popularity of a work against the sense that it is poorly written or even meretricious? The teacher can hardly take up the stance of a publisher of popular fiction interviewed in a television programme who said blandly: 'I don't read the books, but even if a book was bad and I knew there was market for it – terrific!'[9] In the simplest terms, the crucial question for the teacher is: Do you read or recommend stories of which you disapprove if you believe that children will enjoy them?

The problem has been neatly illustrated by discussion of Roald Dahl's *Charlie and the Chocolate Factory*. In writing about the book, Ann Merrick, a graduate teacher, said she found the characters 'crudely delineated' and Charlie himself 'a cipher', that there is a mixture of sentimentality and violence that will 'appeal to the worst in children' and the language is 'exaggerated . . . limited and repetitive'. Nevertheless she also recorded that she would continue to use the book as a class text with children, 'for the mutual pleasure we receive . . . sharing the experience of an enjoyed story'.[8] We have to recall that in judging a book, we are essentially judging the experience of reading it. If the teacher's response is unfavourable, then it is hard to see how she or he can *share* an enjoyable experience, one of *mutual pleasure*, with children, however enthusiastic they may be. To do so suggests an insincerity which would ultimately be damaging. Of course, a teacher's response is likely to be *different* from children's, but the sense of pleasure, of a worth-while experience, in engaging with a good children's novel should be common, though differently formulated. C. S. Lewis is frequently credited with the familiar assertion that no book is worth reading at the age of 10 unless it is also worth reading at 50. First of all, adults have to exercise their own judgement. Unless they are prepared to discriminate between good and less good writing for children, to identify the marks of quality as opposed to those of dead, unimaginative, stereotype writing, then their guidance can be of no real help.

It is necessary to distinguish between those books which a teacher or parent *gives* to a child and those which are simply *available*. A collection like a school library will contain books suitable for a whole range of different ages, abilities and interests. When a teacher recommends a book to an individual, though, or chooses a novel to use with a whole class, that choice carries a hidden authority. Children will understand that this indicates some degree of approval. Teachers who find Enid Blyton's adventures trivial and unattractive in their attitudes may not ban them from the library, on the grounds that we all require some rubbish in our reading diet, but they would hesitate before giving them out for class reading.

In a nutshell, there is so little time for close reading of fiction in school that it should surely all be devoted to books that are, at least, good of their kind. It cannot be pretended that there is universal agreement about what these are, any more than about the Great Tradition of adult literature. Views of the 'best' books for children change. The books which Sarah Trimmer recommended for children's reading in the 1800s were so out of fashion 80 years later, when Charlotte Yonge produced her list of *What Books to Lend and What to Give* that hardly any reappear there. Seventy years later, the *Sunday Times* list of *The One Hundred Best Books for Children* included only a few of Charlotte Yonge's. And 20 years later still, the lists of our times show again how ephemeral the choices of the past seem to be.

Meanwhile we are living in a time, sometimes described as a Golden Age of children's fiction, when the range of choice is wider than it has ever been, but also when the increase in critical writing about these books has left many teachers uncertain about values. Too many diametrically opposed views are promulgated. Is *Swallows and Amazons* one of the few great classics or an outmoded, bourgeois tale of limited appeal? Do the fantasies of C. S. Lewis embody a desirable code of behaviour or are they regressive and authoritarian? It is to the good that teachers are being forced into critical activity, that judgements of the 'best' titles can no longer simply be taken over second-hand? We must all make our own lists and justify them.

IS THE BOOK LIKELY TO BE POPULAR?

In some classrooms, the fact that the teacher has selected a book can be the kiss of death. Many investigations at different ages have concurred in the conclusion that children prefer what they themselves have chosen and that this preference is reflected in a greater readiness to persevere with the book.

> Books borrowed from the public library were completed more often than those borrowed from the school library, and books borrowed during free time at school were completed more often than those borrowed during regular school library periods. Students prefer books from the library and book clubs to those given them in class.[9]

If the instinctive resistance to what is, in a sense, imposed on them is to be overcome, then it is clearly important to be able to predict what will 'go' with a given group.

This is not always as easy as it seems. We sometimes make the crude mistake of interpreting the need for 'relevance', or of 'beginning where the children are' as meaning that their reading matter should be confined within the actual world and experiences they know (instead of being relevant to their stage of development or, indeed, their interests). We can create our own unreliable stereotypes of the sort of reading that boys (or girls) like. We can pay too much attention to the latest fashionable vogue, or to the list of 'popular' topics and genres in generalized studies of reading interests. Not all boys of 13 prefer books on 'war, travel and mystery' (or girls 'animals and simple love stories').

The problem is intensified by the difficulty of establishing just what children's tastes are. It is impossible to disentangle the two sources of reading: the books and comics which children choose for themselves and those which they are given to read by parents and teachers. The twin sources seem neatly illustrated by the fact that the most popular books for 14-year-old readers in the mid 1970s seem to have been *Little Women* and *Skinhead*.[10] The lists of what children read ('Either the same old classics or rubbish!' exclaimed a teacher at a meeting in Hull) are a mixture in differing proportions of what we think they *ought* to read and what they themselves *wish* to read, and both of these are continually changing.

In one article, Stephen James made a comparison between the private reading of able boys in O-level forms, eight years apart. The striking fact was the almost total difference in the books mentioned by each group; only *Brave New World* was mentioned by both. In 1965 the most widely read book was *Lord of the Flies*; Ian Fleming was easily the most popular author; the 'daring' choices were *Lady Chatterley's Lover*, *Fanny Hill* and *The Perfumed Garden*. In 1973 the most widely read book was *Skinhead*, and Richard Allen was the most popular author; the other 'daring' choices were *Chopper* and *Confessions of a Window-Cleaner*. Most of the readers described the books that they chose to read, both in 1965 and 1973, as 'very boring', 'senseless', 'awful' and 'trash'.[11]

Although researchers claim to have found 'a close conformity of interests to grade level' at primary age, 'Developmental shifts vary with students' sophistication', their intelligence, emotional maturity and susceptibility to mass media.[12] The many studies of children's reading interests analysed by Mott and others[13] are largely concerned with the types of books that are popular, and broad differences between the reading tastes of children of different sexes, abilities and backgrounds. As Purves and Beach write, 'Little sophisticated research exists on *why* specific titles or writers are popular . . .'[14] Faced by the enormous variety of individual response, teachers should perhaps not build too much on the anticipated popularity of a particular topic or theme as a criterion for selection.

WILL THE BOOK BE USEFUL

In discussing texts together, many teachers centre their arguments on this criterion: the book's 'teachability'. Can it be handled conveniently, divided into episodes, presented effectively, linked with other activities? How will it relate to the overall English programme (or, indeed, to the total work of the group)? Will it be a fruitful source of other activities, lending itself to discussion, improvisation, writing in different modes? Will it be possible to establish fruitful comparisons with children's own experience and with their previous reading? Will it fit well into a developmental programme?

In-service groups have suggested there are significant curricular discriminations that have to be made between possible works of fiction, as well as critical ones. For example:

(i)   When a novel has to be read by a group over an extended period of time, certain ones are more difficult to 'teach' than others because there are long, or because the plot is complex, or because there are confusing sub-plots involving too many characters, or because of confusing jumps in chronology.

(ii)   Certain authors and works seem naturally to 'go' in class: they have an immediate effect, they stimulate response or controversy, in a way that others do not.

(iii)   Some books provide an enjoyable group experience, something which can be shared and discussed. Others are inherently more personal and better suited to private reading.

(iv)   The topics and themes of some books are more obviously 'relevant' than those of others, either because they are concerned with experiences and ideas common in the class at the time, or because they can be related to work being done in other areas of the curriculum, or because they are 'about' the topic which is currently linking a number of lessons.

(v)   In a class with the full range of ability, some work may be too difficult or sophisticated in a literary sense, even with editing, to enable the pupils to share the experience of reading together.

The best book is not necessarily the one which will provide openings for the greatest number of 'things to do with a book',[15] but practical utility is clearly a significant criterion.

IS THE BOOK SUITABLE FOR THESE CHILDREN?

So far the choice of fiction has been considered in such broad terms as literary merit, popularity and utility. Such generalizations as 'A splendid book for third years' may be of some help, but teachers recognize that matching that book with a particular third-year group is not as simple as it sounds. More than 50 years ago one large-scale study suggested how wide was the range of reading interests and abilities at any age and how inappropriate were many of the works chosen for study. Only a quarter of the students at any age were really suited by the material chosen for them to read in English. Even if the books were selected on the principle of 'what is best suited to the average ability of the grade, about 50 per cent of each grade would be given material unsuited to their needs'.[16] Nowadays we might be less happy with such a neat distinction between *suitable* and *unsuitable*, but the underlying problem of assessing what is appropriate for a group remains to disturb us. Again, the teacher is faced with different, overlapping issues, of which three essential ones can be discussed here.

> the relative difficulty of the text
> the likely emotional impact
> the attitudes conveyed

THE RELATIVE DIFFICULTY OF THE TEXT

What do we mean by saying that the language of a novel is simple? We have heard a good deal recently about testing *readability* levels, in a linguistic sense,[17] and about the horrors of giving children books in which the language is too difficult for them. Unfortunately most of the standard measures of readability reveal a serious misunderstanding of the nature of fiction reading. No single measure can cover all the possible contexts in which reading will go on and all the responses that may be made to a story. The obsession with surface linguistic simplicity rather than with depth ignores the fact that readers are prepared to devote more effort to texts that seem of interest and that give pleasure or understanding. Consistently easy, boring patterns (as in some early readers) can become virtually unreadable. Readability measures tend to ignore such qualities as vividness, precision and organization, as well as qualities of content.[18]

Readability in the true sense depends on diagnosing the kinds of problem which are presented by a text and the ways in which they are to be solved. Little has yet been written about diagnosing the readability level of narration in terms of its structure, conventions, emotional range or stylistic complexity. Statistical measures do not yet take into account, for example, the fact that junior novels typically contain fewer shifts of viewpoint and perspective than books for older readers. Nor do they allow for shifts of register, the frequency of archaisms and allusions or the density of literary mannerism.

Simplistic views of textual difficulty underlie many of the attempts to re-write great novels for less-able and less-experienced readers. Quite apart from the critical issue of whether such an adaptation is the 'same' book as the original, there is a questionable assumption about the relation between simplicity of material and the reader's *desire* to read. Controlled vocabulary and regular constructions may not necessarily make reading more effective if the language seems dull and threadbare and the content boring and undemanding. Investigations seem to demonstrate that children at all levels of intelligence display superior comprehension when reading material which is interesting, and that interest is also associated

with faster reading speed. Too many adaptations simply destroy the qualities of a novel that make it enjoyable.

Take, for example, this scene from a recent simplified version of *Jane
Eyre*, in which, according to the publishers, 'the language . . . has been
carefully structured'.[20] Jane, at Lowood School, suffers at the hands of
Mr Brocklehurst.

> Suddenly I dropped my book. It fell with a loud crash. Everybody turned
> and looked at me.
> 'Careless girl!' exclaimed Mr Brocklehurst. He looked at me. 'Ah!' he
> said, 'I know that child, she is the new pupil. I have something to say about
> her. Come here!' he ordered. My legs shook under me. I could hardly walk.
> Two girls pushed me towards Mr Brocklehurst.
> 'Stand on that chair!' I climbed up on to a high chair.There I stood in
> front of the whole school.
> 'Ladies, Miss Temple, teachers, and children!' began Mr Brocklehurst,
> 'Do you see this child? She is young – very young. But already, the Devil is
> in her. Girls! Don't play with her. Don't speak to her! Teachers! Watch her
> carefully. This girl, this child, is a . . . *liar!*'
> 'Shameful!' exclaimed Mrs Brocklehurst and her daughters.
> 'Yes,' he went on, 'her kind Aunt has told me about her. She is a wicked,
> thankless, shameful child!' To Miss Temple, he said, 'Let her stand there
> for half an hour. Let no one speak to her for the rest of the day!'
> Mr Brocklehurst then left with his family.

What kinds of modification have been practised to make this text more
accessible for less able readers? On the surface they may seem to be
chiefly semantic and syntactic changes. An *obtrusive* crash becomes simply
loud, 'a word to say respecting her' becomes 'something to say about her',
the *Devil* replaces the *Evil One*, and 'don't play with her' is a precis of the
original: 'You must be on your guard against her; you must shun her
example: if necessary, avoid her company, exclude her from your sports,
and shut her out from your converse.' Complex words like *hypocrite, de-
formity, salvation* and *pathos* and allusions like those to heathens praying to
Brahma and the healing pool of Bethesda are omitted. Syntactically, the
average sentence length is about six words as opposed to about 35 words
in the original. More striking is the regularity of the first 20 sentences.
None is shorter than four words or longer than nine (whereas the original
varies between two or three words and over 90). The constructions are all
simple and regular; subordinate clauses are avoided.

Such simplifications are designed to make reading easier, if somewhat
monotonous. Other changes, though, alter not only the language but the
situation. To change *slate* to *book* and *stool* to *chair* seems unnecessary from
the point of view of verbal difficulty. Was it felt that slates and stools would
be unfamiliar to modern child readers? To make the change not only

destroys much of the setting of the original, but also affects the situation. To drop and break a slate is both noisier and a graver offence than dropping a book. To stand on a chair does not raise Jane to the same exposed position as having to be lifted on to a 'very high' monitor's stool. To call it 'a high chair' only creates visions of what a baby sits in.

The basic technique of simplification used in this *Jane Eyre* passage is simple omission. Nearly 1000 words of Charlotte Bronte's are reduced to less than 200. What is omitted, apart from Mr Brocklehurst's rhetoric, includes much of what brings the scene alive. We lose the repeated references to Jane's sensation of being exposed to view ('every eye upon me', 'their eyes directed like burning glasses upon my scorched skin', 'exposed to general view') and of her feelings at the injustice of it. We lose the precision with which her position on the stool is captured: 'at the height of Mr Brocklehurst's nose', lifted above the extravagant dresses of his family. We also lose the important shift in Jane's reactions from paralysing fear, through 'an impulse of fury' to cool determination to endure ('the trial . . . must be firmly sustained', 'in perfect possession of my wits'). The ironic observation of 'the black marble clergyman' with his 'sublime conclusion' and the artificial behaviour of the females simultaneously applying pocket-handkerchiefs to their 'optics' before they 'sailed in state from the room' all disappears.

What purports to be simplification of the text by controlling vocabulary and syntax is actually a much more radical modification. The book is reduced to an unsubtle string of events, lacking vivid realization, in which subtleties of reaction are eliminated and characters are reduced to stereotypes. Such a bland abridgement, removing all problems, complexities and uncertainties, leaves little room for the reader to 'construct' the story or to care very much about what happens. The novel has become like a book in a formal reading scheme, where turning the printed words into speech is all-important.

This is not necessarily to decry the notion of producing books of high interest and low reading level, especially for teenage readers. However, those written especially to satisfy both of these criteria have to be judged by their success as narrative fiction, and not just by the controlled level of the text. If what has been suggested in chapter two about the way in which we read is true, then a reader's ability to tackle a novel cannot be assessed by isolating one element of his or her experience – the linguistic one. Experience of life and experiences of fiction are equally important. The section of chapter three *The development of response to story* showed in simple terms how children grow in awareness of what 'reading a story' means. Systematic analysis of books in such terms has hardly begun, but it seems clear that works for children could be arranged in a rough rank order of difficulty in such different respects as these:

(i)   the clarity or otherwise of the story-line.

(ii)   whether the chronology is straightforward, or the time-scheme is differently handled

(iii) the management of viewpoint: the variety of 'voices' in which the story is told

(iv) the extent to which the events *are* the story, as opposed to having sub-textual significance

These considerations demand a teacher's attention, just as much as the average word length and sentence complexity.

THE LIKELY EMOTIONAL IMPACT

Is this story appropriate to the children's range of maturity? Will it be relevant to their present stage of development? The dynamic interplay between personal response and understanding is a complex one, but there are potential difficulties for children in trying to perform into meaning situations of which they have no direct experience – falling in love, going to war – especially if they are forced back on stock responses. There are emotional issues here. How acceptable or challenging will they find the author's viewpoint and style of presentation? Might any of them be seriously disturbed by the treatment of conflict, violence, sexuality or death? Is the book likely to aid or hinder their understanding of themselves and others?[21] At a time when ideas of what is permissible in children's literature – in terms of topics and attitudes – are changing fast, it is clear that teachers' critical and pedagogic judgements of such issues are inseparable. They have to be concerned with:

(i)   the degree of responsibility or exploitation with which the story treats emotionally charged issues.

(ii)   whether there are subjects or attitudes which children should simply not be permitted to encounter at this age

(iii) the extent to which teaching presentation may colour, influence or distort the 'meaning' of the book and children's responses to it

We can focus on two debatable aspects of this global problem.
How far, and in what circumstances, should children be encouraged to read stories which – in the teacher's opinion – might frighten or upset them or which have to do with naughtiness, wickedness or evil?

(A) The potentially frightening

From an early age most children become aware of pages in books – illustrations or even passages of text – in which they want to be passed over, to remain unopened, because they contain something frightening. When I worked with 13-year-olds on their ideas of fear, it was significant that beneath their superficial stock reactions to conventional frighteners – spiders, snakes, skulls and so on – they revealed a bewilderingly large range of highly individual personal fears. Despite the insights of psychoanalysis, we are still far from reaching any conclusions about what is likely to frighten children in books (or, for that matter, on television).

The distinction between the fear which is potentially beneficial and that which is possibly damaging or corrupting is difficult to establish. This has been brought alive at a number of conferences where teachers have passionately disagreed about whether or not they would use, for example, Catherine Storr's book *Marianne Dreams* or Betsy Byars' *The Pinballs*. We can only speculate about whether such stories increase anxiety in children by creating fears, or whether they simply give a focus and release to anxieties which already exist in a less formulated way.

Fear of any kind can certainly be enjoyable. The screams from any fairground, the popularity of double horror film bills, and the cries of 'Can we have another of those ghost stories?' all testify to the same fact. What is the distinction betweeen this enjoyed or sought fear and genuinely disturbing emotion? Two fairly obvious distinctions can be made. First, the enjoyed fear is nearly always shared, it is a group experience in which individuals exchange reactions and egg each other on to respond. It would be different to go on the ghost train late at night in a deserted fairground. Second, the medium of enjoyed fear is usually stylized: it obeys conventions which distance it from actuality, the horrors are extravagant or 'camp'. The Himmelweit research on television suggested that children were more disturbed when the settings for violence or horror resembled those familiar to them.[22] This raises questions about whether the greater realism of children's books may increase the chances that young readers may be affected by scenes of cruelty or violence described in them.

We may feel less easy today than in previous centuries about the notion of deliberately frightening children into good behaviour, but in general it seems unrealistic as well as misguided to try to protect children from everything that might frighten them. The argument now is more likely to be that they are impoverished if they are cut off from this part of human experience – even if such protection were possible – and that learning to cope with fear and pity is an essential part of preparation for adult life. Because of the limitations of their experience, young children do not fully 'realize' the implications of horrible things they see or read about. John McGreesh, examining the way in which children of different ages wrote about the Aberfan disaster, pointed out that younger children wrote descriptively from the outside, that they were unable to enter into the sufferings and grief of those who were involved. By the age of 15, many of the children were able to empathise and to recognize the impact of the events on those who were involved and those who looked on. McCreesh suggests that there is a need to 'deepen and extend a child's imaginative awareness' of what is involved in tragic events. 'To educate the child in tragedy is in many ways to educate the imagination.'[23]

There is no shortage of books which manage to present the dark or threatening forces of life in a way that is appropriate for young readers. Evil can be personified in the villains, the black figures who have to be opposed and overcome by the 'goodies', as in John Christopher books, or in Leon Garfield's stories. It can be embodied in fantasy, as by C. S. Lewis in the Narnia books and Alan Garner (*Elidor*). Death can be confronted in manageable terms through *Charlotte's Web* or *Tuck Everlasting*. The threat to human existence can be shown in uncontrolled natural forces with which men have to struggle: Salkey's *Earthquake* or *Hurricane*, the avalanche of Rutgers Van der Loeff, Ivan Southall's forest fire, or Paul Berna's flood. Children can be shown struggling to survive after a shipwreck (*The Cay*), or on a dangerous journey (*Children of the Oregon Trail*), in the aftermath of war (*The Silver Sword*), or in the Australian outback (*Walkabout*). The threat of danger can be shown as arising from human prejudice or from social forces which threaten people's happiness or fulfilment, as in Nina Bawden's *Carrie's War*, Betsy Byars' *The Pinballs*, Robert Cormier's *The Chocolate War*, Rumer Godden's *The Diddakoi*, Harper Lee's *To Kill a Mockingbird*, or the Joan Lingard books. In such ways as these, good writing for children helps them to come to terms with the fears that are an inevitable part of being human.

(B)   The influence of bad behaviour

To what extent should children be allowed to read of naughtiness, violence, wickedness, evil? Does it harm them by encouraging them to imitate undesirable behaviour, and actually make them more naughty or wicked? Or does it help them, either by showing them how undesirable such behaviour is, or by allowing them to sublimate the urge towards violent or anti-social acts by engaging them in fantasy? Phrased like that , such questions are naïve because they suggest that simple answers can be given. In some cultures, assumptions do seem to have been made. Felicity Ann O'Dell has pointed out, for example, that whereas stories about naughty children are a regular part of English children's literature, they are very rare in the books given to Soviet children, and where they do exist the culprits have to be shown as penitent and reformed by the end of the story. Heroes and heroines are much more likely to display noble, socially desirable qualities on which readers can model their own behaviour.[24]

Such a directly didactic view, that lessons may be taught and values transferred through stories, is held in common with the authors of moralistic tales for English children who wrote in the late seventeenth and eighteenth centuries. Writers like Maria Edgeworth, Mrs Sherwood and Hannah More wrote stories of children who are shot, burned or drowned because they are naughty, who are taken to see hanged criminals or corpses or people on their deathbeds, or who are severely punished for their wickedness – all with a morally improving aim. This purpose animated even the earliest reading matter. Sarah Trimmer produced for Charity Schools an initial reader, with a highly controlled vocabulary, subtitled *Short Stories of Good and Bad Boys in One Syllable Only* with tales of the naughty girl who played with fires and was burned to ashes or the stone-throwing boy who was 'Put in the Cage and Beat a Great Deal'.[25] It was assumed that there was a direct connection between the values expounded in a book and those learned by a child. Mrs Sherwood and more recent Russian story-makers follow in the tradition of Plato, who suggested in *The Republic* that it was necessary to select and supervise stories, to ensure that only those which reinforced the 'appropriate' opinion should be used. Entertainment came a poor second to instruction. Such a view probably attributes too much power to the author or teacher in predicting pupil response. In fact, there is a good deal of evidence that children find the satisfactions *they* want in stories (like the student who, as a girl, read pony books as disguised pornography).

Many an inexperienced but well-intentioned teacher has chosen a book because it seems to be 'against' some evil like war or intolerance or fox-hunting, or 'for' enlightened attitudes towards the treatment of criminals or relationship between the sexes, only to be disappointed in the result. Pupils are well aware of teachers – and books – that have too manifest an intention about them, and their frequent response is to distance themselves by retreating into stock reactionary or philistine attitudes. Literature does not preach ready-made truths; it provides an opportunity for readers to find or 'make' truth for themselves.

There is another inevitable problem in the conflict which exists in our society between different sets of values. A child may be offered contrasting norms of behaviour by parents, by television, by Sunday School, by friends, by the school, and by books and comics. Indeed, different teachers within the school may have conflicting expectations and sets of values, and the same may be true of any collection of books for children. The lack of consensus about how and how far children may be influenced by their reading is not aided by emotional assertions, by such simple activities as counting the number of crimes or 'violent' episodes (usually undefined) in a book, or by paying too much attention to the claims of young criminals that they got the ideas 'from a book'. There are major variables in the actual presentation of the events in a text, in the manner in which it is mediated in a classroom situation, and in the individual reader's response. Whether *Grandad with Snails* or *The Machine Gunners* or *My Darling, My Hamburger* encourage 'copy-cat' bad behaviour or aid self-understanding or provide a sound social and moral lesson will depend not only on what is 'there' on the page but on the kind of reading that they get and the sort of setting in which that reading is placed.

How far should the selection of books for children shelter them from language or behaviour which parents or teachers might consider undesirable? Words like *censorship* may raise hackles, but there clearly are texts which one would not give to young children. In times of moral and social change, though, the problem is where (and why) one draws the line.

For example, contemporary books for children no longer automatically present adult figures of authority – parents, teachers, police, clergymen – as the paragons that they used to be. The Social Services are shown in a bad light in *My Mate Shofiq*, and the police in *The Machine Gunners*. In fact, the ending of that book would have been unthinkable a few years ago. Is there a fear that children may imitate the behaviour of young Nicky?

> 'C'mon son,' said the police sergeant to Nicky. 'You're going to tell me all about this. You're a cut above the rest of this riff-raff, you know. Your father was a ship's captain. God knows what he'd have said.'
> Nicky took a deep breath.
> 'Get stuffed,' he said.[26]

Does the appearance in print of spoken words like *bugger, sod* and *frigging* in *The Machine Gunners* disturb us, either because we fear noisy classroom reaction or because we anticipate that parents will complain? Can we object if pupils use in their work the salty language which Robert Westall puts into the grandmother's mouth when she is talking about Hitler?[27]

The most emotionally-charged area in children's books is the one which deals with sexuality. The increasing outspokenness of books by Judy Blume and others has produced problems for publishers and teachers. Jessica Yates has pointed out examples of the sort of censorship which has been imposed – doubtless for the best of motives – by Puffin on a number of children's authors. References to girls as being the dominant figures in sexual games with boys, for example, were deleted from Jean MacGibbon's *Hal*.[28] Some teachers may be disturbed by books which acknowledge the facts of homosexuality, even lightly, like John Donovan's *I'll Get There, It Better be worth the Trip* or Deborah Hautzig's *Hey Dollface*. They may be uneasy about novels which present girls falling for older men, like Peggy Woodford's *Please Don't Go* or Pamela Sykes's *Early One Morning*.

It is impossible to reduce to simple rules the vexed issue of what should or should not be admitted for study or for private reading in school. Mak-

ing decisions about particular texts for particular situations at particular
moments is part of the critical and methodological activity demanded of
English teachers. Blanket judgements are unhelpful at a time when the
boundaries are continually shifting; books have to be considered individually, in an imaginative attempt to predict their likely effect on response.

THE ATTITUDES CONVEYED

Who decides which attitudes are to be censored? English teachers are
horrified by the news of American school boards banning novels like *Brave
New World* or *The Catcher in the Rye* from schools, but are teachers themselves necessarily more trustworthy as arbiters? We may assume that children self-censor violence and sexuality for which they are emotionally
unprepared, but social and political attitudes do not get self-censored. We
have to ask: how far are children's views of society, and of groups within
it, affected by what they read? McClelland[29] and others since have
suggested that internationally children's literature reflects the particular
values of a civilisation, and that reading is one of the ways in which children are socialized within a culture. The kind of content analysis which
became popular in the 1960s was much concerned with the sorts of
stereotype presented in stories, and thus with the attitudes that might be
fostered.

Analysing a representative range of novels seemed to expose some of
the unspoken assumptions about race, sex and class which children might
swallow along with the story. What would be the result of reading juvenile
fiction in which the heroes were invariably white, middle-class and hand-
some and the villains frequently coloured, ugly and working class?[30] One
large-scale survey found that fewer than one in 10 American children's
books of the early 1960s contained any black characters at all and that
those books which did contain black figures generally showed them as
servants or in other humble positions.[31] It seems that such findings have
had an influence on publishing practice. A comparison of American picture books published before and after 1965 showed that the later books
showed a greater number of characters from black, chicano, chinese and
other racial groups, and that they were more likely to be shown in roles
equal to those played by whites.[32]

Concern with the way in which racial/cultural stereotypes were presented in school manifested itself in the 1970s in England in ways that can
be broadly characterized as negative and positive. Although the two went
hand in hand, the negative approach was to remove 'unsuitable' books
from the classroom, the positive to increase the understanding of
teachers, publishers and others of the need for more appropriate books

and approaches for a multi-ethnic or multi-cultural society.[33] The critical approach to existing children's literature was probably most clearly expressed by Bob Dixon.[34] He attacked particularly the popular stories of Biggles and Dr Dolittle as embodying a jingoistic fixation on race, seeing coloured characters as either villainous or comical and absurd, and using pejorative terms to describe them. Unlike some of the more extreme critics who followed him, Dixon paid careful attention to the poor quality of the writing in the books he discussed and said that the solution to the problem lay not in censorship but in better teaching. Unfortunately, not all comments were equally scrupulous. In an otherwise balanced examination of the topic, Gillian Klein concluded that every book had to be measured against 'our specific criteria' for detecting racial bias, and 'if it fails there can be no place for it on any book list, still less in the classroom or on library shelves'.[35]

To isolate one critical issue in this way as outweighing all others is disproportionate, and it also assumes that the criteria can be applied uniformly. In fact, of course, attitudes are largely culturally determined and people's responses differ: what seems enlightened to one reader is tokenism to another. There was considerable dispute over a number of the suggested titles in Judith Elkin's revised list of *Books for the multi-racial classroom*.[36] A number of teachers have said that they found *The Cay* was a book which contributed positively to children's attitudes towards blacks. On the other hand, I have seen lessons in which it was read with all-white classes in a Hull comprehensive school when the book seemed to increase prejudices: old Timothy was perceived as unsympathetic and his style of speech ridiculous. Viewpoint is crucial. In this book, as in *My Mate Shofiq*, coloured characters are seen through the prejudiced eyes of white boys, and the critical issue is whether the initial prejudice may be more strongly conveyed than the later shift of opinion with which the books deal. In cases like these it seems impossible to make simple decisions that the book is either beneficial or harmful in terms of racial attitudes. That one issue has to be incorporated in a much broader critical and methodological judgement.

The complaints about sexist stereotyping, which also seemed to gain their earliest expression in the United States, developed here in the 1970s with the publication of booklets like *Sexism in Children's Books* and the formation of the NATE Working Party on Sexism. The purely statistical arguments (because women account for just over half the population they should also supply half the characters in stories and illustrations and 'Women politicians, artists and scientists should be mentioned as much as men') seem dubious. Barnum made a similar discovery that the aged are discriminated against in children's literature, appearing much less frequently than they should in relation to their actual proportion of the population, and generally being shown as disadvantaged in the roles they play.[37] This has not led to any general cry that children's books are 'ageist'. Similarly the complaint that women's roles are unrealistically portrayed and limited in range has to be balanced by the analysis of men's roles in picture books which shows a similar distortion of the real world.

The more convincing reasons for alarm are those based on the nature of children's responses, and on the speed with which stereotyped attitudes about typical sex behaviour are established.[38] Male figures in fiction seem dominant. In an Exeter survey, when children were asked to name their favourite character in fiction, more than half the girls chose men or boys, whereas only seven per cent of the boys chose women or girls.[39] Other studies, including one in Hull, produced very similar results. We do not have enough information to decide the relative importance of different hypotheses to explain such attitudes. It may be that there are too few books with girls as central characters, or that male characters are more usually shown as dynamic and active while female stereotypes seem less interesting, or that social conditioning makes boys unlikely to choose female characters. If girls are encouraged to see themselves as submissive and domesticated, as Dale Spender has argued,[40] and boys are urged to be adventurous, to repress emotion and to be successful, then fiction may be one element in a much more complex pattern of formative social pressures.

Unfortunately, as with racial prejudice, a concern with the evils of sexism can become obsessive. The Children's Rights Workshop, apparently advocating the compulsory use of non-biased materials (if we can agree on them) argued that 'we can no longer base critical assessment solely on literary merit. Content and values, explicit or implicit, deserve similar critical attention.'[41] This seems to suggest that literary judgement is somehow *not* concerned with 'content or values', whereas separating any one element like sexist presentation from our overall critical judgement is dangerous. Some reviews of children's books tend to isolate this issue, and to suggest that simple role-reversal is enough to make a story valuable, delighted when Mum wears trousers, drives a tractor, goes on night shift, or takes the boys fishing, and when Dad cooks the meal, washes up and pushes the pram.

However sympathetic we may be to calls to purge schools or children's libraries of works that are 'objectionable' in one respect or another, it is necessary to question the concept of reading and of education generally on which such calls depend. They imply a view of education as the acquiring of specified attitudes, if not the acquiring of prescribed knowledge. They also imply an authoritarian mistrust of the professional capability of teachers. Beneath a superficial, though doubtless real, concern for values, once centred on religion or morality, now on class, race or sex, the motivation is propagandist: to control the way in which children think, rather than to encourage them to judge social issues critically for themselves. They follow in the tradition of Sarah Trimmer, with her deep suspicion of novels for young people, and the notorious attack on the moral dangers attending on a reading of *Cinderella*, a subversive tale which:

> . . . paints some of the worst passions that can enter into the human breast, and of which little children should, if possible, be wholly ignorant; such as envy, jealousy, a dislike to mothers-in-law and half sisters, vanity, a love of dress,&c., &c.[42]

It is perhaps significant that more recent complaints about *Cinderella* see it as a sexist tale which needs rehandling.

CONCLUSION: THE REASONED CHOICE

The problem for the teacher is to balance the different, sometimes conflicting, claims of the various criteria when choosing and using books with children. Too much emphasis on the literary merits of the text, or on an academic presentation of it, may produce damaging reactions from students, because it limits the way in which the novel can be read. An otherwise interesting article by Brian Hollingworth, for example, ends with this restrictive judgement: 'the English teacher's concern must be in ensuring sympathy with the original intention' of the authors's text.[43] The tone is magisterial: the teacher's concern *must* be (always?) in *ensuring sympathy* (how?) with the *original intention* (can we know it?). On the other hand, too much emphasis on pupils' immediate enjoyment can imply an endorsement of the trivial, the indulgent or the escapist. It can ignore the fact that there are different kinds of enjoyment to be gained from fiction, and the fact that a teacher's recommendation of a text implies a degree of approval. Too much stress on the curricular, pedagogic value of the text may reduce the story to a launching-pad for writing or talk, to a lead-in for a 'theme' or issue, or even to a query for linguistic analysis or formal exercises. There have been articles with such significant titles as 'Using children's novels as starting-points . . .'[44] Over-much concern for the social or political effects of the work on readers may mean a utilitarian restriction on choice, or the distortion of texts to propagate a message, illustrate a theme, or exemplify certain values which the teacher is concerned to approve or demolish.

To sum up, then. All teachers have to make their own choices – nobody else can do it for them – and they have to balance these conflicting criteria as well as they can. In doing so, it is surely more important to choose books that positively have qualities that will make for development (emotional, moral, conceptual) rather than those which simply lack objectionable features. Our judgements are always being called into question, because one of the marks of true literature is that it is frequently subversive: it undermines our accepted ideas. Drawing on discussions with teachers, a simple list of questions can be proposed, keyed to the sections of this chapter, which a teacher might consider when contemplating using a particular novel in class:

1 The teacher's overall view of the purposes of reading fiction

(i)   Why do I want to read this book with them?
(ii)   What do I hope that the reading may achieve?
(iii) What range of personal responses do I anticipate?

2 Literary judgements

(i)   What are the chief merits of this work that I hope students will discover for themselves, and how can I help them to this discovery without telling them directly?
(ii)   How important are the difficulties it presents, and how can these best be dealt with?
(iii) Is the quality of the writing good enough to extend the pupils without being too demanding?
(iv)   Is there any information which members of the group *must* have if they are to appreciate the book and, if so, how can it best be conveyed?
(v)   How vivid/original/dull/cliché-ridden are the situations/characters/dialogue/relationships?
(vi)   How can the pupils' developing response to the text best be assessed?

3 Awareness of children's tastes

(i)   What is it about this book that is most likely to make it popular?
(ii)   How can this book best be related to what I know they enjoy?
(iii) What mode of presentation is likely to increase their enjoyment?
(iv)   How far will it appeal to both boys and girls and to different levels of ability?
(v)   Does it display the qualities that generally seem appealing (e.g. a character with whom they can associate, a plot which creates anticipation, vivid physical detail) and is there *variety* of appeal?

4 Curricular principles

(i)   How far is it necessary to 'teach' this book, rather than just letting the children read it themselves?
(ii)   In what different ways might I teach it, and which seems most likely to be successful with this group?
(iii) In what ways will it lead naturally into other activities without distortion?
(iv)   In what ways does it relate to the total English programme?
(v)   How far will it fit into a developmental reading programme, enabling helpful comparisons to be made with other texts, and aiding literary learning?

5   **Matching the book and the children**

    (i)   Why do I propose to use this book with this particular group at this time?

    (ii)   What problems of language, concept, narrative technique, allusion may interfere with children's enjoyment, and how should I overcome these?

    (iii)   How effectively will it speak to their basic hopes and fears?

    (iv)   In what ways may it help them to understand themselves, their dilemmas and choices better?

    (v)   How far is it likely to aid their appreciation of the humanity of people of other ages, sexes, races, backgrounds?

    (vi)   Does it offer vicarious experiences of aggression, danger, fear or suffering in a controlled way that they can contemplate?

    (vii) Will any aspects of the book need particularly careful handling or preliminary 'de-fusing'?

    (viii) How would I justify my choice of this book in the face of criticisms (from a headmaster or parent, say)?

    (ix)   Are there any individuals in the class for whom this book may prove upsetting, and how might I deal with this?

11 Developing Response to Fiction

PLANNING THE READING PROGRAMME

To ask which books should be read in school, and when and how, raises urgently those problems of reconciling freedom and control. How do we balance the needs of the individual pupil with those of the group, or our awareness of the variety of responses with the need to organize learning coherently?

Reading programmes are concerned with discovering what it is that makes children want to read and with creating a policy and environment that provide those incentives. Like theatre managers who want 'bottoms on seats', we want books in hands. This means that we are concerned with such prosaic matters as comfortable places for reading, attractive book jackets, the state of local bookshops and libraries, and simply providing time in a crowded day when children can read quietly. The teacher is concered with pushing books: introducing them, reading 'tasters' from them making appropriate suggestions for individuals, extending the range of available titles, lending and selling books, encouraging pupils to share their enjoyment.

As well as supporting individual reading for pleasure, though, the teacher has to be concerned with those group activities, those shared experiences of texts, which seem best suited to extending the range of children's responses (in breadth and depth). By definition this has to be a planned activity. Many teachers on this side of the Atlantic view with suspicion any suggestions of a fiction-reading 'programme', and the reasons for this need to be examined:

(i) Planned instruction in literature has become unfashionable, because it seems to go with an implied separation between language and literature and because it carries overtones of traditional formal syllabuses. Certainly the model of school fiction which equipped each class with one novel for each term (sometimes even for a whole year) and which frequently embodied a dubious sequence of reading (*Ivanhoe* before *Animal Farm*, *Midsummer Night's Dream* before *Macbeth*) had to be remade.

(ii) The swing away from the class reader towards group reading or individual choice has been intensified by the increase in mixed-ability teaching. Rigid programmes of reading are seen as likely to force inappropriate material on reluctant readers.

(iii)   The emphasis on aspects of children's experience as a focus for the English programme, usually manifested in different kinds of thematic structure, has involved a different principle in selecting reading matter. The influence of topic-based collections like *The English Project* or of such course books as *Reflections*, and the increasing tendency for schools to produce their own materials, has involved a shift towards short passages and extracts linked by topic.

(iv)   The excellent principle that teachers should use books which they themselves value has led in some schools to the less admirable practice of teachers having 'their' own sets, which they teach to children of different years, without any reference to what they have previously read (or may read in the future).

Without wishing to return to a situation in which a fiction-reading programme can be taught in virtual isolation from other English activities ('It's Friday afternoon, so get out your novels') we can hardly be happy with the unsystematic free-for-all that has sometimes replaced it. In some schools children have been given the same novel to read in different years, have encountered nothing but problem-centred inner-city fiction for three years, or have never compared one text with another (one teacher even exclaimed to a third-year group, 'I'm not interested in what you did last year; it's what you're doing with me that matters!') Although we cannot determine in advance which will be the valuable literary experiences for individuals, we can at least create situations in which they are likely to occur. Development of response must depend on sequence. It is from our previous reading experiences that we learn what kind of reading is demanded by the new texts we encounter. The wider our acquaintance with fiction, the more aware we become of the range of ways in which narrative may develop.

Literature itself is not a collection of isolated works, each one to be read from scratch. Reading grows on reading, both in a personal and in a social sense. It is not simply that one book makes another comprehensible. The very existence of different attitudes and outlooks in books forces the reader towards a continual remaking and refining of values and judgements. A child's views of what the Second World War may have been like, based on reading, say, *The Exeter Blitz* by David Rees, will be likely to shift in different ways, and to grow more complex, after reading *What About Me?* by Gertie Evenhuis, *Conrad's War* by Andrew Davies, or *Friedrich* by Hans Peter Richter. In the sixth form, views on appropriate relationships between men and women may have to accommodate *Mansfield Park* as well as *Wuthering Heights, Little Dorrit*, and *Sons and Lovers*. Socially, also, older students will become aware that a continuous process of reinterpreting and remodelling literary works goes on: that the pool of available readings and associations gets progressively wider and deeper, including views and attitudes that could not have been possible for the author's contemporaries. Their own responses develop as they accept and reject the ideas they hear in class discussion, or from their teacher, or from reading books of criticism, incorporating them into their 'own' interpretation.

Twenty years ago Ralph Tyler demonstrated the importance of sequence in learning, and specifically in the teaching of reading at all levels. Ideally, each new learning situation should incorporate features of earlier learning, provide new ones, and carry the student to a higher level of understanding, skill or appreciation:

> . . . truly effective sequential practice means that each subsequent practice goes more broadly or more deeply into the subject than did previous practice. Only as each new practice requires the learner to give attention to it because of new elements does it serve effectively as a basis for continued learning.[1]

Tyler went on to illustrate what this might involve in such abilities as anticipating and predicting, responding empathetically, and developing mature interests. An unstructured reading programme runs the risk of lacking sequence not only in the material offered but also in the abilities that are being developed and in the corresponding teaching style.

In recent years, many English Departments have been grappling with the problem of evolving structures that are simultaneously firm enough to embody developments in children's responses and in teaching methods but flexible enough to allow individual teachers and pupils freedom of choice. At Toot Hill Comprehensive School, Bingham, a four-stage developmental model has formed the basis for a coherent, classified list of suggested reading for each of the four phases.[2] In John Foggin's department an 'ideas bank' of teachers' guides has been developed for the novels in stock, detailing the appropriate level, the reasons for using the book in class, the issues introduced, the kinds of preparation required, ways of presenting the book, activities arising from it, and links with other work and other reading. The intention is not simply to give help to over-worked or inexperienced teachers, but progressively to establish a coherent fiction policy.[3] In Judith Atkinson's department, members of staff have combined to produce illustrated pupils' booklets to accompany the novels in use. Stage by stage during the reading these provide tested ideas for individual, pair and group activities – talking and improvising, writing in different modes, modelling and drawing, framing questionnaires and preparing displays – frequently accompanied by examples of work done by other children. Again, the intention is not simply to provide teachers with a useful resource, but by involving them in the development of these materials to help them become more aware of developmental patterns.

In departments like these, the actual pattern of work and the emphasis behind it may change frequently. For a month there may be an emphasis on silent, freely-chosen reading, or on the close study of specific texts, or on a class reading a novel together. The teaching unit may change too, with teachers working as a team to offer different reading options and approaches to small or large groups or to individuals. There is no single 'best' way of balancing the needs to provide both shared and individual approaches to texts, intensive and extensive reading, free choice and teacher selection. There is, however, an increasing awareness that planning should aim at developing fiction-reading abilities and the awareness of 'story-grammars' cumulatively, and attempt to group books in such ways that children can make significant links between them. Such links, of course, can be of many kinds (of theme, of genre, of viewpoint, of style, as will be suggested in what follows) but it should at least be possible to establish points of comparison and contrast between any text taken with a group and those read immediately before and after it. Ideally any sort of programme should be firm enough to exemplify some identifiable pattern at the children's level, yet flexible enough to be modified in the light of changing needs and interests.

Such general principles for incorporating fiction in the work of a class can fit very different kinds of structural organization. A teacher could plan work with a group for a month or a term, for example, in such varied ways as these:

(i)   Using a chosen novel as 'core' reader, from which all English activities – talking, writing, acting and so on – will arise.
The novel could be supplemented by
(a) shorter works, selected by the teacher for close study
(b) group study of different additional texts
(c) free individual choice from a class library collection

(ii)   Using a particular theme as the 'core' for English work, approached by
(a) groups, each with a different text related to the theme to read and introduce to other groups (to whom the books may then be made available)
(b) teacher-selected stories and extracts on the 'core' for detailed study, with follow-up reading by individuals or groups from sources provided by the teacher
(c) 'launch' presentation (a film or other audio-visual introduction of the theme), followed by the choice of a number of sub-divisions of the theme, each with its own appropriate set of readings to be followed by those in the group formed from those who chose that sub-division. Final bringing-together of the work of the groups

(iii)   Using a selected genre or style (the ghost story, say, or humorous writing) as the basis for reading, writing and other activities
(a) a cluster of related stories for close study in class with a choice of

other stories keyed to the written assignments chosen by individuals or groups

(b) a programme relating film or videotape extracts in the same genre or style to the texts for reading

(c) starting with individual or group choices from a selection representing the chosen genre, and later drawing together for discussion and the close reading of a few shared texts

(iv) Deliberately balancing a fiction-reading programme against a thematic structure to provide variety. If the work of the class is organized in lengthy units which concentrate on current issues of social concern drawing largely on contemporary materials (race relations, poverty in the inner city, crime and punishment), then some teachers may choose to work in parallel on very different reading material: a programme of fantasy, say, or of historical stories and novels, or of humorous writing

(v) Combining a structured course in close reading, based on short stories and undertaken by the whole class, with periods of silent, individual reading of novels chosen by pupils from a class collection

In any considered planning there are two basic patterns, which can conveniently be called *clusters* and *ladders*. Examples of the kind of organization which these involve can be briefly outlined.

CLUSTERS

The underlying principle is the simple one that literary awareness seems to develop most easily through comparison and contrast. It is easier to focus on the cruelties of Miss Minchin in *A Little Princess* by putting her alongside Miss Murdstone, say, in *David Copperfield*. The assumptions about the boy narrator of George Layton's *A Northern Childhood* can be articulated by relating them to those which we make about the girl narrator of Jane Gardam's *A Long Way from Verona*. Clusters simply bring together books or stories which offer different treatments of similar topics or characters, or which employ the same genre or stylistic devices. The following examples illustrate the principle. They are not intended to be borrowed ready-made, since every Department will frame clusters to fit its own needs and emphases.

(A) A subject or situation cluster

This is probably the grouping which makes it easiest for children to establish their own points of contact between the books and stories they have read. It is important that the teacher should avoid suggesting that books are simply 'about' a single subject, or that responses to other features are to be ignored. As an organizational pattern, though, this does seem to make for unprompted comments on connections, in which the perceived differences are more significant than the relatively obvious similarities.

For example, a teacher may choose to bring together novels, or sections from some of them, which deal – among other things – with the tensions between individual children and their peer groups. Children may be encouraged to discuss the different treatments of the causes of conflict and the responses to it in books like Betsy Byars, *The 18th Emergency*; Louise Fitzhugh, *Harriet the Spy*; Rosa Guy, *The Friends*; Gene Kemp, *Gowie Corbie Plays Chicken*; Joan Lingard, *Across the Barricades*. Why do we laugh at the protagonist's situation in some cases and not in others? How far do we view the situation from both sides? What is implied about ways to relieve the tension? Similarly, the specific threat of violence may be a chosen situation to link together books that are otherwise very different, like Bernard Ashley, *A Kind of Wild Justice*; Roger Cormier, *The Chocolate War*; Ezra Jack Keats, *Goggles*; Robert O'Brien, *Z for Zachariah*; Johanna Reiss, *The Upstairs Room*; Hans Peter Richter, *Friedrich*; Robert Westall, *The Machine Gunners*.

There are obvious dangers in making the subject or situation too wide. A cluster based simply on 'war' or 'young love' or 'the future' may be appropriate for thematic organization, but will be less likely to promote discussion about the nature of fictional treatment unless it is somehow narrowed. It might be interesting to consider, for example, what different *specific* aspects of adolescent feelings for the opposite sex might become the focus by selecting different pairs of novels from this short list: Honor Arundel, *Emma in Love*; Lynne Reid Banks, *My Darling Villain*; Anna Fine, *The Summer House Loon*; Josephine Kamm, *Where do we go from here?*; Ursula le Guin, *A very long way from anywhere else*; Julius Lester, *Basketball Game*; Mary Stolz, *Ready or Not*; Pamela Sykes, *East, West*; John Rowe Townsend, *Good-night, Prof, Love*; Paul Zindel, *My Darling, My Hamburger*. Equally, a group of teachers might discuss whether there is any point in bringing together a cluster of books like these which deal with the isolated 'special' child, and what the possible dangers of doing so are: Rumer Godden, *The Diddakoi*; John Griffin, *Skulker Wheat*; Ivan Southall, *Let the Balloon Go*; Rosemary Sutcliffe, *The Witch's Brat*; Patricia Wrightson, *I Own the Race Course*.[4]

(B) A genre cluster

Although the prescriptive study of genres (what marks off a particular literary form?) has ceased to be fashionable, the practical study of supposedly typical examples has returned in many schools as a result of methods followed in media studies. Considering and evaluating the methods used in different cops-and-robbers programmes on television (from *Dixon of Dock Green* through *Z Cars* to *The Sweeney* and *The Professionals*, say) suggests that the pattern of work can be extended to include stories of a similar kind. A class can look at a group of westerns, or sports stories, or historical adventures, or science fiction. In a cluster of such fantasies as Penelope Farmer's *A Castle of Bone*, Alan Garner's *Elidor*, John Gordon's *The Giant under the Snow* and C. S. Lewis's *The Lion, the Witch and the Wardrobe*, children can discuss how convincingly the transition from real to fantasy worlds are handled, what devices are used to make movement more convincing, and how far the fantasy is used to point particular morals. A related cluster might be a group of *time* fantasies, including such books as Lucy M. Boston's *The Children of Green Knowe*; Helen Cresswell's *A Game of Catch*; Ruth Park's *Playing Beatie Bow*, Philippa Pearce's *Tom's Midnight Garden* or Catherine Storr's *Marianne Dreams*. The variety within such a generalized genre title as 'animal stories' could be considered by bringing together Russell Hoban, *The Mouse and his Child*; Jack London, *White Fang*; Bill Naughton, *A Dog Called Nelson*; Robert O'Brien, *Mrs Frisby and the Rats of Nimh*; John Steinbeck, *The Red Pony*; E. B. White, *Charlotte's Web*.

Comparisons between the way in which different animal stories or love stories work – what they have in common and what is individual – can sharpen the ability to respond and can help to discriminate between more and less successful pieces of writing. To distinguish between genres could be an artificial exercise, but can be considered practically. How far do parodies, like Thurber's *Fables of Our Time*, depend on manipulating our expectations of genre? How successful are books like *Conrad's War* (or, with older students, *Slaughterhouse 5*) which set out to break down the divisions between genres? What happens if you try to rehandle short stories according to different sets of conventions?

LADDERS

Clusters are a teacher's short-term organizationl patterns; *Ladders* are a department's long-term ones. Their aim is to make reading easier by planning certain texts in sequence.[5] The assumption is that complex novels, involving difficult concepts or stylistic features, are more easily approached if students have previously encountered such features in simpler texts. Novels for younger readers make use of the same literary devices as books for adults, but usually changes in viewpoint are firmly signalled (often by a break in the text), interior monologue is distinguished (by being printed in italics, say), and major symbols tend to be labelled. Awareness and enjoyment of unfamiliar devices can thus be helped by using appropriate children's novels.[6] On a larger scale, the interlocking of past and present, and the uncertainty about how far a character's view-point can be trusted, which is found in a sophisticated adult novel like Henry James's *The Turn of the Screw*, can be more accessible to readers who have encountered Alan Garner's *The Owl Service*. Garner's novel itself may be easier for those who know Joan Aiken's *The Shadow Guests*, which, in turn, may build on reading of the more direct handling of the theme for young readers by Penelope Lively in *The Ghost of Thomas Kempe*. Similarly, the complexities of irony in Jane Austen can be made more manageable if the teacher can refer back to shared experience of novels like Paul Zindel's *The Pigman*. The conflicts in that story between good intentions and actual results, between the way in which young narrators perceive events and the reader's understanding of how Mr Pignati sees them, between immediate and recollected valuations of the experiences, between humorous language and tragic events are all essentially ironic.

Because of the personal, idiosyncratic nature of response, there can be no suggestion of a rigid hierarchy of texts that all pupils should follow in order to reach the ultimate work of great literature at the top of the snakes-and-ladders board. The novels should all be worth reading at their own level. Nevertheless any allocation of texts within a school goes on the principle that they can be arranged in a rough rank-order of general difficulty. The establishing of ladders is intended to select particular sources of difficulty and to choose a reading sequence that will gradually diminish the problem. The obstacles to enjoyment of a novel could be defined in a variety of ways, like these:

(i)   Management of narrative:
          the clarity or otherwise of the story-line
          the way in which the time scheme is handled
          the management of viewpoint; the variety of 'voices'
(ii)   Presentation of character:
          the relative complexity of individual characters
          the number of viewpoints from which they are seen
          the level of motivation and complexity of response
(iii)   Mood and location:
          the importance of tone and setting
          the significance of symbolism
          the underlying cultural assumptions
(iv)   Language:
          the level and difficulty of vocabulary and syntax
          the importance of allusions and references
          the sense of an individual style

Ladders, then, are possible groups of work from which appropriate selections can be made at different levels of reading maturity. Like clusters, they can be considered in terms of narrative patterns, or character presentation, or genre or style. Two brief examples of different kinds of ladder follow.

(i) Numerous works centre on characters' fantasies, or on switching between illusion and reality. Some of these imply the gradual enlightenment of the protagonists, others suggest that the dream world is a universal human need. Texts which are frequently used in secondary schools could be organized in such a rough sequence as this:

Lower School: Alan Ayckbourn, *Ernie's Incredible Illucinations*
                 Prudence Andrew, *Una and Grubstreet*
                 Phillipa Pearce, *A Dog So Small*
Middle School: James Thurber, *The Secret Life of Walter Mitty*
                 Keith Waterhouse, *Billy Liar*
                 John Rowe Townsend, *Goodnight, Prof, Love*
Upper School: William Golding, *Pincher Martin*
                 Jane Austen, *Northanger Abbey*
                 Jane Austen, *Emma*

(ii) Major literature requires of readers that they should be able to respond imaginatively to situations which demand moral decisions, to discuss them coherently and to evaluate them. Ladders to develop this ability would have a huge range of choice on every rung, but – taking examples that might be found in an English stock-room – pupils might encounter at different stages, and make connections between, books like these. In the first years of secondary school Bernard Ashley, *Terry on the Fence* or Louise Fitzhugh, *Harriet the Spy*, followed by Nina Bawden, *Carrie's War* or William Mayne's *Earthfasts*; in the third and fourth years Bette Greene, *The Summer of My German Soldier*, K. M. Peyton's *Flambards* books or Ivan Southall, *To the Wild Sky*, followed perhaps by Robert Cormier, *I am the Cheese*, S. E. Hinton, *That was Then, This is Now*, William Mayne, *A Game of Dark* or Paul Zindel, *The Pigman*, which could lead to or be read alongside short stories of Lawrence or Katherine Mansfield and novels by, say, Graham Greene, Aldous Huxley, Iris Murdoch or George Orwell.

GETTING THE NOVEL READ

There rarely seem to be major problems about presenting a short story in class, but using a novel with a whole group is notoriously difficult. When everybody has a copy of the same book, there only seem to be five basic methods:

(i)   Everybody reads the novel silently at their own speed, at home or at school (or both), and at pre-arranged points ('get to the end of chapter five by Monday') there is discussion or other activity.
(ii)   The novel is read aloud by the teacher in instalments, while the pupils follow.
(iii)   The novel is read 'round the class', by pupils taking it in turns to read sections aloud.
(iv)   The book is read 'dramatically', with pupils taking the parts of different characters and reading the words they speak in dialogue, with the teacher or another pupil acting as narrator.
(v)   The book is pre-recorded on tape, by the teacher or another reader, possibly with 'dramatized' sections, and played back while pupils follow.

All methods have their disadvantages. Any form of reading aloud governs the speed at which the book can be taken and frustrates the eager readers who want to hurry on. Any form of silent reading makes it difficult to monitor whether or not the text has actually been read, and deprives the less fluent readers of the help of hearing the text presented clearly. Any method which involves reading by children may spoil the effect of the book for others because of their inability to read clearly and vividly. To avoid using child readers loses one way of encouraging their direct involvement and deprives them of one opportunity of practising reading aloud (though it has to be said that there are much better ways of giving them practice than this, and ways that do less damage to first impressions of a novel).

This does not mean that there are not better and worse methods. Enquiries both among children and among graduate student teachers with experience of all these methods produce the same responses. Reading round the class is almost universally detested: it spoils the story, it distracts attention from the text to 'my turn', it publicly embarrasses the weak readers and makes them dislike reading, it encourages the fluent to 'show off', it prevents the eager from reading on and getting involved in the story. What is preferred (again, almost universally) is variety. No method is popular if it is practised all the time, becoming monotonous and predictable. An example of the favoured approach to an established classic, like *Treasure Island* for example, would be for the teacher to launch the book, reading the first part aloud, to set a section for silent reading and discussion, then to play a dramatized section from one of the available recordings, to set groups to *prepare* their own dramatized readings of forthcoming sections, which can alternate with sections that are silently or teacher read, and so on.

The other decisions which have to be made about presenting the text concern timing and editing. In general, students seem to find it more helpful if the novel is read quickly, rather than being spread over a long period like a term. (In one school known to me the reading of *Kidnapped* was supposed to extend over the entire third year!) All of a form's English lessons for a week or two may be devoted to a quick reading of the text, or several periods may be used in a block to get the reading launched, after which the novel returns only at intervals, until a final block rounds it off. Much depends on the skill with which the breaking into episodes is done. There is evidence that nineteenth-century readers found a novel read in instalments to be more enjoyable than the same work in book form, and the popularity of television serials also suggests that interruptions, with their prolonging of tension and their invitation to predict what will happen, can increase enjoyment, providing that continuity is not lost. In general, it seems helpful to distinguish between those stories with a complex plot or character development, which demand swift and continuous reading to keep the thread, and those which are essentially episodic, dividing neatly into self-contained instalments. In the episodic category come books like *The Silver Sword, The Boy who was Afraid, Joby, Grandad with Snails*. There seem no great disadvantages in tackling these over a month or two with one section being read each week. Recapitulation is no major problem.

How far should the teacher edit the text? Large-scale editing involves the cutting of whole pages and sometimes re-arranging sections. Small-scale editing is concerned with words, references and allusions that may cause difficulty.

In the large-scale, there seem several justifiable reasons for editing, remembering that if children are given the complete text then those who wish to do so can always check for themselves what has been omitted.

(1) Cutting the beginning. Television plays as well as modern novels have made readers impatient of leisurely openings, and teachers may wish to get quickly to the action of classic books they are reading. Nobody would cut the vivid openings of *Treasure Island* or *Great Expectations*, but a reading of *Tom Brown's Schooldays* would be better starting at chapter five, with Tom's arrival at Rugby, and similar cutting (possibly accompanied by a brief synopsis) might be used with novels like *The Thirty-nine Steps*.

(2) Cutting secondary episodes or digressions. A first acquaintance with *Oliver Twist* may do better without most of the sentimental Rose Maylie scenes; *Three Men in a Boat* can lose the guide-book sections and concentrate on the humour. Some teachers practise differential editing of this kind, reading the first part of a section aloud and then suggesting that fluent readers should complete the section for themselves, while less able readers are given selected pages (the main narrative thread, not the secondary matter) to read.

(3) Re-organizing the structure. Rather than cutting the beginning, there may sometimes be a case for starting later in the story and then introducing the earlier part in a kind of flashback (e.g. starting *Oliver Twist* at the point when Oliver arrives in London and is introduced by the Artful Dodger to Fagin's gang, and keeping the workhouse and undertaker scenes until later).

The purpose of small-scale editing is to keep the story going without diminishing understanding. Too many teachers still treat texts as a quarry for comprehension and vocabulary questions, losing the impetus of the narrative while they ask children, often unsuccessfully, 'What is a culverin?' 'What does *tenebrous* mean?' 'Why does the author liken him to King Midas?' 'Whereabouts is the Sargasso Sea?' In preparing a text, a teacher may – as appropriate – substitute simple words for difficult ones, or add a simile or gloss in implied spoken brackets after the original word, or paraphrase a technically difficult paragraph in a sentence or so.

The advantages of editing over buying simplified versions of a text are that the extent of the simplification is in the hands of the teacher, that it can be adapted to the perceived response of the group, that the more difficult words may be learned by being defined in context, and that the original text is still available for those who can cope with it. There may be some merits in the American practice of having different versions of the 'same' text, of differing degrees of difficulty, for groups to read within a class, but the organizational difficulties as well as the economic ones are hard to overcome.

As will be suggested later, thinking about getting the book read should be accompanied by thinking about getting parts of it *re*-read. Effective sections, chosen for their 'performance' qualities rather than for purely literary ones, can be rehearsed and presented as prepared readings, and the interpretations (preferably recorded) can be discussed. Other parts can be presented dramatically by groups. At fourth-year level, groups can be invited to select their own readings to illustrate particular features of the novel, and to present these with commentary. The idea of savouring and sharing enjoyed moments should be encouraged.

THE SEQUENCE OF LESSON ACTIVITIES

There are significant differences between what happens when children read for themselves and what generally happens when a teacher organizes that reading in class. In a lesson, the pace of reading is controlled, it may well be interrupted by questions and comments, and once the reading is over certain responses are likely to be demanded from the readers. The now extensive repertoire of recordings in which children in teacherless groups talk about texts show conclusively how differently they operate as compared with groups that are teacher-led. Studies of children at different ages suggest that they develop certain modes of response before others. A group of small children in Hull read a passage about a cat and, asked to discuss it, instinctively began with anecdotes about their own cats or cats they had known. Rather older children re-tell the reading in terms of their own experience, validating some parts and questioning others, treating the difficult sections as a kind of puzzle from which meaning has to be dug. For example, a third-year group talking about Ray Bradbury's short story *The Pedestrian* related the events to their own lives and values ('I thought he must be queer when he went along talking to the houses', 'I'd have made a run for it') and questioned aspects that puzzled them ('Why did he leave all the lights on?', 'Could they really do that by remote control?'), but they eventually posed questions that a teacher might not have asked: 'Are we supposed to sympathize with the man?', 'What is it really saying about the future?' and (in reply to a comment, 'I don't like science-fiction') 'But is this really science-fiction?' Talk of this kind frequently seems rambling, circling and repetitive, because it is not moving to a predetermined conclusion which the teacher controls.

In fact, though, those models of fiction-reading currently in favour and discussed in chapter two would suggest that these young readers are making explicit what is, in fact, their normal process of response to reading. They are bringing meaning to print by linking their own experiences to the text, by seeking to frame their own hypotheses to explain what seems difficult and by responding positively to those ideas that have most significance for them. Frank Smith has reminded us:

> Readers approach texts from their own point of view, with intentions of their own rather than those of the author. And readers comprehend when their own intentions are satisfied, when the questions they ask of the text are answered because their expectations are fulfilled.[7]

The problem for the teacher is how to take into account what children bring *to* a book, as well as what they get *out* of it. How can a lesson accommodate these different intentions and expectations which will dominate the responses of two dozen assorted young readers? Our experiences continually flesh out this problem. A discussion goes off in a totally unexpected direction, the meticulously planned work dies on us, an almost random, marginal idea becomes hugely successful (work on graffiti arising from *The Eighteenth Emergency*, lists of favourite foods from *The Pinballs*, collections of hideous tortures or terrible jokes).

One possible strategy is to separate out a core of planned activities (which the whole group will follow) from a cumulative list, progressively built up as the reading goes on, of ideas sparked off by the text, from which individuals can select those that interest them most. The dangers for the teacher lie in the two extemes. One is a refusal to think ahead, for fear of cramping spontaneous, heaven-sent inspirations. Thinking on the feet can be exhilarating, but activities are not to be randomly selected, without thought for the function they are to fulfil and the developmental level of the students. The other extreme is to pre-plan not only what is to be done but how the pupils will (or, at least, ought to) respond, and to build successive stages of work on that *anticipated* response. Instead of allowing children time to articulate their own tentative reactions, some teachers hasten to impose their own ideas and judgements, often by the questions they frame. They want an agreed, consensus view, because the links in the lesson depend on it. Divergence or originality would threaten the plan. Such teachers also signal what they see as significant and what kinds of response are to be taken as irrelevant. The further up the secondary school, the more likely it is that personal engagement with the text and straightforward description and savouring will be seen as inappropriate.

The practical implication of the work summarized in this volume is that at *all* ages there is a case for attempting to bring the natural sequence of response into shared reading. Although they do not take place in isolation from each other, the movement from personal engagement through 'enacting' or describing the text to interpretation and evaluation can suggest stages in a lesson, at A-level as well as in the first year. Most important of all is the need for *time* in which children can begin to formulate their own responses and to share them in an informal way with one another. The extending and deepening of these responses through a variety of activities, the movement towards more considered interpretation and evaluation, are later stages in bringing together the members of the group.

What might a structure based on these principles look like? This very simple outline suggests one possiblity that could be used over different time scales: a double period spent on a brief short story or a longer sequence for dealing with a more extended text. The six stages, of which the first and last may or may not be included, lay stress on different responses in turn: personal enjoyment, perception, interpretation and evaluation.

1　Possible pre-reading activities
2　The first reading
3　Encouraging individual responses
4　Sharing and developing responses
5　Assessment and evaluation
6　Possible final readings or presentations

Each of these can be briefly expanded by indicating some of the questions which they raise for the teacher.

1   Possible pre-reading activities

(i)   Are there themes or issues which might be better introduced before the story is encountered?
(ii)   Will there be a preliminary 'trailer' to create interest?
(iii)   How can an appropriate atmosphere be created for the reading?
(iv)   Is it necessary to establish a context for the reading?
(v)   Should it be linked in any way with previous reading? If so, how?
(vi)   Is there any essential information (allusions, vocabulary) which students *must* have to understand the reading?

2   The first reading

(i)   How will it be presented? (teacher reading, recording, dramatically, etc.)
(ii)   Will it be uninterrupted, or with pauses for prediction, retrospection or speculation?
(iii)   Will it be complete?
(iv)   Is any editing necessary?

3   Encouraging individual responses

(i)   How far – if at all – should the teacher intervene at this stage?
(ii)   What methods are most likely to encourage immediate personal responses? (Picturing, jotting, marking the text etc.)
(iii)   How can perceptions of the reading be tried out? (relating to personal experiences, re-telling, anecdotal parallels, selecting key passages)
(iv)   How can immediate responses be more clearly formulated? (e.g. pairs or groups seeking clues, identifying questions to answer, finding points of focus)

4   Developing and sharing responses

(i)   What kinds of collaboration focused on particular passages would be most appropriate?
(ii)   What aspects of the narrative (story line, characters, mood, viewpoint, style) need particular attention? What activities will be most helpful for this?
(iii)   What forms of imaginative rehandling in talk or writing might be used?
(iv)   Would there be reasons for extending into other media? (art work, improvisation, recording etc.)

5   Assessment and Evaluation

(i)   How can helpful contacts with previous reading be established?
(ii)   What are the central issues on which judgement of this text will depend?
(iii)   What are the key questions which have to be asked about this text?
(iv)   What aspects of narrative technique – if any – should be considered?
(v)   In what terms can these students be expected to 'value' their experience of this story?

6   Possible final readings or presentations

 (i)   What is the best way of rounding-off this work or bringing together
         group activities?
 (ii)   Should there be any formal outcome (display, compilation, etc.)?
 (iii) What reasons are there for and against a re-reading of the text in some
         form?

THE RANGE OF ACTIVITIES

What might be happening with novels in those English classrooms not
committed to reading round the class, 'doing' comprehensions and
spoon-feeding information about set texts? Apart from the illustrative
case studies, this book is not concerned to describe methods in detail. One
continuing theme is the danger of advancing generalized ideas of 'how to
teach' a particular story or novel, as though they can adopted ready-made,
without further thought, by teachers in very different situations. What can
be done is to give an analytic overview of a variety of activities and
approaches currently in use, organized particularly to illustrate what different purposes they may serve in developing response. It is the teacher's
responsibility to decide in any situation which of these will be most
appropriate, and how, and why, and in what sequence they will be
employed.

Those activities which we practise in teaching fiction can be classified
in very different ways. We can see them in conventional terms as marked
by the kind of action they demand: reading, writing, talking, drawing, acting, and so on. We can arrange them on a continuum from 'closed' (concentrating on the text as such, and nothing else) to 'open' (using the text
solely as a springboard for personal, creative activity). We may categorize
them in terms of those features of fiction to which they draw particular
attention (the story-line, the characters, the setting). Here they are related
to particular phases in that simple teaching sequence outlined at the end
of the last section, to suggest how certain activities can best be keyed to
successive moments in development of response.

In what follows, therefore, the emphasis is on those stages in the sequence (three to six) directly concerned with response. The first two
stages can be swiftly dealt with. The function of pre-reading activities
(stage one) is essentially to influence pupils' reactions to the reading so
that they will be more sympathetic, alert or informed. Teachers may concentrate on making the text more accessible, by giving 'tasters' or trailers,
by leading in with simpler work by the same author (short stories by Lawrence or Joyce before *Sons and Lovers* or *A Portrait of the Artist*), by discussing expectations of the book based on the title or on a brief extract, or by

hearing what the author said about the book (on schools radio or TV, for example). Alternatively, they concentrate on getting pupils into an appropriate frame of mind for the encounter, by preliminary work or other reading on the themes of the book, by drawing on personal experiences that will relate to the opening episodes, or by improvisations keyed to the action of the book. The second stage, the reading process itself, has already been considered in some detail, particularly in the section *Getting the novel read* earlier in this chapter.

Nearly 100 activities are now briefly presented according to the natural sequence of developing response. For clarity, stage four is sub-divided into two sections, separating the first limited sharing of responses from more directed and structured work. The rounding-off stages of the work (five and six) are combined here, so that what follows is organized like this:

1	Emphasizing personal response	(stage three)
2	The first sharing	(stage four a)
3	Developing and structuring response	(stage four b)
4	Summarizing responses	(stages five and six)

1   Emphasizing personal response

It has been argued that in the traditional literature lesson children are pushed too quickly through the stages of learning. Not enough importance is attached to those first, intense, instinctive reactions to the story or the chapter of a novel. Not enough space is allowed for children to sort out what it is they have actually experienced in reading. In their case studies, Judith Atkinson and Mike Town are both aware of the dangers when teachers intervene too quickly or structure too tightly, and when children are not given the opportunity for 'individual reflection'. So, before anything else, there normally needs to be time in which these immediate, instinctive responses of readers can be allowed to become more considered and coherent before they are ready to be shared. To make this kind of time explicit in the lesson helps to validate and legitimize personal response. It makes clear that our stress is on *making* rather than *finding* meaning in the text.

When groups are used to the idea that there will be a period of reflection after the reading of a short story or episode from a novel, they seem to require less and less guidance as they become more confident in formulating their own reactions to what seems significant in the text to them as individuals. If the idea is a new one, though, they will require help in discovering that personal reactions, not 'right' answers are wanted. They may be encouraged to formulate their ideas by marking the text or jotting down thoughts in rough. The more there is physical involvement with the text – checking back, re-reading, pointing to words, underlining sen-

tences – the better. With groups that are hesitant, it is sometimes helpful
to give out duplicated copies of four or five comments on *Uncle Ernest*, say
(drawn from other classes or years), ask them to decide which is closest to
their own opinion, and revise it if necessary to make it a still more accurate version of their own feelings. The chief purpose of this is to reassure
them that a range of possible reactions is possible, and that others are not
worried at expressing them. Among the familiar ways of emphasizing personal response are the following:

(A) *Rough jottings*
(i)   At the most open, pupils can simply be invited to put down in a few
      words their immediate personal reactions to the story or episode, the
      things they particularly liked and remembered or to make a quick
      lightning sketch of what seems essential to them in it. Some exam-
      ples of such snap reactions to stories were given at the beginning of
      the first chapter of this book.[8]
(ii) The teacher may deliberately encourage students to set up parallels
      between the story and their own lives: does this remind you of any-
      thing that has happened to you? Have you ever felt like this? What
      would you have done in this situation? Younger children find it
      easier to work by recalling incidents in this way, making the connec-
      tions between themselves and the text explicit.
(iii) Alternatively, the focus may be placed on the reading experience
      itself: how did you *feel* when we were reading this? Why? What par-
      ticularly caught your imagination? What do you like/dislike most
      about the story? At a more advanced level, pupils might be invited to
      consider *how* they read the story (how far they empathized, iden-
      tified) or what connections – if any – they see between their response
      to the story and their response to the author.
(iv) Rather more formally, children may be asked to choose a new title
      for the story (and to consider why their choice is a good one), jot
      down in a sentence or so what the story particularly says to them, or
      to identify the key questions which the story arouses in their minds.

(B) *Reading journals*
Increasing interest has been shown recently in encouraging students, particularly in year four and later, to keep their own logs or journals, in which
they record their personal impressions of novels *as they read them*, as a preliminary to later, more considered, talking and writing about the book.
Those who are interested should read David Jackson's account of a girl's
journal, made while reading John Branfield's *Nancekuke*.[9] Her first entries
emphasize personal engagement, as she tries to establish links between

her own experience and the book, and tentative judgements. As her reading progresses, she seems to give more to interpreting the book, predicting how it may come out and how the characters will interact.

(C)   *Marking the text*
If pupils have their own copies, or if key sections can be duplicated, marking these can provide a simple way of embodying personal response. With groups that have not been used to doing this, it will probably be necessary for the teacher to make suggestions at first. For example:

(i)   Selecting key words and phrases. Students can be asked, 'What do you think is the most important word in this story? Underline it each time it is used.' The same thing can be done with phrases. The teacher may ask them to pick a quotation, not more than a sentence in length, that sums up for them the point of the story and circle it, to lead to later discussion.

(ii)   Picking out clues. What words tell us that the opening of *1984* is set in the future? reveal the narrator's character? suggest that something unpleasant is going to happen? Particularly with stories that have some surprise in the ending (*The Landlady* by Roald Dahl, say) children can be asked to pick out and underline those phrases earlier in the story which, with hindsight, now indicate to them what was going to happen.

(iii)   Dividing up the narrative. 'How would you break this story into separate sections? Draw a line between them and give a title to each section.'

(iv)   Establishing distinctions. This can be done at a variety of levels, as a preparation for later discussion. At a simple level, dividing description from narration; at a more complex level, one mood from another, or reality from fantasy, (e.g. *The Secret Life of Walter Mitty*); at an advanced level, direct from implied authorial comment. Coloured pens can be useful.

2   The first sharing

Particularly when the impact of the book is strong, when we feel 'lost in' or 'carried away by' it, we are frequently not aware of just what is happening to us as readers. As when we have been moved by a film, or by events in real life, we feel a need to talk about the experience, to discover what it means for us, to distance ourselves a little from it, and perhaps to seek the confirmation of our own feelings in the reactions of others. Because children's initial responses are also likely to be tentative and uncertain (and may be intense and private), the movement towards sharing is usually better if gradual, small-scale (pairs or very small groups), and without a sense of teacher-judgement. Again, the organizational approach may range from the free and open ('Well, what do others think? Just compare your reactions with your neighbour's') to ones which focus on some particular aspect or activity. This is the early stage of the process that Leavis calls 'an appeal for corroboration', a 'mutual check' and openness to other responses.[10] All five case studies give examples of the ways in which children learn from one another, and Keith Bardgett, Mike Town and Judith Atkinson particularly draw attention to the ways in which pupils seem to talk themselves into greater understanding.

(A) *Finding points of focus*

Small-scale exploration in talk can be used to isolate what are key points for the pupils in coming to terms with the story, and these can serve as a basis for class discussion or other activity.

(i)   Open-ended comparison of immediate, personal reactions in pairs, identifying points of agreement and difference, savouring and re-telling favourite moments, relating to their own experiences.

(ii)   Pairs or small groups compiling a short list of questions which *they* think require answering, to form the basis for group discussion.[11]

(iii) More formally, groups choosing one character each, and discussing that person's role in the story, feelings and reactions to others, to establish where there may be disagreements about motivation.

(B) *Recapitulating: the story till now*

This is a desirable activity when a novel is being read in instalments, but too often proceeds by highly selective teacher question and answer, the end-product of which is incoherent and yet implying that there is one 'right' view of what is significant in the past action. There are different ways of shifting this emphasis:

(i)   The word limit approach. Ask pairs to combine: 'What would the two of you tell someone who had just joined the class and had missed all the story up to this point? What is it essential to know if you have only fifty words to do it in? (Giving different pairs different word limits can sometimes produce interesting results.)

(ii)   Explaining the events to someone who wasn't there, from the point of view of someone involved. One of each pair tells the partner in the first person about escaping from the camp in *The Silver Sword*, or about attempts to sell *The Pearl*, and the other asks questions about details left unclear.

(iii) Serial narration. Groups are formed with the same number of pupils in each as the number of chapters that have been read. Each is allocated a chapter, and given five minutes to prepare a brief résumé (or to pick out two or three key sentences that sum it up). They then present their summaries in turn to form a serial version of 'the story so far'.

(iv)   Critical comparisons. Each pair or group writes a brief summary, and
       larger groups are then formed to compare and discuss these. The con-
       sideration of what seems essential knowledge (and why) is more impor-
       tant than agreeing on any particular formulation.

(C)   *Anticipating: what next?*
The Schools Council project, *The Effective Use of Reading*,[12] has made prediction, as it is called there, a familiar technique. It is frequently practised
with a whole class, and sometimes as an isolated activity for its own sake.
Here we are concerned with it particularly as a group activity at appropriate stages in the reading of a novel. In such work, it may be helpful to
distinguish different kinds of anticipation, which involve different sorts of
discussion. For example:

(i)   Short-term: What is going to happen next? *Now* what will he do? How
       do you think she will respond to that?
(ii)   Long-term: How is this all going to turn out? Will the book end happily
       or unhappily? Is he eventually going to prove a sympathetic or an unsym-
       pathetic character? Will she get what she wants?
(iii) Problem-solving, encouraging speculation and guessing about specific,
       practical problems raised in the narrative: how might they set about rais-
       ing the money? How do you think she could escape? With older stu-
       dents, the formulation may be more deliberate: how do you think that
       this author will arrange for the heroine to escape?

3   Developing and structuring response

The teacher's role becomes more directly significant from this point on.
It involves diagnosing what aspects of the story to concentrate on, in light
of the observed reactions of the children, selecting appropriate activities
and deciding which parts of the work might be undertaken by the whole
class together and which in groups. The case studies illustrate ways in
which teachers may emphasize what it is that an author *does* (Paul Francis), or what can be learned from comparisons between texts (Judith
Atkinson and Mike Town), or what recreating the experience can achieve
(Keith Bardgett and John Foggin). It is at this stage that particular aspects
of narrative can be identified for special attention.

(A)   *Keeping track of the novel*
There are a number of continuing activities, each appropriate to different
kinds of novel, that can help to give a sense of shape to the narrative and
to avoid losing the thread if the reading continues over a period of weeks.
The formal summary is an unpopular (and frequently unhelpful) way of
achieving this, and visual, representational methods have the advantage

that they can be easily displayed, shared and added to as the reading progresses. Among such methods are:

(i)   With younger children, creating a comic-strip or story-board version of the story (which usefully involves group discussion of precisely which key moments demand a new picture).

(ii) The simple chronological table of events, map of the places mentioned in the story, family tree of the characters involved and so on, according to the kind of novel and the age of the students (e.g. a map of Ged's journeys in *A Wizard of Earthsea* or features of the island in *Lord of the Flies*, justifying details from the text).

(iii) From the fourth year, a wall chart on which are accumulated key quotations for each of the major characters or themes. Different groups can each be given one character or aspect to keep up to date.

(iv) Diagrams of a sociometric kind, showing the names of characters, and linking with lines those that have some relationship or direct influence on another. (This is a useful way of showing how certain characters are central, and how some minor characters are still significant.)

(v)   Particularly with set texts, charts showing the incidence and influence of characters in the book. Some developments of this 'modelling' technique have been described by Josephine Hall.[13]

(B)   *Concentrating on the story-line*
      To focus attention on particular aspects of the text it will sometimes be necessary to introduce additional material (as in some of the following suggestions):

(i)   Sequencing (one). In pairs or small groups, sorting out the 6 – 12 stages of a piece of narrative that has been cut up and jumbled, and comparing results.

(ii) Sequencing (two). Ask groups to give each of the first 10 or 12 chapters an appropriate title, and to write it on a slip of paper. Each group then gets another group's slips, and endeavours to sequence them.

(iii) Openings. By examining different first paragraphs (e.g. *Animal Farm, Saturday Night and Sunday Morning, The War of the Worlds*) consider what different sets of expectations are raised for the story that is to follow.

(iv) Narrowing options. Considering how the range of possible developments decreases as a story goes on, and identifying the key moments at which the options are crucially narrowed. This is probably best done first with short stories, like Sansom's *The Vertical Ladder*, but can also be applied to novels.

(v)   Finding the 'clue'. Groups or pairs pick out the indicators that prepare for the ending, especially in suspense, ghost or crime stories or the 'evidence' that supports a particular reading (e.g. the 'real' and 'unreal' qualities of Ted Hughes' *The Rain Horse*).

(vi)   Endings. Creating an ending for a story that has been left incomplete
         by the teacher; or choosing one from a number of possible endings pro-
         vided, and discussing the choice; or rewriting an ending to change its
         effect (a serious climax into a comic anti-climax, or vice-versa, e.g. in
         W. W. Jacobs *The Monkey's Paw* or Saki *The Unrest Cure*).
(vii)   Alternatives. At key moments of choice, groups consider 'What else
         might X have done? What would probably have been the result?' Ideas
         are shared to see what the range of possibilities is.
(viii)   What has changed? By comparing the beginning and the ending of the
         story, groups have to discuss and list those things which have remained
         unchanged throughout the story and those which have significantly
         altered.
(ix)   What if? Imagining that a key event had turned out differently, and
         improvising in talk or writing how the story would have continued.
         (What if Jim Hawkins had not been in the apple barrel that night? What
         if Jack, not Ralph, had been originally elected leader in *Lord of the Flies*?)
(x)   Changing the time-scheme. Groups making a rearranged outline of a
         chronological first-person story as for flashback treatment in film or
         TV.

(C)   *Concentrating on viewpoint*
  (i)   This concept can be simply introduced to younger children
           through pictures of the same object or place taken from differ-
           ent positions and distances. To what extent is the object the
           'same'? What are the advantages of having more than one
           view?
  (ii)   Another method of introduction can be through group impro-
           visations. Pupils can be given characters and a situation within
           which they argue about an issue from their character's view-
           point. Then they read a story which rehearses the topic from
           one particular standpoint. The other characters can then be
           asked how they react to this version, and how *they* would tell
           it. (For example, students can be mother, father, son and
           grandmother improvising the 'generation gap' issues before
           reading the initial breakfast scene from *Billy Liar*.)
  (iii)   Students can be asked to pick out indications of an omniscient
           narrator's attitude to characters and events, and to consider
           how the characters themselves might see them. Similar inci-
           dents from *Tom Sawyer* (where Mark Twain is the narrator)
           and *Huckleberry Finn* (where Huck is) might be compared.
  (iv)   The advantages and limitations of a first-person narrator can
           be considered. Episodes can be rehandled through the eyes of
           a different character (how Marv Hammerman sees *The
           Eighteenth Emergency*, or Estella describes the first meeting

with Pip in *Great Expectations*, or the old man tells about the destruction of his greenhouse by a gang of boys in *Grandad with Snails*).

(v)		Events narrated more or less as they take place can be considered as they might appear to the narrator later in life. (How would Holden Cauldfield at the age of 50 describe some of the events in *The Catcher in the Rye*?)

(vi)		At a more advanced level, where is the narrator 'placed' in certain scenes, and how does this affect our reading?

(vii)	Experienced students can seek the points of transition from apparently 'external' description to revelations of what is passing in a character's mind, or is being seen through a character's eyes, and discuss how effectively, or otherwise, these transitions are made.

(D)	*Concentrating on the characters*

(i)		Straightforward 'picturing' of the character: 'Imagine that he/ she has just walked into the room . . .' What does the character look like, behave like, make you feel? Some pupils may be encouraged to make rough sketches before writing word pictures.

(ii)		Interviews. One pupil in each pair plays the interviewer and the other takes the role of a major character in the book, being asked about his or her life and opinions. Try interviewing Mr Farthing, Atticus Finch.

(iii)	Describing characters from the point of view of other characters at key moments. Students representing these characters can be asked, for example, 'What's your real opinion of young Smith (In Leon Garfield's novel)? Why do you feel like that?' Or characters can prepare statements to the police about Lennie in Steinbeck's *Of Mice and Men* or Vic in Stan Barstow's *The Desperadoes*, or school reports on Gowie Corbie or the boys in *Thunder and Lightnings*, or consider how a staff meeting would view the friendship between Danny and Tyke Tiler.

(iv)	Writing an extract from a character's diary or journal or letters, reflecting and commenting appropriately on events in the story.

(v)		Creating an additional incident about a major character, with an emphasis on consistency. Younger pupils can usually 'slot in' an additional adventure in an episodic book like *The Silver Sword, A Dog called Nelson* or *Grandad with Snails*. Older students can be asked to project beyond the ending of the book:

create an incident involving Billy Fisher, Hal or Tyke Tiler when they are 10 years older; say what happened to Long John Silver after his escape.

(vi)   In novels where dialogue is important, sub-text exercises can be used ('When they say this, what are they really thinking and feeling?').

(vii) At a more formal level, making a simple table of the major methods of character revelation (what is thought/said/done by the character; what is said/revealed in other ways by other characters; what is said/implied by the author) and filling in as much of the grid as possible with details about a chosen character in the story.

(viii) Giving groups prepared lists of personality characteristics, each of which has to be attributed to one or other of two (or three) characters in the story (e.g. George and Lenny in *Of Mice and Men*, Bernard and Shofiq in *My Mate Shofiq*). After discussion, in which groups try to justify their decisions, they can be asked to prepare similar lists of traits for other characters in the novel.

(ix)   Selecting two characters and asking groups to list in what ways they are alike and in what ways they are different. Alternatively asking individuals to consider which of the characters they themselves are most like, and in what ways they are similar and different.

(x)   Groups preparing a list of references or a diagram to show the moments in the novel where a chosen character seems to change or to develop.

(E) *Concentrating on language and style*

(i)   Filling in the blanks. Pupils can be given short, key passages of text with words systematically deleted (cloze), and be asked to fill these in with the most appropriate words and later to discuss the results in groups. For studying fiction, it may be better not to delete words at regular intervals (every tenth, say) but to concentrate on omitting key words, or certain classes of word (verbs, adjectives) or 'mood' words.

(ii)   Restoring the text (one). A variant of cloze is to give out the text with certain significant words replaced by others. For younger children these can be words that obviously do not fit the context; for older pupils they may simply be feeble words (got, nice). The activity is in two stages: (a) deciding on the 'wrong' words, and the reasons for identifying them (which may be helped by saying e.g. that there is one in each sentence

and 10 in all) and (b) replacing them with more effective
words after the fashion described above in 'filling in the
blanks'.

(iii)   Restoring the text (two). More radically, passages of text can
be distributed in a rewritten form in which an inappropriate
style (journalistic, genteel, over-idiomatic) has been used, and
pairs can be asked to identify where the language seems inappropriate and then to attempt to rehandle it as they think it
'ought' to be, before comparing with the original.

(iv)   What is the text doing? Distribute a list of possible effects
which a fiction text may achieve (or aims which an author may
have) and a set of page-references (or duplicated extracts)
drawn from the novel. Pairs or groups classify the passages
according to the chief effects (not necessarily just one) which
they seem to be achieving, and discuss the results.

(v)   Writing 'in the style of'. When studying an author with clearly
marked stylistic qualities, pupils can be asked to write an early
childhood memory after the fashion of Laurie Lee, a description of an eccentric character like Dylan Thomas, or dialogue
like Hemingway.

(vi)   Modernizing. Passages from older texts can be rehandled by
groups, not in the sense of paraphrasing, but of bringing into
our own time the objects, references, life styles, allusions, as
well as the language. The bullying of Jane Eyre at Lowood
School or Oliver Twist's introduction to crime can be updated
in this way, from then to now and from there to here.

(vii)   Critical examination of changes in text. From the fourth year
onwards two sorts of comparison seem helpful: (a) between an
author's original and revised drafts (e.g. Joyce's successive
versions of passages from the stories in *Dubliners*), and (b) between the original versions of texts and 'simplified' versions
produced for schools (what is gained and what is lost?).

(F)   *Concentrating on form*

(i)   Comparison of versions of the story in different forms. Works
like *Billy Liar* exist as novel, radio drama, play, film and
musical, and the varied adaptations can be compared and
evaluated to establish what are the demands of these different
ways of presenting narrative. It is particularly interesting to
examine parts of the texts where the original author has
rehandled a novel in a new way (e.g. Orwell's radio version of
Animal Farm or John Steinbeck's film script for *For Mice and
Men*).[14] Pupils can consider the points at which films like *To*

Kill a Mockingbird or *Brighton Rock* vary from the original novel, and discuss why the changes have been made.

(ii)   Translating story into radio play. This is probably the easiest form of re-creation for students to attempt, and has the advantage that the results can easily be recorded and assessed by the group. If models are needed, BBC Schools Radio is a good source of brief dramatizations (of short stories, as well as novels) which can be used in the classroom. Episodes from books like *The Pearl*, *The Machine Gunners* and *The Seventeenth Emergency* seem to convert fairly easily.

(iii) Translating story into play or script for film or TV. Writing for a visual medium, 'showing' instead of describing, provides a different kind of technical challenge. Fourth-year students in groups can script the death of Lennie scene from *Of Mice and Men* or an episode from *Kes*, and then discuss the problems and their attempted solutions.[15]

4   Summarizing responses

Especially if a good deal of time has been spent concentrating on certain aspects of the text or on a close examination of key passages, the concluding stages of the work should enable readers to reconsider their response to the novel as a whole, to relate it to their other reading and to consider how it can be recommended to and shared with others. After group activities, there is a need to bring the whole class together again for the final stages. Particularly in Judith Atkinson's case study there is an awareness that we rarely give children enough chance to return to and to savour favourite passages, or to share them with each other. In what follows there are no separate 'evaluative' activities as such. Certainly it is at this late stage that children should be expressing considered judgements of what they have read, but the argument throughout has been that evaluation is a developing process not to be separated from other modes of response. Testimony of what the text means to individuals, evidence of a direct personal encounter, should arise, be shared and reformulated in the whole range of these activities.

(A)   *Possible rounding-off activities*
(i)   The public enquiry, trial or post-mortem. All the class can be given roles to play in the public enquiry, with teacher as Chairman, into the mine disaster of *Bonnie Pit Laddie*. Witnesses can be called in 'The Case of Billy Casper: who is to blame?' a television documentary, or 'For and Against Jack' in *Lord of the Flies*.

(ii)   News coverage of the events. With a book like *The Machine Gunners*, children can be asked to think about the different ways in which the dramatic events might be reported by different news media. Groups can produce facsimiles of reports in *The Daily Mirror* or the *Sun*, *The Times* or *Guardian*, the local paper, ITV News, BBC radio news, and the local radio newsflash, and compare these.

(iii) Providing the 'missing' documents. This is a variant of (ii), in which groups compose the letter referred to but not printed in the text, the police report, the reference that Ogion would have made about Ged in *A Wizard of Earthsea* or the Doctor about Tom Brown.

(iv)   Planned pattern of shared group work. Topics can be planned for group work which will combine into an organized view of the whole text. For example, different groups could be set to examine each of Billy Casper's relationships (with his mother, his brother, Mr Farthing, the headmaster, the hawk) and to analyse it with an accompanying series of key quotations. Each group can then report back to the others or display its findings.

(v)   Extending beyond the text. Improvisation can be used to explore what might happen after the book ends, based on understanding of the book as a whole.[16] Alternatively, the continuation can be in written form (Now that you've read about Ged's adventures when he was young, write a story about his later adventures in other parts of Earthsea) and these can be collected and shared.

(vi)   Debating the central issues. It is difficult to suggest how formally groups should be encouraged to come to grips with major critical issues. In some form, however, it is likely that groups will want to discuss such issues as whether *Lord of the Flies* shows us what boys – and human beings generally – are really like, or whether *Z for Zachariah* convinces us by its picture of the future.

(vii) What is important about this story? Groups are given 10 statements about the story, and have to choose which three they think are most important. The results can then be discussed by the whole class.

(B)   *Relating to other reading*

It is important for the deepening of response that points of contact should be established between the story and other works previously read or deliberately introduced at this stage.

(i)   Direct comparisons with other works read by the group. Students can explore different responses to the first person narrators of, say, *Great Expectations, Huckleberry Finn, A Portrait of the Artist* or *Catcher in the Rye*. They can compare the way in which openings of certain novels introduce thematic concerns: *Bleak House* or *Hard Times, Far from the Madding Crowd* or *A Passage to India*. They can discuss the conflict of different systems of values in novels like *Kes, Eagle of the Ninth, Walkabout* or *The Go-Between*, or the importance of the setting to characters like Fagin, Mr Polly, the Morels, Arthur Seaton.

(ii) Stories can be related to those on which they are directly modelled or with which they are intended to conflict. Passages from *Coral Island* can be put alongside *Lord of the Flies*; sections from Richardson's *Pamela* related to *Joseph Andrews*.

(iii) Groups can be asked to compile their own sets of readings from other works on major themes from the book (attitudes to school, colour prejudice, feeling for animals).

(iv) Comparing the protagonist's behaviour and attitudes in key situations with those of similar figures in works of a different period or country (the bullied child in *Tom Brown's Schooldays* and *My Mate Shofiq*; the concern for the threatened animal in *Charlotte's Web* and *The Peppermint Pig*; the family adventures of E. Nesbit's Bastables and Arthur Ransome's Swallows).

(v)   Suggestions for further reading. 'Tasters', lists and displays of other books that might now be appropriate for children.

(C) *Presenting and sharing*

(i)   Creating a display based on the novel for classroom, library or foyer, including posters, alternative book jackets, reviews, selected quotations and related objects. *The Machine Gunners* lends itself to such a display, with items like gas-masks, ration books, medals, tin-hats and interviews with those in the family who have war-time memories.

(ii) A brief, taped 'promotion' of the book, including extracts or dramatizations, that can be preserved on cassette for playing to other classes, or by individuals.

(iii) For younger children with 'journey' books (*A Silver Sword, A Wizard of Earthsea*) creating board-games based on the narrative which other groups can play.

(iv) Art work based upon the book: a cover design, the choice of about five significant episodes to illustrate for a school edition, the making of group collages to illustrate the major themes of the book.

(v)   Preparing a Jackdaw-style folder of materials about the author
        and the story for use by a form a year younger.
(vi)   Writing letters to a friend or pupil in another school recom-
        mending the book.
(vii)   Groups are given a key episode each, and are asked to prepare
        a way of presenting it effectively to the rest of the class, using
        drama, art, reading, commentary, interpretation, as they wish.
        The showing of these prepared presentations can round off
        work on the text.

CONCLUSION

This book has argued that a more detailed knowledge of how children
respond to stories, and how that response develops as they grow older,
should underlie all that we do with fiction in schools: our programmes of
work, our choice of texts and our classroom methods. The development
of response demands to be seen as beginning with our earliest engagement with stories and continuing throughout life. At present the process
is hampered rather than aided in many children by misguided classroom
practices, by forcing inappropriate reading on them and by the pressure of
examinations with their accompanying break in methods of approach to
the text.

How might the situation be improved? The five case studies and other
examples in the text have been an attempt to suggest more helpful
approaches. Readers of this book – like those of any text – will have
responded to these suggestions in very different ways: nodding in agreement or growling in exasperation, skipping, making comments, questioning and considering. However imperceptibly, they will have been influenced as we always are by our reading. Our responses to such written
accounts of teachers' experiences will not be very different from the way
in which we react when we hear about them face to face in the staff-room.
We may be led to reflect on our own practice, or decide to test out these
ideas, or begin to work out variations on them. We may push further back
to consider the implications of our own reading experiences, or to enquire
more closely into how our pupils read and respond.

Ideally, though, such developments will not be wholly private, internal
ones, but will be shared with others. The age of isolated English teachers,
all in their own rooms doing it their way, is passing. What might happen
if a number of teachers in a department wanted to move toward more
effective, response-centred fiction teaching? However different their
situations, the processes would probably be the same: *enquiring* into the
present state of affairs, *experimenting* with possible ideas and *organizing* for
change.

Enquiring.
This book grew out of the urgent feelings of a number of teachers that they simply did not know enough about how their children read. Any coherent departmental fiction programme needs to build on detailed awareness about the amount and variety of reading that is going on in the school. This might involve questionnaire surveys of reading habits, interviews with individuals about how and what they have been reading, or repeating some of the simple school-based investigations described in part one. Students on teaching practice are often happy to be involved in such enquiries. Responses to fiction is one of those topics particularly suited to small-scale 'cottage industry' research, and most departments can identify aspects in which they are interested and which they can examine for themselves. It may be desirable to widen further and to establish contacts with parents about voluntary reading, and to enlist their help. How long is it since book provision in the school was given serious examination? Is there adequate choice (in class sets and form libraries) for different ages, interests, abilities, sexes? Is the school library's fiction stock keyed to the work being done in the department? Are pupils – as well as teachers – asked what proposals they have for books that might be acquired? Do any members of staff have responsibility for assessing new children's fiction as it appears, or at least for checking reviews in search of likely titles?

Experimenting.
Good teaching is based not only on sound principles, but on trial and error. Curriculum change proceeds largely on the basis of witnesses who say, 'This worked for me, so perhaps you might try it.' Beyond the stage of individuals trying out new approaches, there are a number of ways in which a team can give support to its members. Some departments have experimented with several teachers presenting the same novel in different ways (or different novels in the same way) and pooling their experiences. Some have systematically attempted as many as possible of 'Twenty-four things to do with a book' and reported back. Some have recorded teacher-led and small-group discussions of the same sections of text and analysed the results. Where timetables permit, teachers can pair off to share lessons: either with one teaching while the other observes children's responses, or with the two planning, working and evaluating as a team. There may be a need to experiment not only with methods but with the choice of books.It can be tempting to use *The Machine Gunners* year after year, because it goes well and because we know which activities seem most successful, but it can be stultifying if we – as well as the children – are not sometimes faced with the challenge of responding to new, unfamiliar texts.

Organizing.

Since the demise of the formal syllabus, many schools work without any formulation of the principles that should underlie the teaching of fiction. Getting a brief agreed statement into writing is a good way of involving the members of a department in thinking about the topic. Arguing about criteria for choice of books and discussing teachers' preferences, is another way of opening it up. This can be followed by a range of activities that will affect the structure of work in the school. A broad programme of key stories and novels can be worked out, making choices available each year that will enable connections to be established with past and future reading. It may be possible to frame a policy for reading in examination forms that will avoid the limiting effects of that assessment, and encourage a continued extension of reading. Members of staff may form working groups to report on those areas of most concern to the department: how to record the reading progress of each pupil in the school, say, or what strategies might be attempted to avoid the falling-off in voluntary fiction-reading at ages 13–14. Groups of teachers in the department can be formed to work together, drawing up materials and approaches for work on particular novels, so that they can be made available to others. Brainstorming sessions can be held to propose ways of pushing books: ensuring adequate time for independent reading and talk about books, developing the work of the library and bookshop, establishing or reorganizing class libraries, using displays, book fairs and visits, building up materials about authors in print and on audio or videotape, bringing authors of fiction into school.

None of these ideas is new. Each of them is already common practice in some schools. They can only be recommended to teachers who are already excessively busy and under stress because most of those who have made the attempt feel that their work has benefited (and therefore their pupils have gained) as a result. The first chapter suggested that, in the words of Chris Woodhead, 'there is at present considerable uncertainty amongst English teachers as to the books and materials which are most likely to succeed with pupils of different ages and abilities.' Perhaps we are now at a stage when it is possible for us to reduce some of that uncertainty.

Notes
and References

Chapter 1

1   G. Bosley, *The Killing* in *New Stories I*, Arts Council of Great Britain, 1976
2   In *The Habit of Loving*, McGibbon and Kee, 1957, and subsequently reprinted in a number of school anthologies
3   John Willett, *Brecht on Theatre* , Methuen, 1964, p. 150
4   Geoff Fox, *Reading fiction – Starting where the kids are*, in John L. Foster (*ed.*), *Reluctant to Read?*, Ward Lock, 1977, pp. 17 ff.
5   APU, *Language Performance in Schools, Secondary Survey Report No. 1*, HMSO, 1982, pp. 40–1
6   D. H. Lawrence, *Hymns in a Man's Life*, *Phoenix II*, Heinemann, 1968, pp. 597–601
7   Norman N. Holland, *Five Readers Reading*, Yale University Press, New Haven, 1975
8   June Downey, *Creative Imagination: studies in the psychology of literature*, Kegan Paul, Trench, Trubner & Co., 1929
9   Homer J. Wightman, *Study of reading appreciation, Journal of Education*, Vol. 82, September 1915, pp. 743–4
10 Alan C. Purves, *Literature Education in Ten Countries*, Wiley & Sons, New York, 1973
11 Norman N. Holland, *The Dynamics of Literary Response*, New York, Oxford University Press, 1969
12 Reported in *English in Education*, Vol. 8 No. 2, Summer 1974, and Vol. 13, No. 1, Spring 1979, and in *The Use of English*, Vol. 29, No. 3 Summer 1978
13 HMI, *Aspects of Secondary Education in England*, HMSO, 1979
14 Gunnar Hansson, *Some types of research on response to literature, Research in the Teaching of English*, Vol. 7, 1973, pp. 260–84
15 Albert B. Somers and Janet E. Worthington, *Response Guides for Teaching Children's Books*, NCTE, Urbana, Illinois, 1979
16 Ted Hughes, *Children's Literature in Education*, No. 1, 1970
17 Simon O. Lesser, *Fiction and the Unconscious*, Beacon Press, Boston, 1957, p. 39
18 Norman N. Holland, *The Dynamics of Literary Response*, Oxford U.P., New York, pp. 340–1
19 E. P. Jackson, 1944; G. R. Carlsen, 1948; Jane Webster, 1961
20 David H. Russell, *The Dynamics of Reading*, Ginn-Blaisdell, Waltham, Mass., 1970, p. 85

21 Patricia Beer, *Doing you Wrong, Times Educational Supplement*, 27 August 1976
22 Kathleen Raine, *Farewell Happy Fields*, Hamilton, 1973, p. 114
23 Fred Inglis, *The Promise of Happiness*, Cambridge University Press, 1981, p. 57
24 D. W. Harding, *The Bond with the Author, The Use of English*, Vol. 22, No. 4, Summer 1971, p. 325
25 A. C. Purves, *Testing in Literature* in Benjamin Bloom et al, *Handbook on Formative and Summative Evaluation of School Learning*, McGraw Hill, New York, 1971, pp. 697 ff.
26 Norman N. Holland, *Poems in Persons*, Norton, New York, 1973, p. 110
27 Geoffrey Yarlott, *'Aims' in teaching literature, Educational Review*, Vol. 10, No. 2, February 1968, pp. 147, 150
28 Chris Woodhead, *Teaching Literature: The Oxford Education Research Group Project, Oxford Review of Education*, Vol. 5, No. 1, 1979, p. 64

Chapter 2

1   In an interview with Katharine Whitehorn, reported in the *Observer*, 27 May 1979
2   Alan Sillitoe, *Raw Material*, W. H. Allen, 1972
3   E.g. M. L. Pratt, *Towards a Speech Act Theory of Literary Discourse*, Indiana U.P., Bloomington, 1977
4   Andrew Sinclair, *The Facts in the Case of E. A. Poe*, Weidenfeld and Nicolson, 1979, p. 53
5   Simon O. Lesser, *Fiction and the Unconscious*, Beacon Press, Boston, 1957, pp. 4–8
6   *A Language for Life*, HMSO, 1975, Para. 9.9
7   Frank Whitehead *et al, Children and their Books*, Macmillan, Basingstoke, 1977. See especially pp. 113, 125–9, 151–3
8   Terry Eagleton, *Walter Benjamin or Towards a Revolutionary Criticism*, NLB/Verso, 1981, p. 72
9   R. L. Gregory, *Psychology: towards a science of fiction, New Society*, 23 May 1974
10 E.g. in Michel Butor, *Inventory*, trans. Richard Howard, Simon and Schuster, New York, 1969; James Moffett, *Teaching the Universe of Discourse*, Houghton Mifflin, Boston, 1968; Jonathan Culler, *The Pursuits of Signs*, Routledge & Kegan Paul, 1981
11 Barbara Hardy, *Tellers and Listeners*, Athlone Press, 1975, p. 4
12 Frank Kermode, *The Sense of an Ending*, Oxford U.P., New York, 1967 Umberto Eco, *The Role of the Reader*, Indiana U.P., Bloomington, 1979
13 David H. Russell, *The Dynamics of Reading*, Ginn-Blaisdell, Waltham, Massachusetts, 1970, p. 207

14   Gill Frith, *Reading and response: some questions and no answers, English in Education*, Vol. 13 No. 1, Spring 1979, p. 31
15   Wolfgang Iser, *The Act of Reading*, Routledge & Kegan Paul, 1978, p. 279
16   Some published examples of such talk can be found in David Jackson, *Continuity in English Teaching*, Methuen, 1982; Jack Ouseby, *Little factories of understanding, Children's Literature in Education*, Vol. 11, No. 4, 1980; and articles by Nancy Martin and others in Robert Protherough, *ed., The Development of Readers*, Hull University, 1983
17   Horst Ruthrof, *The Reader's Construction of Narrative*, Routledge & Kegan Paul, 1981, p. 77
18   Roland Barthes, *S/Z*, trans. Richard Miller, Cape, 1975
19   John Willett, *Brecht on Theatre*, Methuen, 1964, pp. 14, 71, 79, 89, 187, 190, 201
20   Roman Ingarden, *Aesthetic experience and aesthetic object*, in N. Lawrence and D. O'Connor, *Readings in Existential Phenomenology*, Englewood Cliffs, 1967, p. 304; Seymour Chatman, *Story and Discourse*, Cornell U.P., Ithaca, 1978, pp. 41–2
21   F. R. Leavis, *Education and the University*, Chatto & Windus, 1943, p. 70
22   Georges Poulet, *Phenomenology of Reading, New Literary History*, Vol. 1, No. 1, October 1969, pp. 53–68
23   Norman N. Holland, *Poems in Persons*, Norton, New York, 1973, p. 146
24   Wolfgang Iser, *The Act of Reading*, Routledge & Kegan Paul, 1978, p. 109
25   John Dixon, *Growth Through English*, NATE, Reading, 1967
26   Louise M. Rosenblatt, *The Reader, the Text, the Poem*, South Illinois U.P., 1978, p. 11
27   Norman N. Holland, *Poems in Persons*, Norton, New York, 1973, p. 3
28   I. A. Richards, *What is involved in the interpretation of meaning?* in William S. Gray, *Reading and Pupil Development*, Supplementary educational monographs No. 51, October 1940, University of Chicago, p. 49
29   James R. Wilson, *Responses of College Freshmen to Three Novels*, NCTE, Urbana, Illinois, 1966, pp. 39–40
30   D. W. Harding, *The bond with the author, The Use of English*, Vol. 22, No. 4, Summer 1971, pp. 315–6

Chapter 3

1   Mary C. Burch, *Determination of a content of the course in literature of a suitable difficulty for junior and senior high school students, Genetic Psychology Monograph* 4, Nos. 2 and 3, August–September 1928
2   James R. Squire, ed., *Response to Literature*, NCTE, Champaign, Illinois, 1968
3   Margaret Spencer, *By adult standards* in *Reading: Implementing the Bullock Report*, Ward Lock, 1978

4   D. W. Harding, *Psychological processes in the reading of fiction, British Journal of Aesthetics,* Vol. 2, No. 2, April 1962, pp. 133–47
5   HMI, *Bullock Revisited,* HMSO, 1982, Para. 4.6
6   The phrases are taken from Frank Whitehead, David Holbrook, James Britton, A. N. Applebee and Michael Tucker
7   I. A. Richards, *Practical Criticism, a study of literary judgement,* Kegan Paul, 1929 and *Interpretation in Teaching,* Kegan Paul, 1937
8   *British Journal of Educational Psychology,* Vol. 24, 1954, pp. 17–31
9   E.g. Walter Loban, *Literature and Social Sensitivity,* NCTE, Champaign, Ilinois, 1954; James R. Squire, *The Responses of Adolescents while Reading Four Short Stories,* NCTE, 1964; Jerry Ward Ring, *A study of the interpretive processes employed by selected adolescent readers of three short stories,* Ph.D. thesis, Ohio State University, 1968
10 E. D. Williams, L. Winter and J. M. Woods, *Tests of literary appreciation, British Journal of Educational Psychology,* Vol. 8, 1938, pp. 265–83
11 Herbert A. Carroll, *A method of measuring prose appreciation, English Journal,* Vol. 22, March 1933, pp. 154–9
12 Robert S. Zais, *A scale to measure sophistication of reading interests, Journal of Reading,* Vol. 12, 1969, pp. 273–6
13 Bruce H. Choppin and Alan C. Purves, *A comparison of open-ended and multiple-choice items dealing with literary understanding, Research in the Teaching of English,* Vol. 3, No. 1, 1969, pp. 15–24
14 James R. Squire, *The Responses of Adolescents while Reading Four Short Stories,* NCTE, Champaign, Illinois, 1964
15 James R. Wilson, *Responses of College Freshmen to Three Novels,* NCTE, Urbana, Illinois, 1966. Compare P. L. Sanders, *An investigation of the effects of instruction in the interpretation of literature on the responses of adolescents to selected short stories,* Ph.D. dissertation, Syracuse University, 1970
16 Alan Purves and Victoria Rippere, *Elements of Writing about a Literary Work,* NCTE, Urbana, Illinois, 1968
17 J. N. Britton, *An enquiry into changes of opinion, on the part of adult readers . . .* M.A. thesis, London, 1952 and W. S. Harpin, *The appreciation of prose: measurement and evaluation . . . Educational Review,* No. 19, November 1966, pp. 13–22
18 Frank Whitehead, et al, *Children and their Books,* Macmillan, Basingstoke, 1977
19 Jennie Ingham, *Books and Reading Development,* Heinemann, 1981, p. 240
20 Vera Southgate, et al, *Extending Beginning Reading,* Heinemann, 1981
21 Ingham, *Books and Reading Development*
22 A. N. Applebee, *The Child's Concept of Story,* Chicago U.P., 1978
23 Pat Hutchins, *Rosie's Walk,* Macmillan, 1968
24 Janet and Allen Ahlberg, *Peepo!,* Kestrel Books, Harmondsworth, 1981
25 Louise B. Ames, *Children's Stories, Genetic Psychology Monographs,* vol. 73, 1966, pp. 337–396 and A. N. Applebee, *The Child's Concept of Story,* Chicago U.P., 1978
26 Frank Smith, *Writing and the Writer,* Holt, Rinehart & Winston, New York, 1982, p. 193

27 Gordon H. Bower, *Experiments on story understanding and recall*, *Quarterly Journal of Experimental Psychology*, Vol. 28, 1976, pp. 511–34

28 N. L. Stein and C. G. Glenn, *An analysis of story comprehension in elementary school children*, in Roy O. Freedle, ed., *New Directions in Discourse Processing*, Ablex, New Jersey, 1979, pp. 53–120

29 Robert Protherough, *Children's sense of story-line*, English in Education, Vol. 13, No. 1, Spring 1979, pp. 36–41

30 Seymour Chatman, *Story and Discourse*, Cornell U.P., Ithaca, 1978, p. 49

31 Jane Austen, *Pride and Prejudice*, Chapter 58

32 Jane Austen, *Emma*, Chapter 15

33 Truman Capote, *The Thanksgiving Visitor*, Random House, New York, 1968 and Stuart Evans, ed., *The Story Inside*, Hutchinson, 1977. The stories have been broadcast by the BBC in *Listening and Writing* and in *Books, Plays, Poems* respectively

34 E. A. Peel, *The Nature of Adolescent Judgement*, Staples Press, 1971, p. 114

35 Jonathan Culler, *Literary Competence* (1975), reprinted in Jane P. Tompkins, *Reader-Response Criticism*, John Hopkins U.P., Baltimore, 1980, p. 109

36 Alan C. Purves, *Evaluation of Learning in Literature*, Oxford, Pergamon Press, 1979

37 D. W. Harding, *Practice at Liking: a study in experimental aesthetics*, *Bulletin of the British Psychological Society*, Vol. 21, No. 70, January 1968, pp. 3–10

38 Robert Protherough, *Children's sense of story-line*, English in Education, Vol. 13, No. 1, Spring 1979, pp. 41

39 Angela Marie Broening, *Developing appreciation through teaching literature*, Ph.D. thesis, John Hopkins University, 1928, published Baltimore, 1929

40 Dwight L. Burton, *An experiment in teaching appreciation of fiction*, *English Journal*, Vol. 42, No. 1, January 1953, pp. 16–20

41 Peter Lawrence Sanders, *An investigation of the effects of instruction in the interpretation of literature on the responses of adolescents to selected short stories*, Ph.D. thesis, Syracuse University, 1970

42 James R. Wilson, *Responses of College Freshmen to Three Novels*, NCTE, Urbana, Illinois, 1966

43 Sanders, 1970, *op.cit.*

44 Darleen Ann Michalak, *The effect of instruction on high school students' preferred way of responding to literature*, Ph.D. thesis, State University of New York, Buffalo, 1976, p. 96

Chapter 9

1 APU, *Language Performance in Schools*, Secondary Survey Report No 1, HMSO, 1982, pp. 43–51

2 James Britton in J. R. Squires, *ed.*, *Response to Literature*, Dartmouth Seminar Papers, NCTE, Illinois, 1968, p. 8

3 Alan B. Howes, *Teaching Literature to Adolescents: Novels,* Scott Foresman & Co., Glenview, Illinois, 1972, p. 50

4 Barbara Hardy, *The teaching of literature in the university: some problems, English in Education,* Vol. 7, No. 1, Spring 1973, pp. 27–8

5 David Jackson, *Continuity in Secondary English,* Methuen, 1982, pp. 23 ff.

6 APU, *op.cit.* pp. 49–50 Compare the results of the survey described by Audrey Third, *Talking Books, Times Educational Supplement,* 22 October 1982

7 *Bullock Revisited,* HMSO, 1982, Para. 4.4

8 *The Teaching of English in England,* HMSO, 1921, sections 275–83

9 See John Dixon and John Brown, *Response to Literature: What Is Being Assessed?* (forthcoming), John Dixon, *Education 16–19,* Macmillan, Basingstoke, 1979, the beginning of Mike Town's case study and Bill Greenwell, *Alternatives at English A-level,* NATE examinations booklet No. 4, 1982

10 Robert Protherough, *How student teachers see English in the sixth form, The Use of English,* Vol. 33, No. 2, Spring 1982, pp. 40–5

11 Louise M. Rosenblatt, *Literature as Exploration,* Heinemann, 1970, p. 60

12 Roman Ingarden, *Aesthetic experience and aesthetic object* in N. Lawrence and D. O'Connor, *Readings in Existential Phenomenology,* Prentice Hall, Englewood Cliffs, New Jersey, 1967, p. 319

13 F. R. Leavis, *Education and the University,* Chatto & Windus, 1943, pp. 68–9

14 *ibid.,* p. 7

15 *ibid.,* p. 68

16 *ibid.,* p. 138

17 *ibid.,* p. 71

Chapter 10

1 Some small-scale investigations at Hull have begun to examine this topic with reference to younger children. See Jean Williams, *A sample enquiry into what initially attracts eight-year-olds to the books they choose to read,* M.Ed. dissertation, Hull University, 1979, and Vera Wyse, *First impressions: an investigation into some of the factors which children 8–9 say guide their initial selection of freely-chosen fiction and their later decision to continue or abandon their reading,* M.A. dissertation, Hull University, 1981

2 Kate Vincent, *A Survey of the Methods by which Teachers select Books,* Centre for Research in User Studies, Sheffield, 1980, p. 155

3 Nearly four million fewer school books were bought in 1980 than in 1979. See, for example, *The Supply of Books to Schools and Colleges,* The Booksellers Association and The Publishers Association, 1981, and the regional guides to schoolbook spending, Educational Publishers Council, 1980–1

4 Bob Bibby, *Teachers and their books, English in Education,* Vol. 17, No. 2, Summer 1983

5   David Holbrook, *English in Australia Now*, Cambridge U.P., Cambridge, 1973, p. 8

6   Peter Hollindale, *Choosing Books for Children*, Paul Elek, 1974

7   BBC Television, *The Risk Business: The Hype*

8   Anne Merrick, *Children's Literature in Education*, No. 16, Spring 1975 pp. 21–30

9   Alan C. Purves and Richard Beach, *Literature and the Reader*, NCTE, Urbana, Illinois, 1972, p. 103

10 Frank Whitehead, et al, *Children and their Books*, Macmillan, 1977

11 Stephen James, *What O-level boys are reading*, Times Educational Supplement, 20 April 1973. A similar, earlier investigation in the USA found that of 64 novels popular with young readers in 1927 only four remained popular nine years later (W. W. Charters, *Sixty-four popular boys' books*, Literary Journal, No. 63, May 1938, pp. 399–400)

12 Purves and Beach, *op.cit.*, pp. 92 and 20–1

13 J. H. Mott, *Reading interests of adolescents: a critical study of fifty years of research*, Ed.D. thesis, University of North Colorado, 1970; Purves and Beach, *op.cit.*

14 Purves and Beach, *op.cit.*, p. 78

15 Geoff Fox, *Twenty four things to do with a book*, Children's Literature in Education, Vol. 8, No. 3, 1977

16 Mary Crowell Burch, *Determination of the course in literature of a suitable difficulty for junior and senior high school students*, Genetic Psychology Monograph, Vol. 4, Nos. 2 and 3, August–September 1928, p. 225

17 See Colin Harrison, *Readability in the Classroom*, Cambridge U.P., Cambridge, 1980

18 For further details, see Katharine Perera, *The assessment of linguistic difficulty in reading material*, Educational Review, Vol. 32, No. 2, 1980, pp. 151–61

19 E.g. Margery R. Bernstein, *Relationship between interest and reading comprehension*, Journal of Educational Research, Vol. 49, December 1955, pp. 283–9

20 Charlotte Bronte, *Jane Eyre*, simplified by S. E. Paces, Compact English Classics series, Ward Lock Educational, 1982

21 Walter Loban has indicated the lack of comprehension and the dislike shown towards stories outside students' emotional range in *Literature and Social Sensitivity*, NCTE, Champaign, Illinois, 1954

22 H. T. Himmelweit, et al, *Television and the Child*, Oxford U.P., 1958

23 John McCreesh, *Children's ideas of horror and tragedy*, Catholic Education Today, Sept-Oct 1970, reprinted in *The Cool Web*

24 Felicity Ann O'Dell, *Socialization Through Children's Literature*, Cambridge U.P., Cambridge, 1978, pp. 103–4

25 Sarah Trimmer, *The Charity School Spelling Book*, 4th ed., 1798

26 Robert Westall, *The Machine Gunners*, Macmillan, 1975, M books edition, 1980, p. 186

27 *ibid.* p. 59

28 Jessica Yates, *Censorship in children's paperbacks*, Children's Literature in Education, Vol. 11, No. 4, 1980, p. 182

29 David C. McClelland, *The Achieving Society*, Free Press, New York, 1961

30   John P. Shepard, *The treatment of characters in popular children's fiction*, *Elementary English*, November, 1962, pp. 672–6

31   Nancy Larrick, *The all-white world of children's books*, *Saturday Review*, 11 September 1965

32   Thomas D. Yawkey and Margaret L. Yawkey, *An analysis of picture books*, *Language Arts*, May 1976, pp. 545–8

33   E.g. *English in a multi-cultural society*, *English in Education*, Spring 1977

34   Bob Dixon, *Catching Them Young*, Vol. 1, Pluto Press, 1977

35   Gillian Klein, *Racism in books*, *Times Educational Supplement*, 8 April 1977

36   Judith Elkin, *Books for the multi-racial classroom*, Library Association Youth Libraries Group and SLA, 1976

37   Phyllis W. Barnum, *The aged in young children's literature*, *Language Arts*, January 1977, pp. 29–32

38   Moira Monteith, *Boys, Girls and Language*, *English in Education*, Vol. 13, No. 2, Summer 1979, and Julia Hodgeon, *Topsy and Tim rule – OK? English in Education*, Vol. 14, No. 1, spring 1980

39   Geoff Fox, *Times Educational Supplement*, 14 July 1978

40   Dale Spender, *The facts of life: sex differentiated knowledge in the English classroom and the school*, *English in Education*, Vol. 12, No. 3, Autumn 1978

41   Children's Rights Workshop, *Racist and Sexist Images in Children's Books*, Writers and Readers Publishing Cooperative, 1975

42   A correspondent (O.P.) to Sarah Trimmer, *Guardian of Education*, Vol. 2, No. 15, July 1803, p. 448. Mrs Trimmer wrote that she would be happy to hear more from 'so good a judge of what children *ought* and *ought not* to read'

43   Brian Hollingworth, *Literature in use*, *The Use of English*, Vol. 24, No. 3, Spring 1973, pp. 230–4.

44   E.g. *The Use of English*, Vol. 20, No. 3, Spring 1969

Chapter 11

1   In Helen M. Robinson, *ed.*, *Sequential Development in Reading Abilities*, Supplementary Education Monographs No. 90, University of Chicago Press, 1960

2   David Jackson, *Continuity in Secondary English*, Methuen, 1982

3   Compare the scheme produced in a middle school for using *Carrie's War*, reproduced in *Fiction-based English in the Middle School*, booklet 3 of the Wakefield Literature and Learning Project 8–14, 1982

4   Other suggestions, drawing on American sources, are made in an article by L. Jane Stewart, *The cumulative study of literature for the secondary school*, in *Focus: Teaching Language Arts*, Vol. 3, No. 2, Winter 1977

5   The idea is taken from social education, in such books as *Reading Ladders for Human Relations*, 6th ed., Eileen Tway, American Council for Education, Washington, 1981

6   Such points have been illustrated from American novels by Al Muller, *Teaching adolescents to read adult fiction, Journal of Reading*, Vol. 20, October 1976, pp. 28–33

7   Frank Smith, *Writing and the Writer*, Holt, Rinehart and Winston, New York, 1982, p. 97

8   A published example of such jottings in response to the opening chapters of *Great Expectations* is in David Jackson, *Dealing with a set book in literature at 16+, English in Education*, Vol. 16, No. 1, Spring 1982, pp. 17–29

9   David Jackson, *First encounters: the importance of initial responses to literature, Children's Literature in Education*, Vol, 11, No. 4

10 F. R. Leavis, *Education and the University*, Chatto & Windus, 1943, p. 70

11 See John Alcock, *Students' questions and teachers' questions* in Mike Torbe and Robert Protherough, *Classroom Encounters*, Ward Lock 1976, pp. 37–76, and David Jackson, *Our questions and their questions, Teaching English*, Vol. 12, No. 3, Summer 1979, pp. 19–28

12 Eric Lunzer and Keith Gardner, *The Effective Use of Reading*, Heinemann, 1979

13 Josephine Hall, *Charting Literature, The Use of English*, Vol. 31, No. 3, Summer 1981, pp. 23–27

14 Some useful sections are reprinted in Alan B. Howes, *Teaching Literature to Adolescents: Novels*, Scott Foresman, Glenview, Illinois, 1972

15 See George Bluestone, *Novels into Film*, University of California Press, Berkeley, 1957 (which discusses *Wuthering Heights, Pride and Prejudice*, and *The Grapes of Wrath*) and Edward Murray, *The Cinematic Imagination*, Ungar, New York, 1972 (discussing Hemingway, Greene and Steinbeck)

16 See John Seely, *Approaches through drama: Robert O'Brien's Z for Zachariah* in O.U. Inset, *Children, Language and Literature*, 1982, pp.70–2 and accompanying cassette

Subject Index